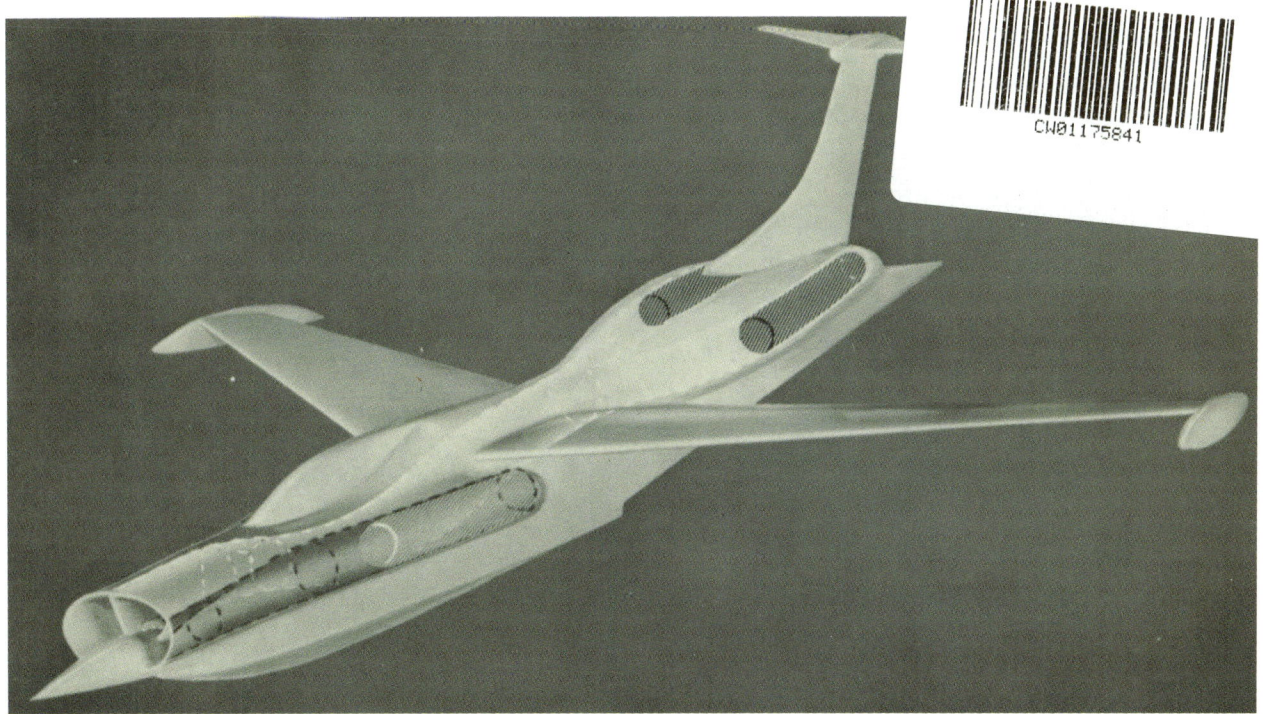
Diagram showing Martin's M-275 supersonic seaplane bomber design from a NACA report.

Introduction

The previous volume described the development of American supersonic bombers that got as far as obtaining an official designation from the Department of Defense. But that is hardly a comprehensive list of all American supersonic bombers; a vast number of them have been designed but got no further than proposals. Some, not even that far. A lack of development does not, however, denote a lack of interest.

This volume will describe a wide range of designs that have been put forward over the course of around three quarters of a century. As with the first volume, the definition of a 'bomber' is a little vague… an aircraft designed from the outset to carry bombs (or missiles meant to strike ground targets). With one rather outstanding exception, the bomber is intended for recovery and re-use.

Given the vast number of supersonic bombers designed, organising them in a sensible manner that everyone can agree on would be virtually impossible. So here the author has chosen a reasonable number and organised them into a few distinct groups: seaplanes, nuclear powered, nuclear powered seaplanes, vertical takeoff and landing, hypersonic.

Scott Lowther
aerospaceprojectsreview.com

Contents

Chapter 1: Nuclear Powered Supersonic Bombers	4
Chapter 2: Seaplanes	43
Chapter 3: Nuclear Powered Seaplane Supersonic Bombers	69
Chapter 4: VTOL Bombers	83
Chapter 5: Hypersonics	107
References	128
General data table	129

Author/artist: Scott Lowther
Publisher: Steve O'Hara
Published by:
Mortons Media Group Ltd,
Media Centre, Morton Way, Horncastle,
Lincolnshire LN9 6JR, Tel. 01507 529529

Typeset by: Druck Media Pvt. Ltd.
Printed by: Acorn Web Offset Ltd, Loscoe Close, Normanton Industrial Estate, West Yorkshire WF6 1TW
All diagrams ©2023 Scott Lowther

Acknowledgements: This book could not have been completed without the assistance of a number of authors and historians, including but not limited to: Dennis Jenkins, Tony Landis, Tony Buttler. Their assistance and contributions are greatly appreciated.

ISBN: 978-1-911703-18-1

© 2023 Mortons Media Group Ltd. All rights reserved. No part of this publication may be reproduced or transmitted in any form or by any means, electronic or mechanical, including photocopying, recording, or any information storage retrieval system without prior permission in writing from the publisher.

Nuclear Powered Supersonic Bombers

By the end of the Second World War the United States was on the verge of fielding bombers that could reach European targets from American bases and return, all on a single load of fuel. Aircraft such as the Convair B-36 had incredible ranges, but the requirements turned the aircraft into flying fuel tanks. The advent of jet engines made the range problem even worse: the new engines could raise top speed, but at the expense of even greater fuel consumption. The use of turboprops would theoretically improve on the maximum airspeed of piston engined aircraft, while increasing the range over that of pure turbojet designs; even so, the improvements were not spectacular.

There were few options for improved fuels, though some hope was held out for propellants such as liquid hydrogen. In the end, the Strategic Air Command was able to raise the range of bombers to truly global, with mission durations measured potentially in days through the use of in-flight refuelling. This has worked well over the decades, but it ties the bomber to slow and vulnerable tanker aircraft.

Another option was studied shortly after the end of the Second World War. Immediately following the detonations of Little Boy and Fat Man the world entered the Atomic Age and for a while it seemed that the friendly atom could do just about anything. It proved that it could cleanly light cities and run factories; it also proved practical to power submarines and aircraft carriers. There were proposals to use nuclear power to create instant ports and sea-level canals across Nicaragua and to send giant space vehicles to Mars and beyond. And it was studied in some considerable depth as a means of powering aircraft.

The basic notion of atomic energy to power aircraft existed in both the United States and Germany during the Second World War, but it seems it was little more than that: notional. Practical reactor engineering design was as yet unknown in the United States, and virtually impossible in Nazi Germany. Nevertheless, things were moving quickly.

In May 1946, the United States Army Air Force awarded a contract to Fairchild Engine and Aircraft Corporation to begin the study of Nuclear Energy for the Propulsion of Aircraft (NEPA). NEPA was instituted to both perform basic feasibility studies and to provide information to the American aircraft engine industry on nuclear issues. At first highly hypothetical, NEPA and its successor programmes would go on to build nuclear powered jet engines and create detailed designs of atomic-powered aircraft. However, in the early years the programme was populated by experts who felt that atomic-powered aircraft were only a few hard-working years away, and others who felt that the whole concept bordered on the ludicrous.

In 1948, the Massachusetts Institute of Technology was brought on board in large part to finally settle the matter. MIT scientists concluded that nuclear flight was possible, though they estimated that it would take 15 years and a billion dollars to achieve. This was when even the United States government felt that a billion dollars was a fairly large sum of money.

Two main engine types were looked at under NEPA. The 'Direct Cycle' ducts air from an inlet directly into the reactor. Air flows through the reactor itself, coming in physical contact with reactor fuel elements. The reactor running at high power generates a vast amount of heat energy; left alone, the reactor would melt. But the air flowing through the Direct Cycle reactor cools the fuel, preventing damage to the hot structure. In the process, the air becomes superheated. This hot blowtorch of air is ejected aft at high speed, generating thrust directly, or flows through a series of turbines, providing the power needed to turn either propellers or a compressor stage.

The Direct Cycle engine is simple and effective and quite efficient; but white-hot oxygen and nitrogen – not to mentions bugs and dust – will do the uranium fuel elements no good whatsoever. A Direct Cycle engine stands a very good chance of ejecting a constant spray of tiny bits of the engine, leaving a radioactive trail wherever the aircraft may go. This is generally considered undesirable, especially when flying over friendly territory.

The Indirect Cycle engine avoids the environmental hazards – as well as extending the life of the reactor – by inserting a heat exchanger between the fuel and the air. The reactor is cooled not by air flowing through it at high pressure and velocity, but by something like liquid sodium metal. The superheated molten metal then flows through a heat exchanger, transferring its energy to air. The heat exchanger is generally located in the part of a turbojet or turboshaft engine normally occupied by the combustors, replacing the chemical fuels contribution to the engine cycle.

The Indirect method is heavier and more complex than Direct, but it has many obvious advantages. Not least of these is that since the liquid metal is very dense compared to air, it can be piped elsewhere, to heat exchangers located far from the reactor. Thus where Indirect systems generally required that the reactors and the jet engine be either integrated units or at least located very close to each other, the Indirect system allows for reactors to be deeply buried in the fuselage while the jet engines can be located far out along the wings.

In addition, while the Indirect system introduces inefficiencies due to the added steps, the fact is that a liquid metal, being many times denser than compressed air, is far more effective at removing heat from the reactor. In addition, a liquid metal is unlikely to chemically interact with the reactor, while white-hot oxygen is quite effective at oxidizing virtually anything.

These two methods allowed for a wide range of possible engine and aircraft configurations. But one thing that remained consistent was that nuclear propulsion for aircraft was monstrously heavy. The reactor was, compared to the chemical fuel, generally relatively light, but the plastic and lead radiation shielding, typically surrounding the reactor and again surrounding the crew, located as far as engineeringly possible from the reactor, were massive. And as powerful as an atomic reactor may sound, in practice they often struggled to produce power outputs equal to those of conventional turbojet engines at full thrust. The result was that the vast majority of the designs for atomic powered aircraft were strictly subsonic. Even then they often required chemical fuel augmentation for takeoff.

Nevertheless, the occasional nuclear powered design was produced that was capable of exceeding Mach One. The designs were often unconventional to say the least.

A note on shielding: most designs included shielding around the reactor, and further shielding around the cockpit. Generally the shielding was a mix of heavy metal such as lead or tungsten and a light plastic like polyurethane or rubber, often with additional water tanks (sometimes with boron compounds dissolved or mixed in as well). This composite was due to the fact that dense metals are effective at shielding against gamma rays, while plastics contain a fair amount of hydrogen which absorbs neutrons. In general the cockpit was placed as far as possible from the reactor, with as much of the aircraft structure as possible between the two to serve as further shielding.

At first glance it may seem that it would only be necessary to place radiation shields directly between the reactor and the cockpit, but the shielding generally fully encompassed the cockpit on all sides including the front. This is because the radiation would be scattered by the air surrounding the craft. A way to think of it is that the reactor was an intensely bright light bulb, and the air surrounding the cockpit was filled with fog: the light bulb may have been well behind the cockpit, but light would still come pouring in from the front due to being reflected by the fog.

The radiation would be reflected by the air molecules in the same fashion and would quickly irradiate the crew if they were not shielded on all sides. This included the windows: they would need to be made of thick leaded glass and Plexiglas in order to absorb the incoming radiation. Further, radiation would be reflected from the metallic structure of the aircraft including wings and the fuselage; anything that could be seen from the cockpit would be a source of incoming radiation. So while some designs featured expansive cockpit canopies, in general those were only the transparent aerodynamic fairings that covered the real windows… thick, small transparencies that protected the crew.

One of the advantages of a nuclear propulsion system for aircraft is also a problem for the aircraft. An aircraft that burns a large amount of fuel weighs considerably less at the end of its flight than it did at the beginning, a detail that allows planes to land at a lower speed than they took off at. Given that landings are naturally more challenging than takeoffs, reducing the landing speed is always helpful. But a nuclear powered aircraft can weigh virtually exactly the same after a two-day mission as it did at the beginning. The plane lands at its gross weight, minus whatever payload it might have dropped. This makes landings difficult in many ways… not only on the pilot, but also the landing gear and the rest of the structure.

In April of 1949 a conference held at Oak Ridge National Laboratory in Tennessee included representatives from the Air Force, the Atomic Energy Commission, the Navy and several industry contractors. The result was the birth of the Aircraft Nuclear Propulsion (ANP) programme, a turn from theoretical studies towards a more engineering development effort. The design of aircraft and engines began in earnest.

Lockheed L-195-A-13

Dating from 1949, the L-195 series was the earliest known serious design effort from Lockheed to develop a nuclear powered bomber. Unfortunately very little technical information is available on this and related designs apart from a few drawings. It is unknown if this was work contracted under the NEPA programme, though it seems likely.

The L-195-A-13 design featured a nuclear reactor mounted well aft, nearly in the tail. This was counterbalanced by an extremely long forward fuselage with a cramped cockpit located near the nose;

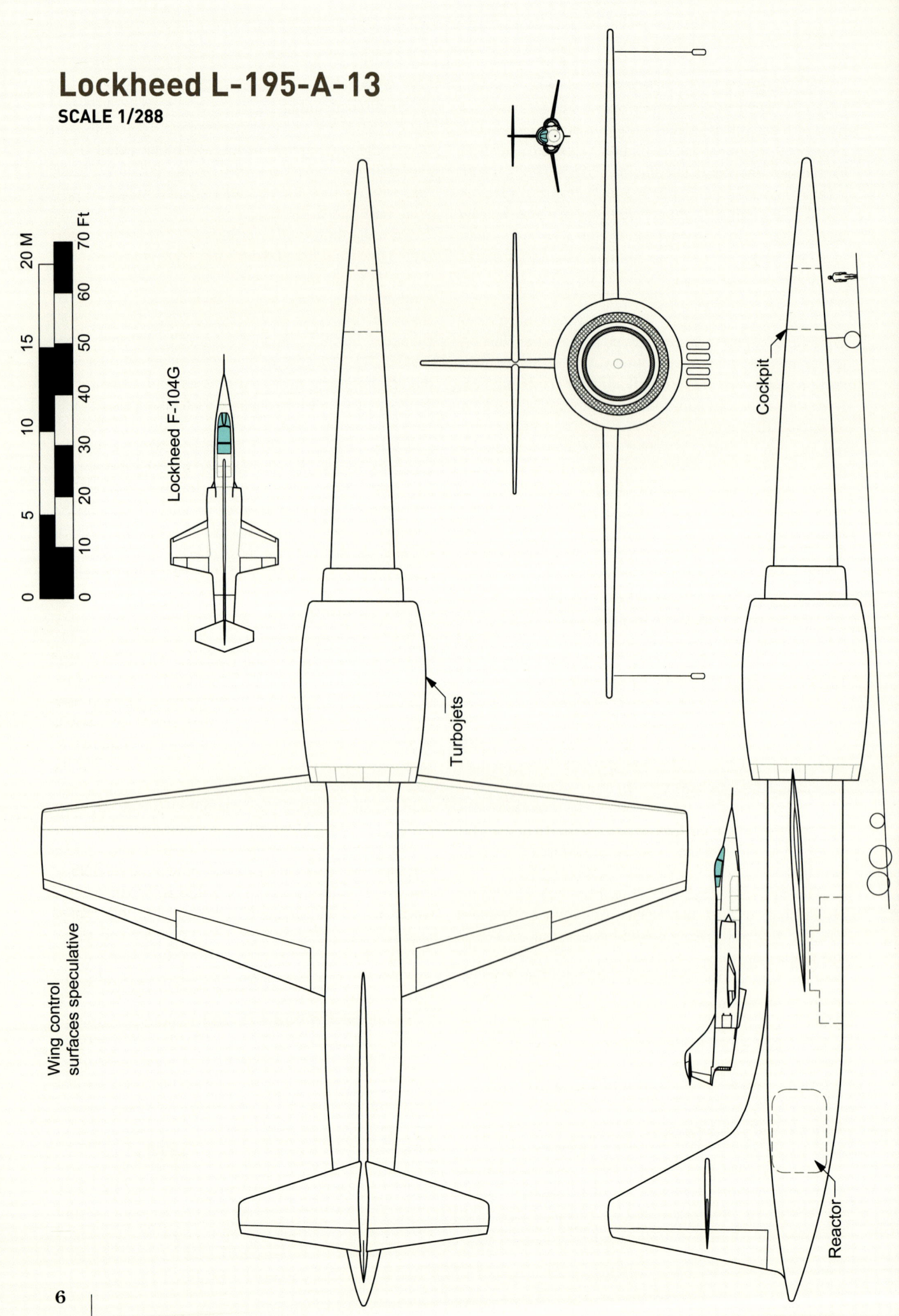

undoubtedly there would have been a massive lead and plastic radiation shield behind and around the cockpit. The turbojets, of uncertain number, were located in an annular cluster wrapped around the fuselage, just ahead of the straight wing. The payload bay was located aft of the engine cluster but ahead of the reactor. This was clearly an 'indirect' system, with long tubes leading from the reactor to the engines. As the engines were all clustered together, the piping would at least have been relatively straightforward and located securely within the central fuselage.

Performance, payload and nuclear reactor data are all absent. It was almost certainly meant to be supersonic given the sleek lines and, importantly, the very thin F-104-like wing. Supersonic speeds may have been achieved only with chemical fuel afterburning. Total length was 225ft.

Lockheed NEPA A-7

From January to March of 1950, a small Lockheed Aircraft Corporation contract (a total of 2.1 man-months… a very minor study) under NEPA resulted in a series of preliminary aircraft designs based on a common core fuselage. A primary feature was described as the 165ft separation distance between the crew cabin and the reactor, providing structural shielding a substantial distance between crew and reactor. The reactor was immediately ahead of a ring of turbojets; this design used eight jet engines.

The fairly enormous generic design was just a planned starting point… many wing areas, wing sweeps, engine numbers, gross weights and maximum speeds and altitudes were considered, but solely as a guide for future study. Designs featured sweep from 0° to 60°; this was not a variable geometry design, but a single basic aircraft that could have a number of different wings attached to it. This was to study performance potential with various planforms, gross weights and thrust levels.

The unswept wing was, unsurprisingly, restricted to subsonic speeds, and even the most highly swept designs did not greatly exceed the speed of sound. Configuration A-7, shown here, had a 60° wing sweep, and had a maximum airspeed of Mach 1.12 at 35,000ft; its maximum speed at sea level, though, was a creditable Mach 0.97. Curiously, configuration A-9 was able to achieve Mach 1.5 at sea level with 45° wing sweep… or above Mach 1.5 at sea level with a wing sweep of only 15°. Given the minimal study, these numbers are likely highly tentative and were meant to be used to help guide future studies.

Fairchild NEPA N-3

Fairchild was the first company to be contracted to work on atomic propelled aircraft, and produced several designs for supersonic atomic-powered bombers. Unfortunately, the available information on these early designs presents configurations that are best described as 'crude'. It may well be that these designs truly were only roughly designed, or it may be that detailed and well considered designs were reproduced with reduced fidelity. A brochure produced by Fairchild in 1951 described a range of nuclear powered bombers; most were subsonic, but two were supersonic.

The N-3 design was a rotund vehicle with a centrally located reactor surrounded by an annular ring of six turbojets, each generating 11,900lb of thrust. In the brochure the engine is described as an 'open' or 'air' cycle, otherwise known as a Direct Cycle type where the air that passed through the compressor then goes directly through the reactor, then out through the turbines. The reactor wall temperature was 2,500°F, while the turbine air inlet temperature was 1,900°F.

The overall configuration, apart from the annular engine cluster, was recognizably '1950s', with mid-mounted thin (3%) tapering unswept wings. The canopy was small but raised, providing a fair bit of visibility for the pilot (and only the pilot). The vertical fin was unusually 'curvy'. No indication is given in the available art or diagrams about the arrangement of control surfaces.

Fairchild NEPA N-4

The propulsion system for the N-4 used a 'compound liquid metal cycle'. This variation of the Indirect Cycle used two loops of liquid metal (lithium in both cases)… one passed through the reactor and into a heat exchanger; another loop of liquid metal passed through the heat exchanger and then into the turbojets, replacing the combustors. The reactor had a wall temperature of 1,840°F (doubtless due to the more efficient liquid lithium heat exchange medium) and a turbine air inlet temperature of 1,500°F. The annular ring included ten turbojets, each producing 6,580lb of thrust, around the reactor. The N-4 was in many ways a lower performance system, but where the N-3 cruised at Mach 1.5 at 35,000ft, the N-4 did so at 45,000ft.

The layout was similar to that of the N-3, but stretched in various ways. The wing was similar, but set low; the vertical tail was larger and straighter, less generally cartoonish in appearance. The cockpit canopy was smoothly faired into the nose contours, providing a poorer view, but also lower drag and likely better radiation shielding. Like the N-3, though, the general impression is of a very preliminary concept.

North American Aviation Sodium Vapour Compressor Jet

In 1952 North American Aviation issued a report describing an unusual type of nuclear turbojet applied to a supersonic bomber, work that had been

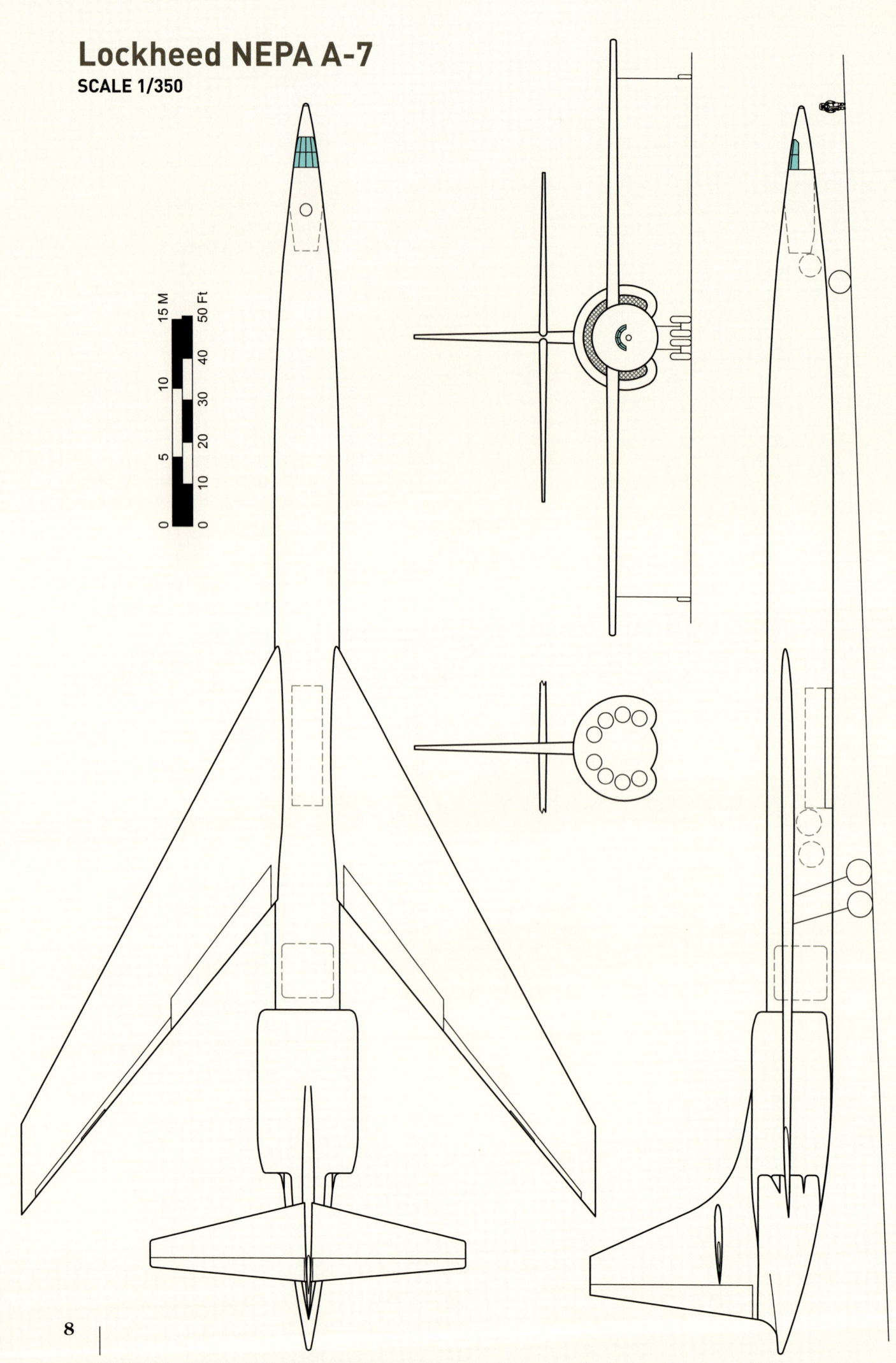

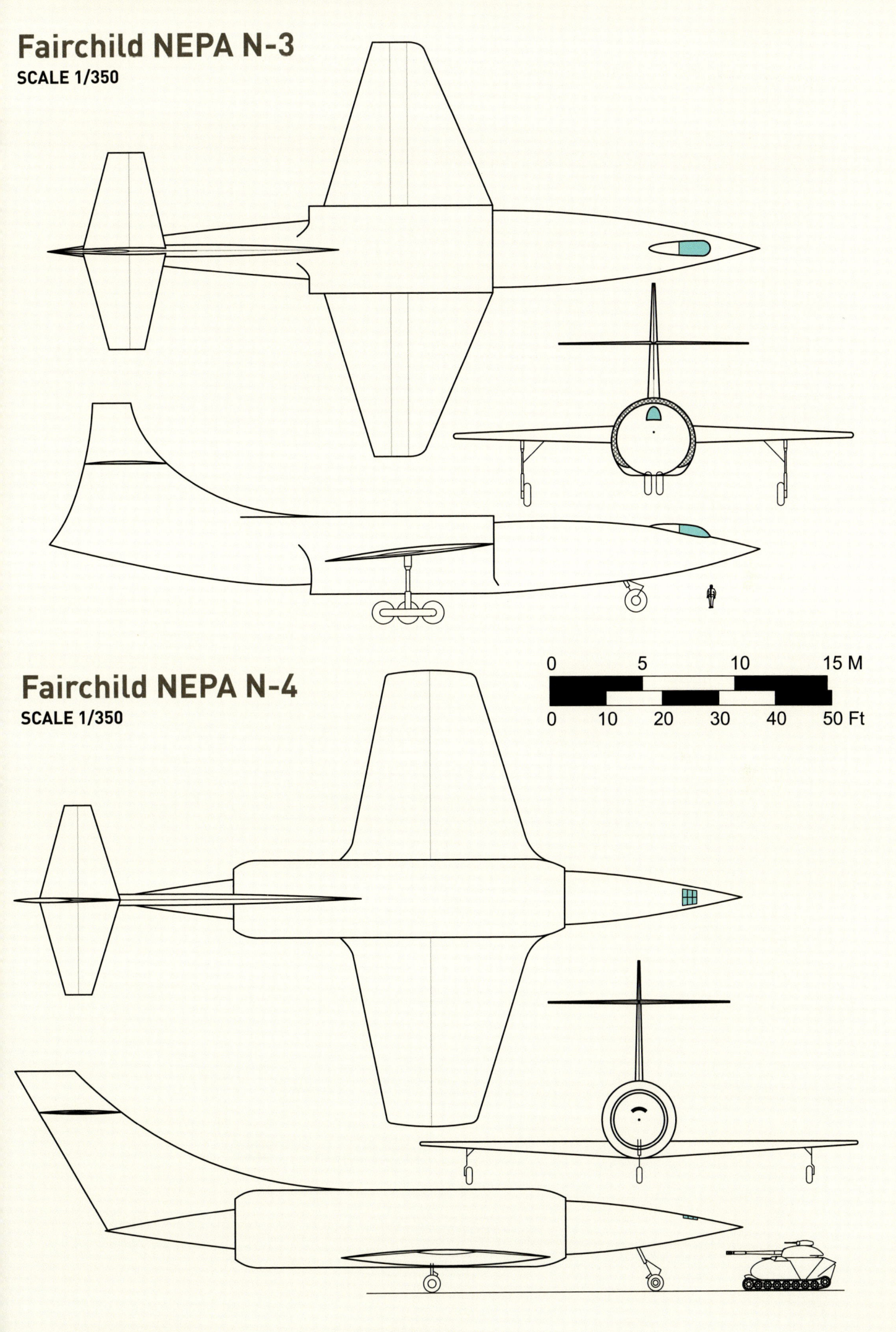

done in 1951 under contract to the Atomic Energy Commission. North American suggested a "sodium vapour compressor jet" as a means of providing the thrust needed for a cruise speed of Mach 1.5.

Sodium metal would not be simply melted but boiled to vapour (at 271lb per second). Sodium would, however, not be the cooling fluid for the reactor; instead, tin would cycle through the reactor to extract heat; a heat exchanger would pass that energy to a loop of liquid sodium. This would require increasing the wall temperature of the reactor from the then-achievable 1,500°F to at least 1,800°F… with the possibility that a reactor temperature of 3,000°F might be necessary (considered attainable with a graphite reactor in a non-oxidizing environment). This uncertainty was due to the technology being in its infancy at the time.

Unlike most nuclear turbojets, the thermal energy from the reactor was not used to replace the chemical combustors of normal turbojets. Instead, the "compressor jets" were composed of compressor stages attached directly to the turbine stages. The superheated pressurized metallic gas would be used to directly drive the turbines; the air flowing through the compressor would, unlike in a turbojet, not pass through the turbine section. The sodium would be a lower pressure mix of vapour and liquid after passing through the turbines; it would be cooled further – and pressure dropped – by running it through a heat exchanger behind the turbojet exhausts. The heat exchanger would superheat the air running downstream of the engines and would serve as a nuclear afterburner. The cooled, lower-pressure sodium would be collected and pumped back up to a higher pressure and re-run through the reactor. The loop would continue indefinitely.

The aircraft carried a single reactor and five compressor-jet engines. A row of three engines side-by-side were topped by two engines side-by-side, fed from a common plenum that was itself fed from two fuselage-side inlets, and exhausting through a common duct through the tail.

The aircraft was of a fairly conventional (for the time) configuration, with thin swept wings and a conventional tail. The forward fuselage was pointed and featureless; a canopy appears to be visible in the available diagram and artwork, but, unusually, the canopy is on the underside of the nose. This indicates that vision for landing was considered paramount. The crew (a rather large number, seven) were housed within a single shielded compartment. The payload was listed as being 20,000lb, but not described further.

NACA Manned Nuclear Designs

The National Advisory Council on Aeronautics spent much of the 1950s looking at nuclear powered flight

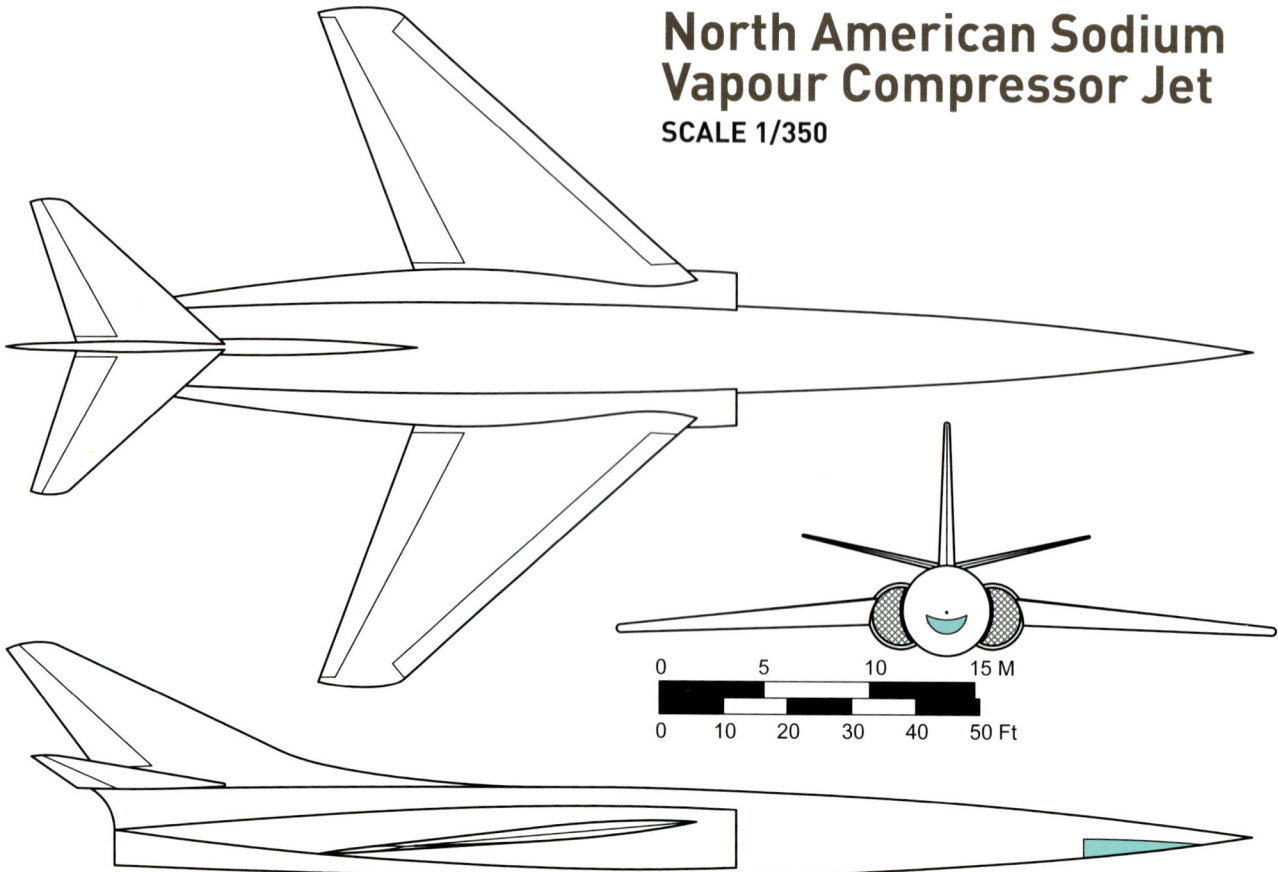

North American Sodium Vapour Compressor Jet
SCALE 1/350

NACA Concepts
SCALE 1/300

from a more theoretical standpoint. The NACA's job was not to do detailed engineering designs of aircraft but to do the basic science; what they learned would then be used by the American aviation industry to produce actual products. But the NACA did from time to time produce aircraft designs; supersonic nuclear powered bombers were no exception to this rule. Two such concepts have come to light.

From February to September 1952, staff at the NACA Lewis Laboratory studied a manned supersonic aircraft powered by a direct cycle nuclear turbojet engine. The configuration was geometrically simple, being much like a stretched and scaled-up Convair XP-92: a cylindrical fuselage with a very long conical nose, backed by an annular inlet for the engine and a long tapering rear fuselage terminating in a circular exhaust. The wings and vertical tail were simple deltas, 4% thick double-wedge sections. There was no elegance to the design, but the form of the aircraft was not the point of the exercise. Instead, the goal was to demonstrate the possibility of supersonic flight (Mach 1.5 at 35,000ft) with the engine envisioned.

The reactor was located in the centre of the fuselage, surrounded by six turbojets. A water shield surrounded the reactor and a lead shadow-shield was placed ahead of it to protect the crew. The compressors at the front of the engines would dump high pressure air into a common plenum and then pass through the water shield and into the reactor; after being heated, the air would leave the reactor into another common plenum at the rear, then pass through the six individual turbine sections, then out the exhaust nozzle. The compressors and turbines would be lined up and the drive shafts would straddle the reactor, passing through the water shield.

A range of vehicle and reactor sizes were studied, all based on the same performance requirements. The design shown here is the 'Case IIA' configuration, a conservative concept based on ceramic fuel elements with a core temperature of 2660° Rankine and a turbine inlet temperature of 2,000° Rankine. The reactor would be 8.5ft in diameter, 3.14ft long and would produce 504,000 Btu/sec of heat.

There was a very sizable cockpit transparency, but that was just the aerodynamic fairing. Behind the very large panes of relatively thin glass or plastic were the much smaller, much thicker windows of the lead and plastic shielded crew compartment. No indication is given of the payload or location of the payload bay, though it would be reasonable to assume it would have been located in the cylindrical section of the fuselage ahead of the inlets.

Even before the 1950s, nuclear ramjets were envisioned under project NEPA. While the bulk of the work done for NEPA and its successor ANP was aimed at nuclear powered turboprops and turbojets, the nuclear ramjet was nonetheless understood to have some potential value. The ramjet's advantage – high speed – did not compare well to its disadvantages – poor subsonic performance, and virtually no low-speed performance. Consequently few nuclear ramjet configurations were proposed for manned aircraft. But 'few' is not the same as 'none'.

A NACA concept from 1957 used two General Electric AC-210 nuclear ramjets located side by side at the rear of the fuselage. This design was done to even less engineering fidelity than the earlier NACA concept if the sole document known on the subject is accurate; only a simplistic top view is known. Consequently, the side and front views reproduced here are fairly speculative.

At the request of the Air Force a preliminary design was performed at the NACA Lewis Flight Propulsion Laboratory for an aircraft capable of cruising at Mach 4.25 with a crew of one while carrying a 10,000lb payload. The NACA report does not describe the aircraft as a bomber, but several details point to that being the role.

This design put the cockpit roughly in the middle of the fuselage, rather that at the forward end. This drove the need for a massive shield surrounding the cockpit, in this case made of lead and water. The pilot had no direct vision to the outside world. Ahead of the cockpit was a cylindrical volume for 'instruments', and ahead of that was another cylindrical volume for 'payload'. The payload is described solely as weighing 10,000lb… a common generic weight for a single nuclear bomb. In this case it seems the bomb would be carried in a vertical orientation.

The nuclear ramjets were optimized for cruise, and would have struggled to produce meaningful thrust below Mach 2.5. Consequently, the aircraft would have required some form of booster; that was left undefined, but likely would have been a sizable vertically-launched rocket system.

Lockheed CL-285-815

The CL-285-815 was one of a series of designs for nuclear powered supersonic bombers produced by Lockheed in 1954. While details on this and other CL-285 designs are extremely lean, what is clear is that this was a somewhat confusing design. It was meant to attain Mach 2.85; this indicates that the long straight outer wing panels were to be jettisoned. This arrangement is quite similar to that of the 'three ship formations' produced by Boeing and North American in 1955 in response to the requirements of WS 110A (see *US Supersonic Bomber Projects Volume 1*).

While the extra wing area would allow the aircraft to loiter or cruise at lower power (and thus radiation) levels,

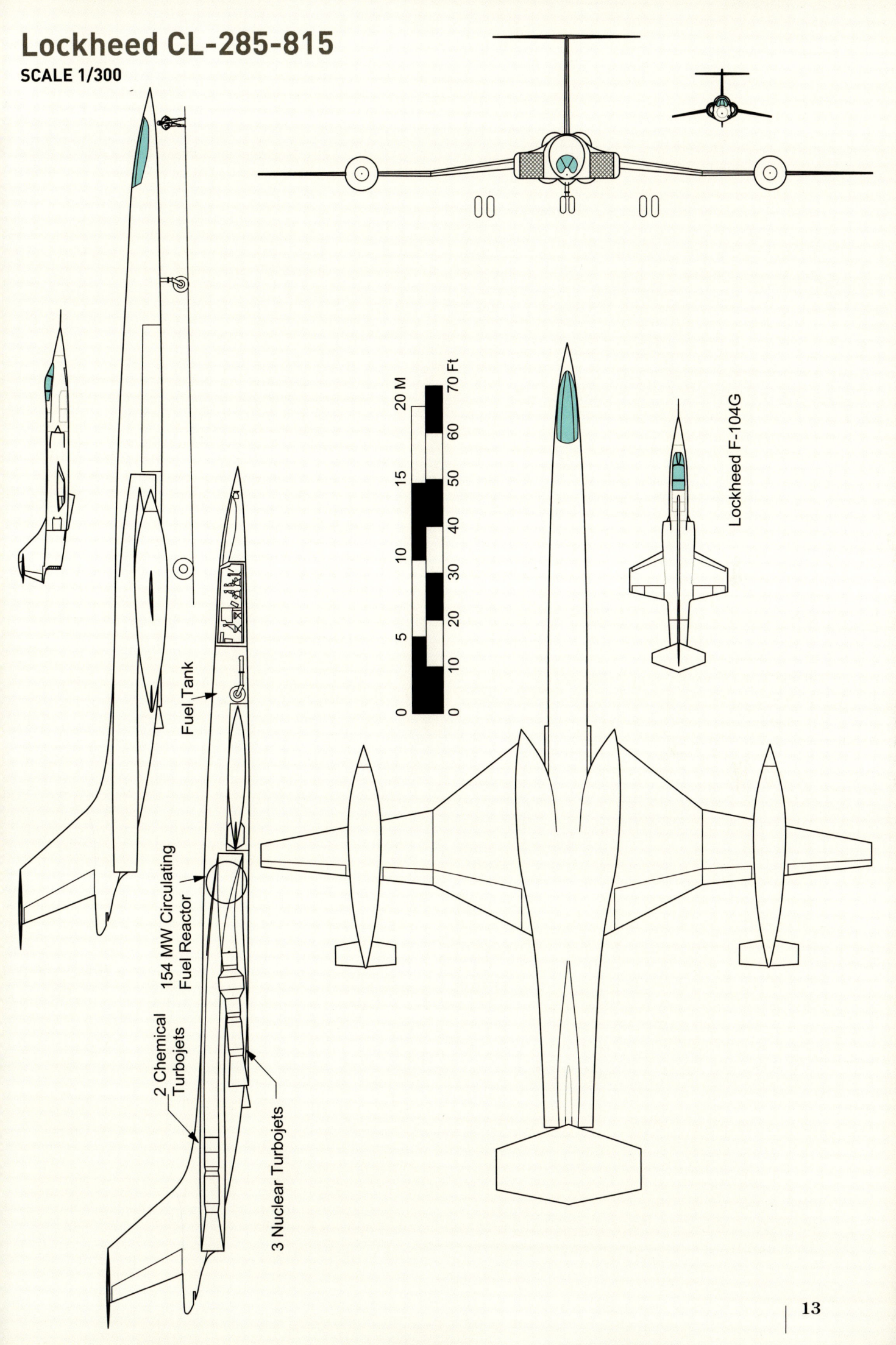

it's unclear what need the craft would have for the large mid-span chemical fuel tanks. It may be possible that the tanks were actually weapons pods, but there is no evidence to support that. The available drawings show the CL-285-815 fitted with a single very large and very aerodynamic gravity bomb, presumably a high-yield thermonuclear device designed for jettisoning at high supersonic speeds. A 30mm gun was located in the tail, along with its own radar, for self-defence. The extreme nose held a forward-looking warning radar; behind and below that, looking forward and downward, was a bombing and navigation radar.

The aircraft had five turbojets. Three were nuclear powered, fed superheated liquid metal from a single 154 megawatt nuclear reactor; two were chemically fuelled. The chemical engines would presumably be used for takeoff and for high speed flight over the target. The crew were positioned in a relatively long but narrow and heavily shielded compartment mounted well forward. The pilot was granted only a relatively small forward window, very likely of foot-thick leaded glass.

To maintain aerodynamic contours, an expansive windscreen ahead of the window was faired into the fuselage. The canopy gives the impression of a cockpit located in the extreme nose, but in fact the cockpit was well aft of the canopy, not underneath it. So even though the outer canopy was relatively gigantic, the actual field of view the pilot would have had would have been fairly minimal.

The CL-285-815 is not described in the available information as a response to WS-125A (programme described shortly...), but the timing would suggest the distinct possibility. Given that WS-125A and WS-110A were contemporaneous programmes, it is just barely conceivable that the confusing combination of design features was because the aircraft was intended as a response to both sets of requirements: perhaps there was meant to be a fully chemically fuelled version that would need the extended wing panels and fuel tanks (fulfilling the WS-110A requirement), and a purely nuclear vehicle that did not need the added fuel tanks. In general, chemical fuel was used by nuclear powered aircraft for a boost during takeoff and again for high speed dash, but the large external fuel tanks were connected to the extended wing panels which would have had to have been jettisoned prior to dash.

Lockheed CL-286-665

Known from a single diagram, the Lockheed L-286-665 was a 1954 design somewhat similar to the CL-285-815. It was equipped with a single 161 megawatt nuclear reactor mounted well aft in a long slim fuselage that fed superheated air to two turbojets; two additional chemically fuelled turbojets were included. The chemical engines were no doubt meant to be used during takeoff and dash, with the plane cruising – likely subsonically – on pure nuclear power.

The crew of five were contained in a heavily shielded cockpit module well forward of the reactor. As with the CL-285-815, the pilots had relatively small forward-viewing thick leaded glass windows; beyond those was a vast transparent fairing. The drawing shows a single fairly enormous bomb carried internally, apparently the same as that used on the CL-285-815. Unlike the prior design, the CL-286-665 had neither extended wings nor external fuel tanks. As with the CL-285-815, it had a 30mm tail gun plus a warning and a bombing/navigation radar in the nose.

GE Supersonic System 6X

In 1955 General Electric made a design study for a bomber powered by nuclear engines capable of sustained supersonic cruising. General Electric was, and remains, a manufacturer of aircraft engines, not a designer of airframes, so the design work was highly hypothetical. The aircraft was a 'rubber design', with variables such as weights, dimensions, number of engines and so on, but several layouts were produced and discussed. One such had the designation '6X', and was the largest of the series.

The 6X featured six nuclear turbojet engines; two in the extreme tail, two each stacked vertically behind and below the root of the wing trailing edge. The engines were powered by a single reactor which provided superheated air to the turbojets. No chemical fuel would be used in either interburning or afterburning. But even without chemical augmentation, General Electric felt confident that a cruise speed of Mach 3.5 was possible above 35,000ft, with the reactor providing 2,500°F air at the turbine inlets.

The overall configuration was vaguely similar to that of the Lockheed F-104, with relatively small, thin (3% thickness biconvex) unswept shoulder mounted wings and side-mounted inlets. The cockpit was at the extreme forward end of the fuselage and was granted extremely large transparencies for a nuclear powered aircraft. This was due to a belief that the shielding directly around the reactor might prove sufficient; the cockpit itself was offered in an unshielded option.

Doubtless the five man crew would have been little comforted by the knowledge that their cockpit was unshielded; at least they'd have a good view of the air around the forward fuselage as it reflected nuclear radiation back at them.

Convair WS-125A

In October 1954, the USAF put out requirements for two supersonic bombers, the WS-110A and the WS-125A. These were intended as replacements for the Boeing B-52; while that aircraft had only just started

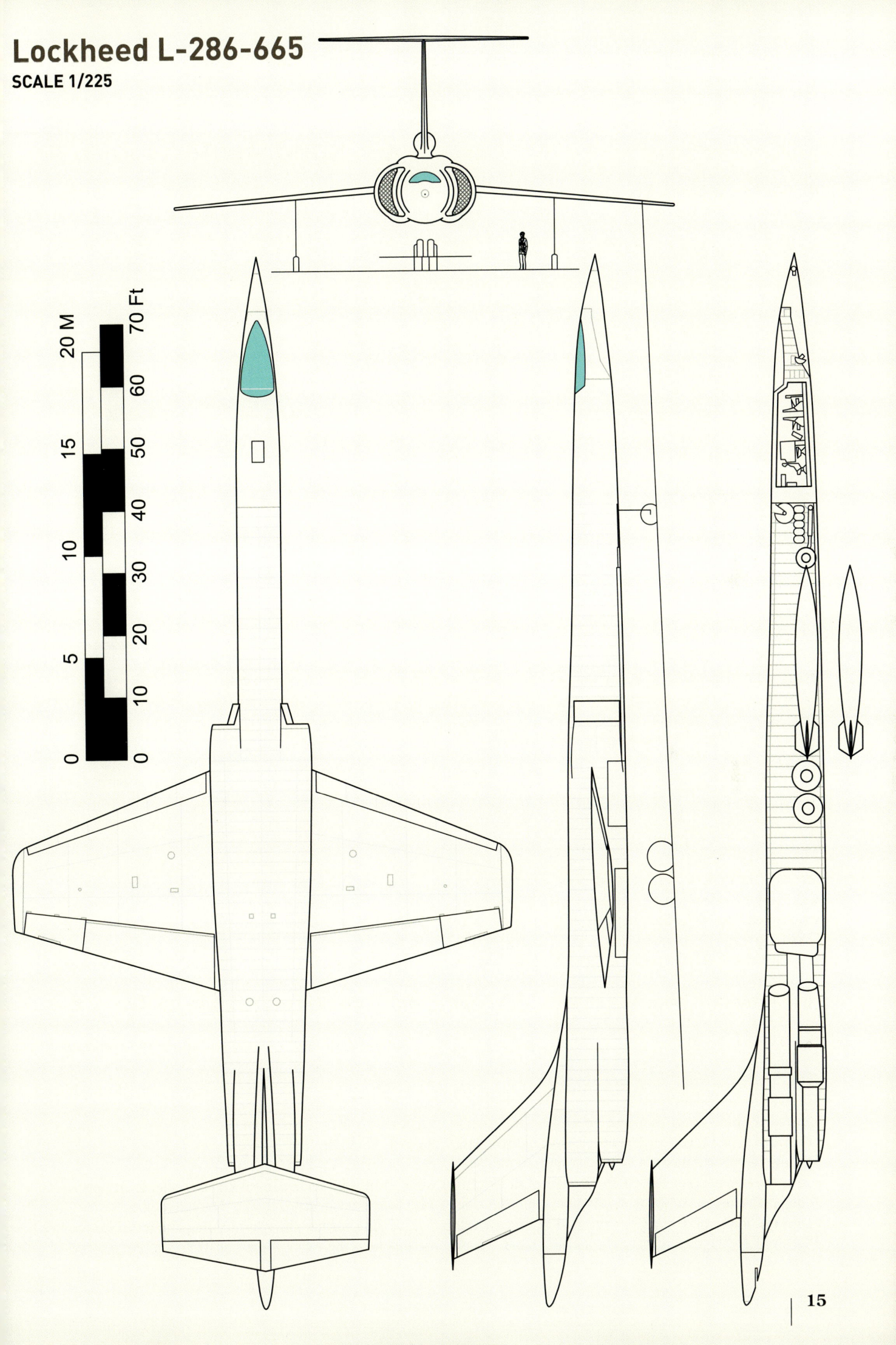

GE Supersonic System 6X
SCALE 1/200

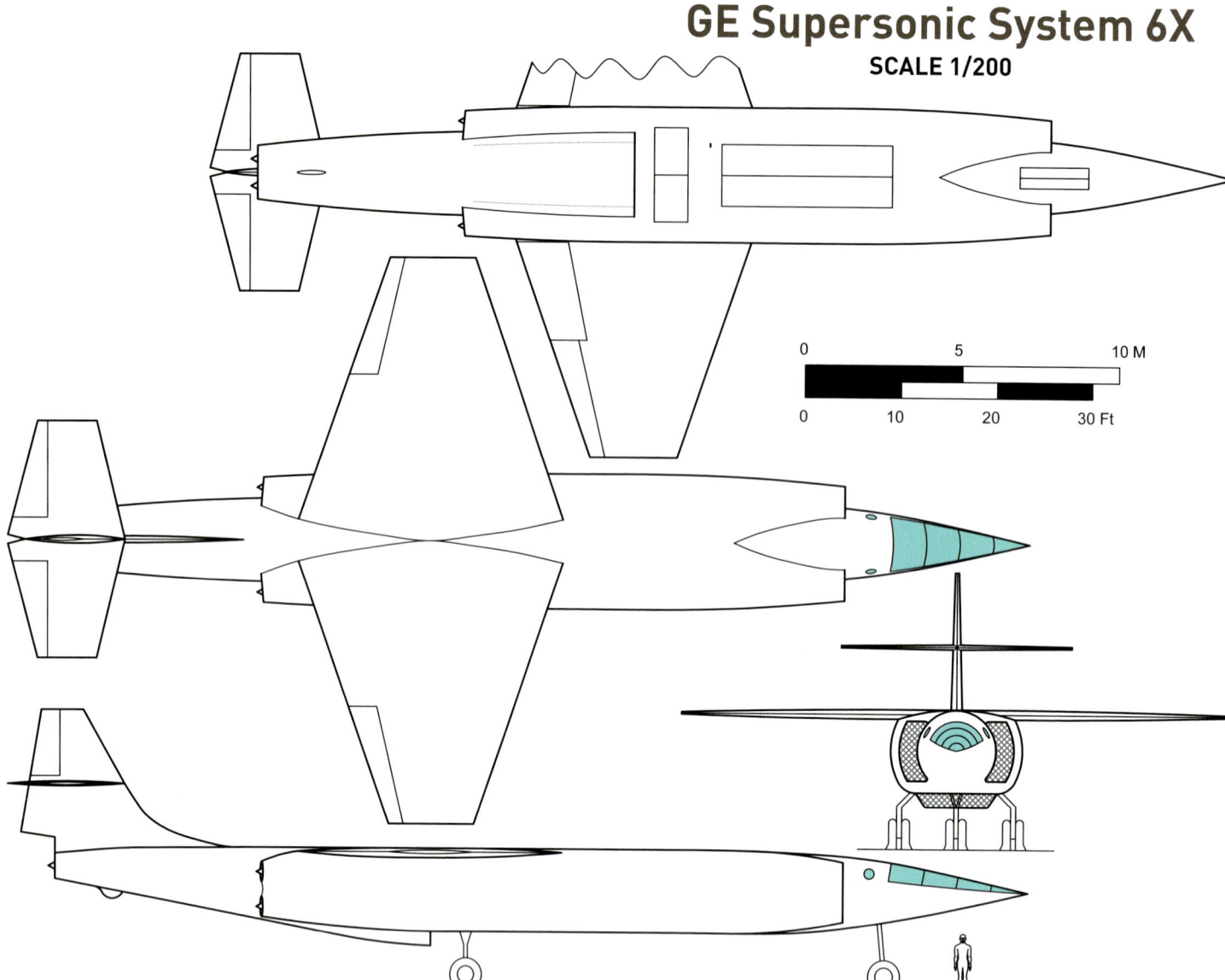

entering service, at the time it was expected that obsolescence would come fast and that by 1965 an entirely new bomber would be needed.

Both the WS-110A and WS-125A were to be supersonic strategic bombers, the main difference being that the WS-110A was to be chemically powered with the WS-125A being nuclear powered. Both were to have the speed of the B-58 and the payload of the B-52.

The Strategic Air Command did not truly want two very different aircraft to replace the B-52, but it was felt that systems developed for the less technically aggressive (and thus safer and cheaper) WS-110A could be applied to the WS-125A. In the end, Boeing, Douglas, Martin and North American decided to pursue the WS-110A, the competition for which resulted in the North American Aviation XB-70 (see *US Supersonic Bomber Projects Volume 1*), while Convair and Lockheed went after – and received contracts for – the WS-125A.

The WS-125A was required to cruise at Mach 0.9 and have a mission radius of 11,000 nautical miles of which 1,000 nautical miles was to be at Mach 2 and 60,000ft altitude. Lockheed and Convair both put forward several conceptual designs, though detailed descriptions of them remain unavailable at this time.

In late 1956 Convair designed a WS-125A – the Model 25 – that appeared as a cross between the B-58 and the B-70. Minimal information is currently available on it beyond a layout diagram. A modified delta wing was married to a very long fuselage and a conventional tail unit. Four nuclear turbojet engines – two General Electric AC-110s – were contained in a pack underneath the rear fuselage, fed by wing root inlets. Additional engines were in individual pods under the wings; these were chemically fuelled, used for takeoff and high speed dash but powered down during subsonic cruise.

The wingtips had different leading and trailing edge sweeps than the main wing, and were supposed to be

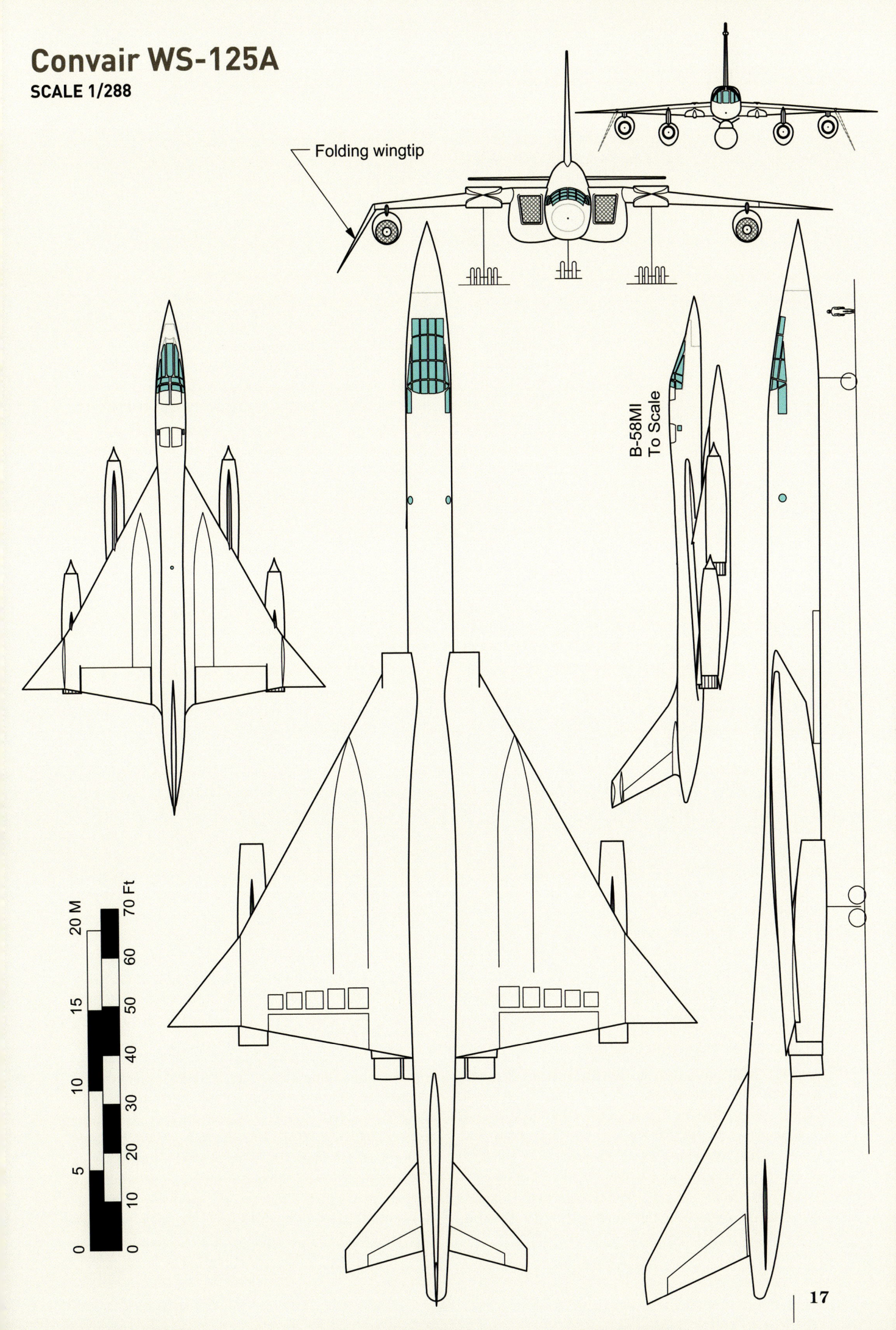

able to fold down in much the same way as the B-70 wingtips. The cockpit canopy was surprisingly large with a number of individual panes. This probably indicates that the crew compartment was a heavily shielded pod within the fuselage. In order to give the pilots a fair view, the external windscreens would have to be quite large. An "Advanced Model 25" was said to have a folding nose to improve pilot visibility during landing, but that feature does not seem to be present in this layout.

As shown in the diagram, the Convair WS-125A was quite a bit larger than the B-58 but shared many configuration similarities. Shown here specifically is the proposed B-58 Model Improved, which used not only similar folding wingtips but also used cockpit canopies of remarkably similar appearance. It seems quite possible that the same designers worked on both concepts.

The extreme range available to the WS-125A meant that even though its bases would be doubtless known to the Soviets, the direction the bombers would come in from would not. The bombers would not need to take a fuel-conserving direct course, but could instead follow a dog-leg pattern far from Soviet air defences. The bombers could then penetrate Soviet airspace from many unpredictable and difficult to intercept vectors. The need to expend chemical fuel for the high speed dash was a limiting factor, as was crew fatigue and radiation dosage. But given the likelihood that these bombers would only be used in the event of all-out thermonuclear war, the crews would doubtless have been considered expendable. The nuclear engines could be used as purely chemical-fuel burners, with the reactor safely shut down; this would greatly restrict the range and duration of the aircraft, but it would permit radiation-free training and ferrying flights.

Lockheed CL-293-64

The earliest known Lockheed attempt to design an aircraft to meet the WS-125A requirement was the CL-293 programme from 1955. Little remains of this effort, but a good diagram of the CL-293-64 is available. A very long and thin fuselage was mated to a BOMARC-like wing and a large T-tail; two circular inlets on either side of the fuselage fed into three turbojets each. This was part of the Pratt & Whitney NJ-2 nuclear propulsion system, powered by a single 320 megawatt nuclear reactor. The diagram does not show the location of the reactor, but it is likely just above the engines in the uplifted fuselage.

The wings feature substantial anhedral and unusual small fences both above and below near the wingtips. The nose is remarkably long ahead of the cockpit. Performance fell below what was required of WS-125A, with the dash phase – Mach 2.5 at 61,000ft, using chemical augmentation – only having a radius of 312 nautical miles. This was well below the 1,000 nautical miles the Air Force wanted. To alleviate this, the CL-293-64 was designed to carry a single ML293-4 airbreathing missile under the fuselage, or a 10,000lb weapon internally.

Lockheed CL-315-1

The CL-315-1 was a refinement of the CL-293. Externally the configuration is much like that of the CL-293, but with somewhat larger squared-off wings. Internally there were important changes, however… there were now four nuclear turbojets and four chemical turbojets. Unfortunately little else is available on this design that was transferred from Lockheed-California to Lockheed-Georgia.

Lockheed 'Blackjack' WS-125A

Lockheed studied many configurations for WS-125A; one of the more unconventional approaches was taken by a concept dubbed 'Blackjack'. Here the subsonic cruise and supersonic dash segments of the mission were broken distinctly apart. A nuclear powered 'tug' aircraft would tow a conventionally powered 'dash' aircraft for the subsonic phase, releasing the dash component to carry out the supersonic strike mission using conventional chemical engines. The 'Blackjack', from July of 1956, was composed of two very different aircraft, the CL-319-35 and the CL-326.

The CL-326 was the tug aircraft, known as the "Combination Airplane". It was a distinctly subsonic airplane fitted with a Pratt & Whitney NJ-2 propulsion system… a single 300 megawatt nuclear reactor powering six turbojets consuming 400lb of air per second each. If ever an aircraft was to be compared with a tugboat, this would be the one. The fuselage was fairly long and slim, but it was married to a horizontal bank of six turbojets, three on either side, with a barely-swept, fairly stubby wing outboard of those. The slab of engines would serve as a substantial wing in its own right, generating much of the lift the aircraft required. A sizable T-tail provided control and stability.

The reactor would have been fitted in the fuselage between the engines, the long forward fuselage providing shielding for the crew of five. The overall appearance is sturdy rather than elegant, but being nuclear powered it hardly needed elegance. In order to tow the CL-319-35, the CL-326 would be fitted with a tow reel in an aft compartment. When serving as a tow aircraft, the Combination Airplane would not carry offensive armament, leaving the strike role to the other aircraft. However, it would be equipped with two supersonic decoy missiles capable of simulating the

Lockheed CL-293-64
SCALE 1/275

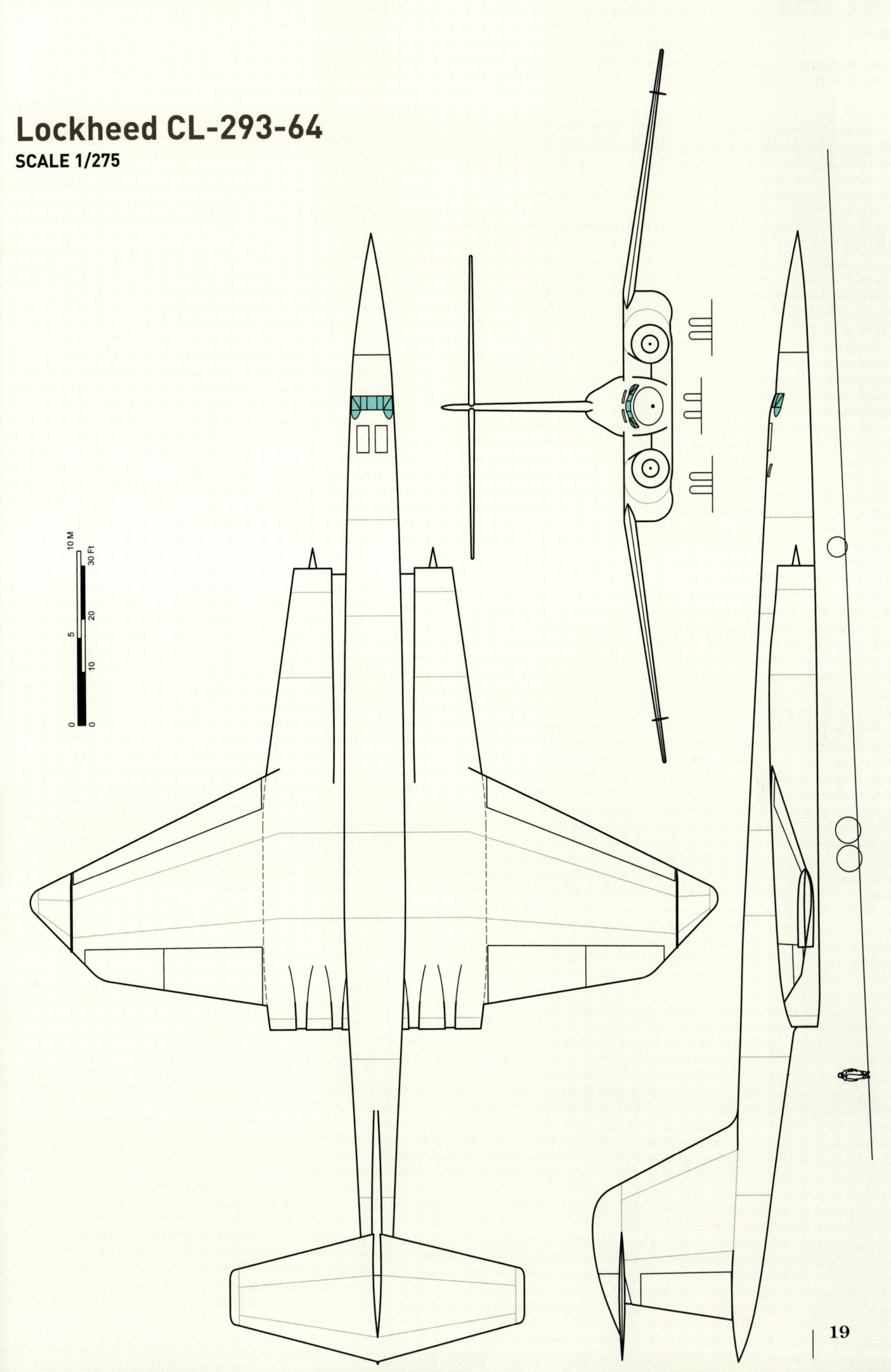

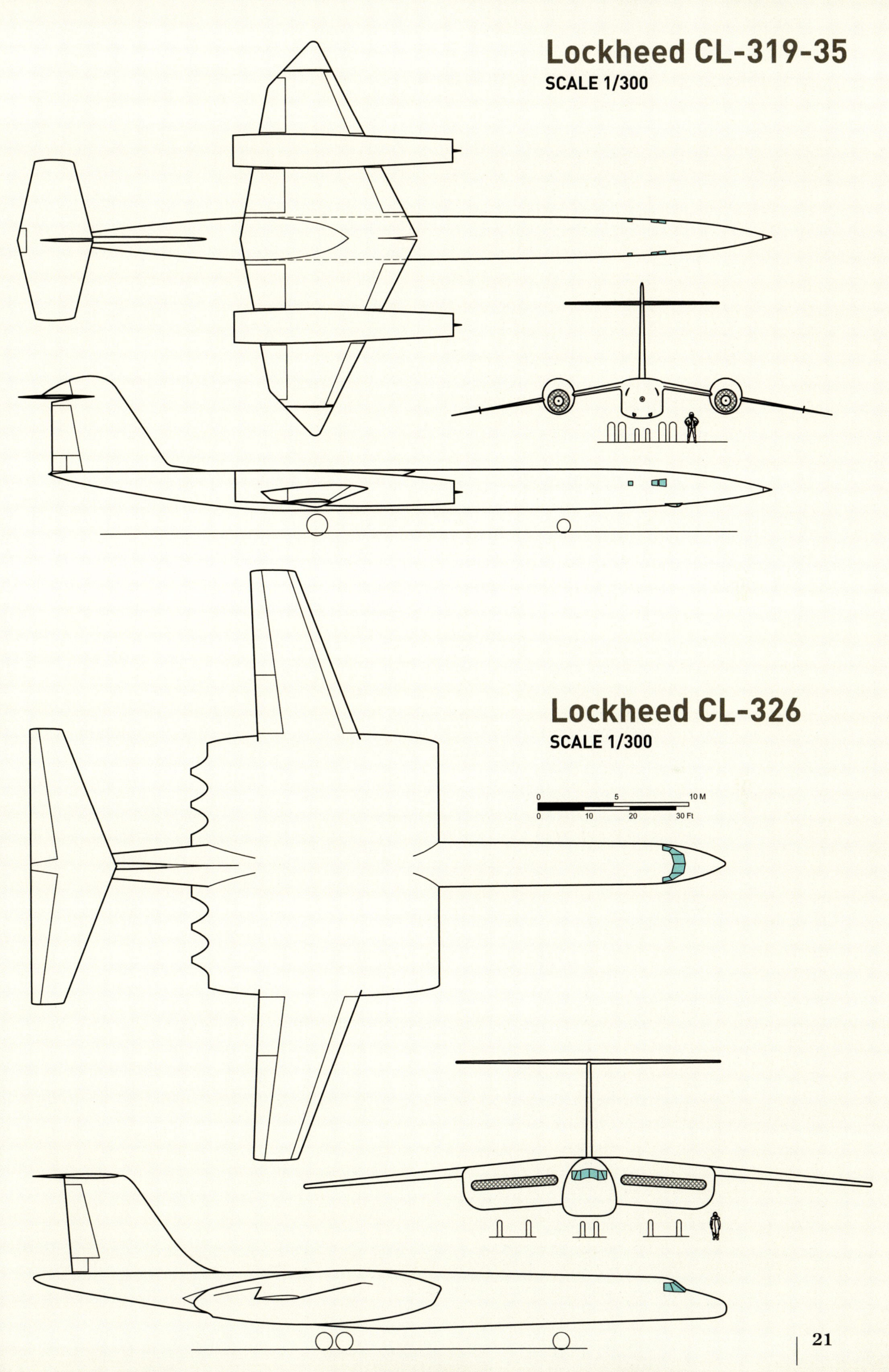

strike aircraft; additional anti-radar missiles could also be carried.

The tug would, in times short of actual war, operate in international airspace, running laps with the strike aircraft; but when the balloon went up the tow plane would go right to the enemy. Nuclear powered and essentially unlimited in range though the CL-326 may have been, the conventionally fuelled strike aircraft had definite range limitations. The tug would get it as close as possible.

The Combination Airplane could also be used as a low altitude bomber in its own right. By removing the tow reel, an aft compartment would be freed up for ordnance.

Lockheed CL-319-35

Derived in part from the CL-293, the CL-319-35 was the chemically fuelled supersonic component known as the "Strike Airplane". It was for the time a conventionally configured supersonic aircraft (bearing a fair resemblance to the British Bristol 188 supersonic research aircraft that first flew in 1962), with low aspect ratio wings fitted with one turbojet nacelle each. The nacelles were large and bisected by the wings; the wings themselves were shoulder mounted and had substantial anhedral. In order to reduce drag, the cockpit was fully faired into the forward fuselage with only a few side-windows for direct vision, and two 'eyes' on the underside providing for landing vision (it's unclear whether these were periscopes or television cameras).

The Strike Airplane and the Combination Airplane would not take off together; they would not even take off from the same airbase. Instead, the Strike Airplane would be based as close as practical to enemy territory; the Combination Airplane further back. The two would rendezvous while en route to the enemy; the Strike Airplane would attach to the tow cable behind the Combination Airplane. Once hooked on, the Strike Airplane's engines would be shut down. The Strike Airplane would then be towed to the enemy, its engines started and the aircraft released to carry out its mission. The Combination Airplane would loiter, flying in circles waiting for the Strike Airplane to return, rendezvous and recouple. The chemical engines would once again be shut down and the bomber towed close to its original base (assuming it still existed).

Boeing Model 722 Studies

While Boeing devoted the bulk of its effort to the WS-110A, it did study nuclear powered bombers both subsonic and supersonic. The company's Model 722 studies are thought to be the designs aimed squarely at the WS-125A requirement; unfortunately not much information seems to be available on them. Diagrams depict a number of Model 722 configurations, but weight and performance data is not included. Dimensions are about all that so far exists on these designs. Given that Boeing is understood to have not turned in a WS-125A proposal, it's entirely possible that the Model 722 designs were little more than basic configurational concepts with little engineering behind them.

Model 722-209 is noted as dating from about 1955 and may be the design intended to be the WS-125A submission. Much like the Convair WS-125A, it had four nuclear turbojets side-by-side in the rear fuselage, likely AC-110s; under each wing was a single chemical turbojet to be used for takeoff and dash. The

Lockheed "Blackjack" WS-125A
SCALE 1/700

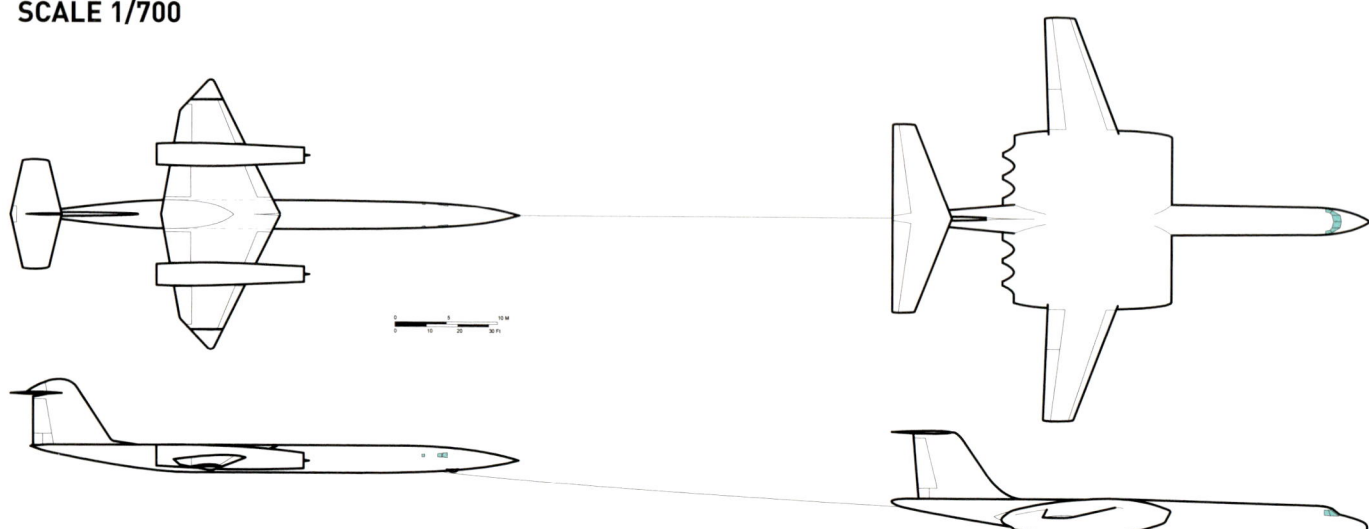

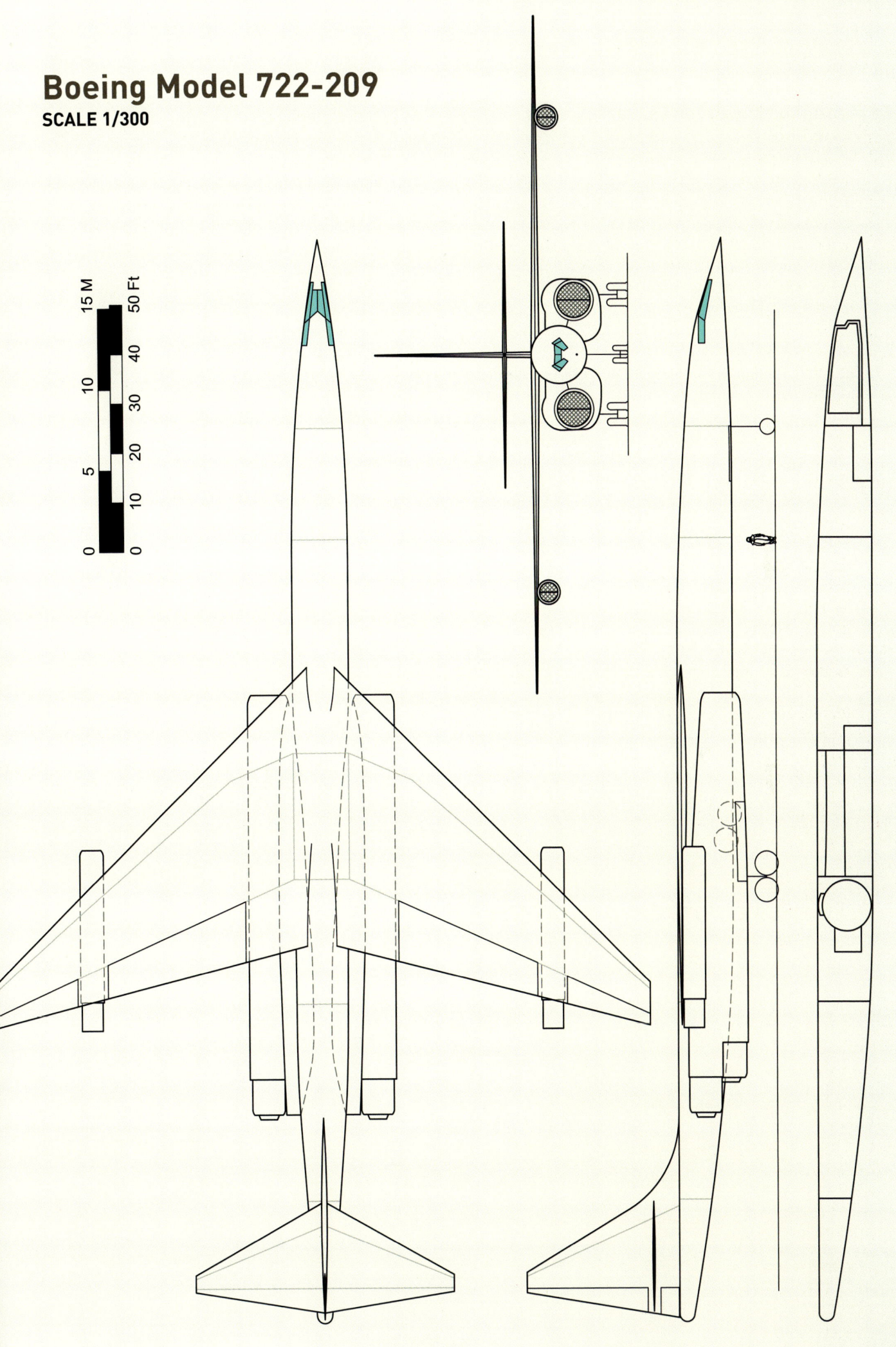

configuration is remarkably like that of its Convair competitor, a result no doubt of convergent evolution – the same requirements, married to the same propulsion technology and aerodynamic understanding, leading to much the same conclusions. The design in the available diagram is not done to the same level of detail and does not include the folding wingtips of the Convair design, rather, simpler swept wings were used. It may be that no detailed report was created for this or any other Model 722 design.

Boeing Model 726 Studies

In 1956, Boeing followed up its WS-125A studies with the Model 726 series. So far all that has emerged on these are diagrams and some basic data, though it is clear that at least some of these designs received a fair amount of effort. Model 726 began as a derivative of the WS-125A, but the designs are wildly divergent and in some cases quite surprising. A major difference between Models 722 and 726 is that the latter had a pair of nuclear turbojets (typically the GE AC-110) while Model 722 had not only four nuclear turbojets but generally two chemical engines as well.

Boeing Model 726-1

Model 726-1 was a fairly conventional configuration. This is not too surprising, given that it was derived – at least somewhat – from the Model 712 Long Range Interceptor. Compared to Model 712, Model 726-1 was scaled up and bloated, with a fairly tubby fuselage married to plain swept wings and a single GE AC-110 nuclear engine which used a single reactor to power two turbojets. A pair of elliptical inlets flanked the fuselage, located below and just ahead of the wing roots. The tail surfaces were fairly small and slim, the vertical stabilizer's narrow tip capped with a long fairing containing antennae.

The internal arrangement isn't available, which makes explaining the seemingly generous window area for the crew – including side windows, not strictly needed for the pilot to land the craft – a bit difficult. Without an interior view it's difficult to say if the surprisingly conventional looking canopy was, like many other nuclear aircraft, simply an aerodynamic fairing well ahead of a thick leaded glass window at the front of the shielded compartment; if this is the case, the side windows may well have been directly to the

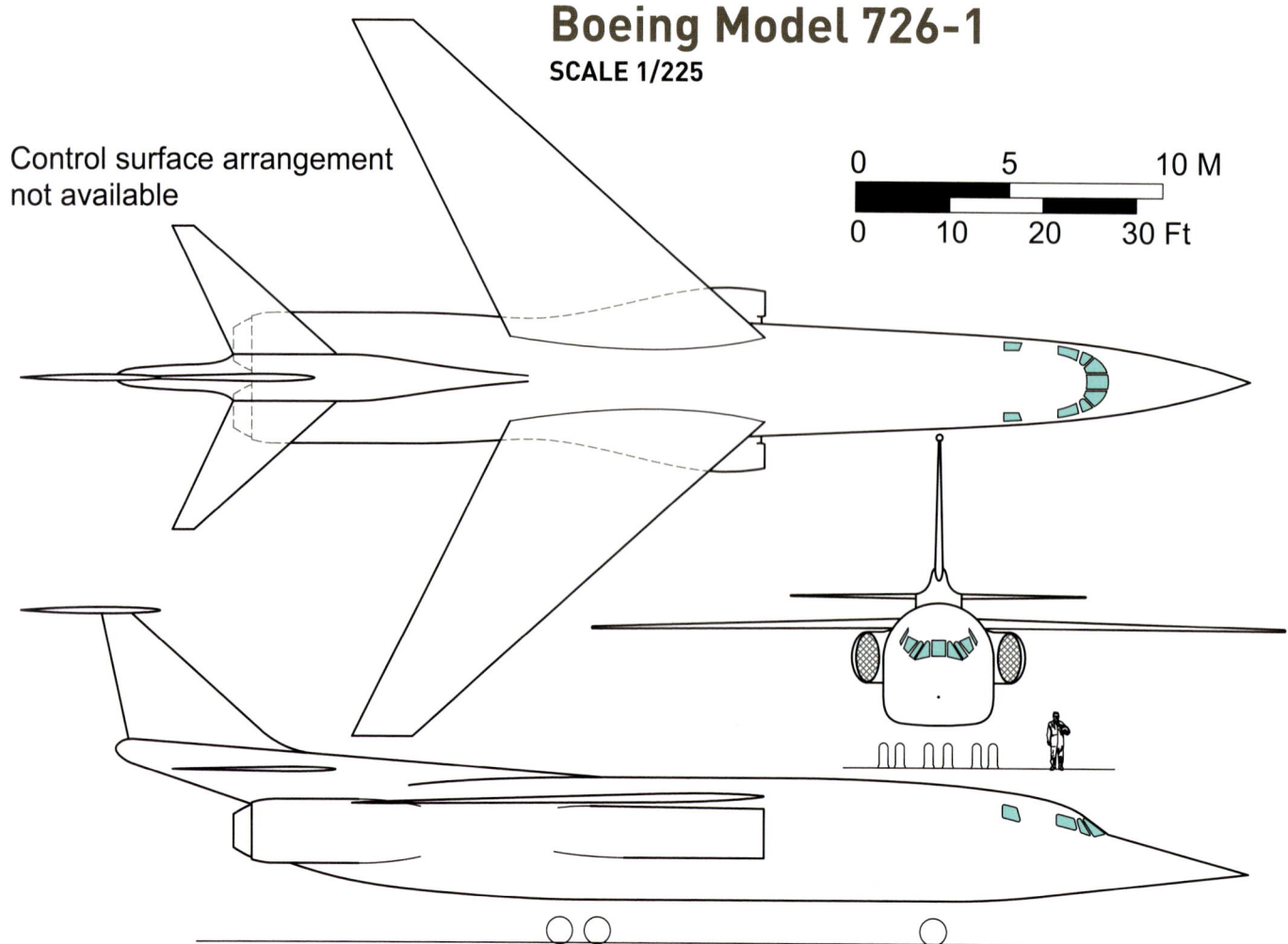

side of the pilot's head. If the visible canopy itself was of thick shielded glass, then the side window would be for the benefit of other crewmen.

It was intended for low level supersonic flight and was submitted to the Air Force as an unsolicited proposal.

Boeing Model 726-3B

This design had a canard and fuselage length was used as a way to gain distance from the reactor for the crew. The 726-3B was a sleeker-looking configuration than the 726-1, with a longer forward fuselage. The pilot and co-pilot sat side-by-side with a third crew position behind them and two more side-by-side further aft still (five crew positions, but the crew complement was only four... the middle seat may have been a place for crew to rest on what could well have been very long missions).

The shielding for the cockpit was fairly thin as such things go, but it was backed up by a jet fuel tank that filled the width and height of the fuselage. The fuel in that tank would be the last to be consumed and would, until it was burned, serve effectively as radiation shielding. Data on this design is almost wholly lacking, but the payload appears to have been one or perhaps two substantial jet-propelled supersonic cruise missiles of some kind. The main wings of these missiles would fold up to facilitate stowage in the bomb bay.

Boeing Model 726-13

Model 726-13 had a particularly odd layout, and according to the available data not designed to any great fidelity. The purpose was to examine the possibility of a configuration that would provide greater safety for the crew in the event of a crash during takeoff or landing. To that end, the crew was ensconced within a heavily shielded cockpit module located far from the reactor... but the cockpit was in the tail rather than the nose. The single General Electric nuclear engine, a single reactor with two jet engines, was located under the nose.

The result was that the bulk of the fuselage, including the weapons bay and chemical fuel tanks, stood between the reactor and the crew, serving as shielding. How the design was supposed to help the crew in the event of a low-speed crash is not clear, unless there was meant to be some means of jettisoning the cockpit module away. However, no indication of that is shown in the available documentation.

Sadly, dimensions are lacking for this configuration. The size of the vehicle was roughly determined from the single clue given about its size... a wing area of 1,245sq ft. No performance data is given, though it's probably safe to assume that it was meant to be modestly supersonic. The configuration has a distinctly 'desperate Messerschmitt end-of-war concept' look.

Boeing Model 726-20

While most of the Model 726 designs used the GE AC-110 engine, which was composed of a single reactor sandwiched between two turbojets, Model 726-20 used two GE AC-107 nuclear engines which had a single reactor integrated inline within a single turbojet. Consequently, Model 726-20 had two separate reactors, each in a nacelle partway out under the wings. Again details are lean. The canopy is different from those of other Model 726 designs; a single transparency serves as an aerodynamic fairing ahead of the small window built into the crew shield. Two small side windows flanked the pilots. With the reactors under the wings rather than in the fuselage, less of the structure and chemical fuel could be used as shielding. This might help explain why the original diagram was relatively crude.

Boeing Model 813-1034

Boeing studied a hypersonic strategic bomber under the Model 813 designation in 1958. While there were design variants, in general they were two-stage vehicles powered by a mix of rockets and ramjets using chemical fuel. However, as a comparison Boeing produced the Model 813-1034 configuration. This variant was different enough as to be virtually unrelated. Instead of being hypersonic, it had a top speed of 'only' Mach 3. Instead of being a two-stage aircraft, it had only the one. And instead of having chemical fuel, it was mixed chemical-nuclear in nature.

Model 813-1034 was a close-coupled canard configuration not unlike that of the Swedish Saab Viggen fighter of about a decade later. It had highly swept clipped delta wings set low on the rear fuselage and similarly clipped delta canards set high on the forward fuselage. To each side of the rear fuselage was an engine nacelle with a translating spike inlet. Each nacelle held a single 104in diameter ramjet engine; inboard of each nacelle, fitting within the rear of the rectangular-cross-section fuselage, were two non-afterburning chemically fuelled Pratt & Whitney J91 turbojets.

The turbojets would serve to get the aircraft from runway to ramjet velocity, as well as providing control for landing. But power for the cruise portion of the mission would come from a single 450-megawatt nuclear reactor within the fuselage, cooled by liquid lithium. The lithium at 1,750°F would exchange heat with liquid sodium-potassium at 1,650°F; this liquid metal would be passed through a radiator in the ramjet, transferring heat to the air at 1,350°F.

Boeing Model 726-3B
SCALE 1/175

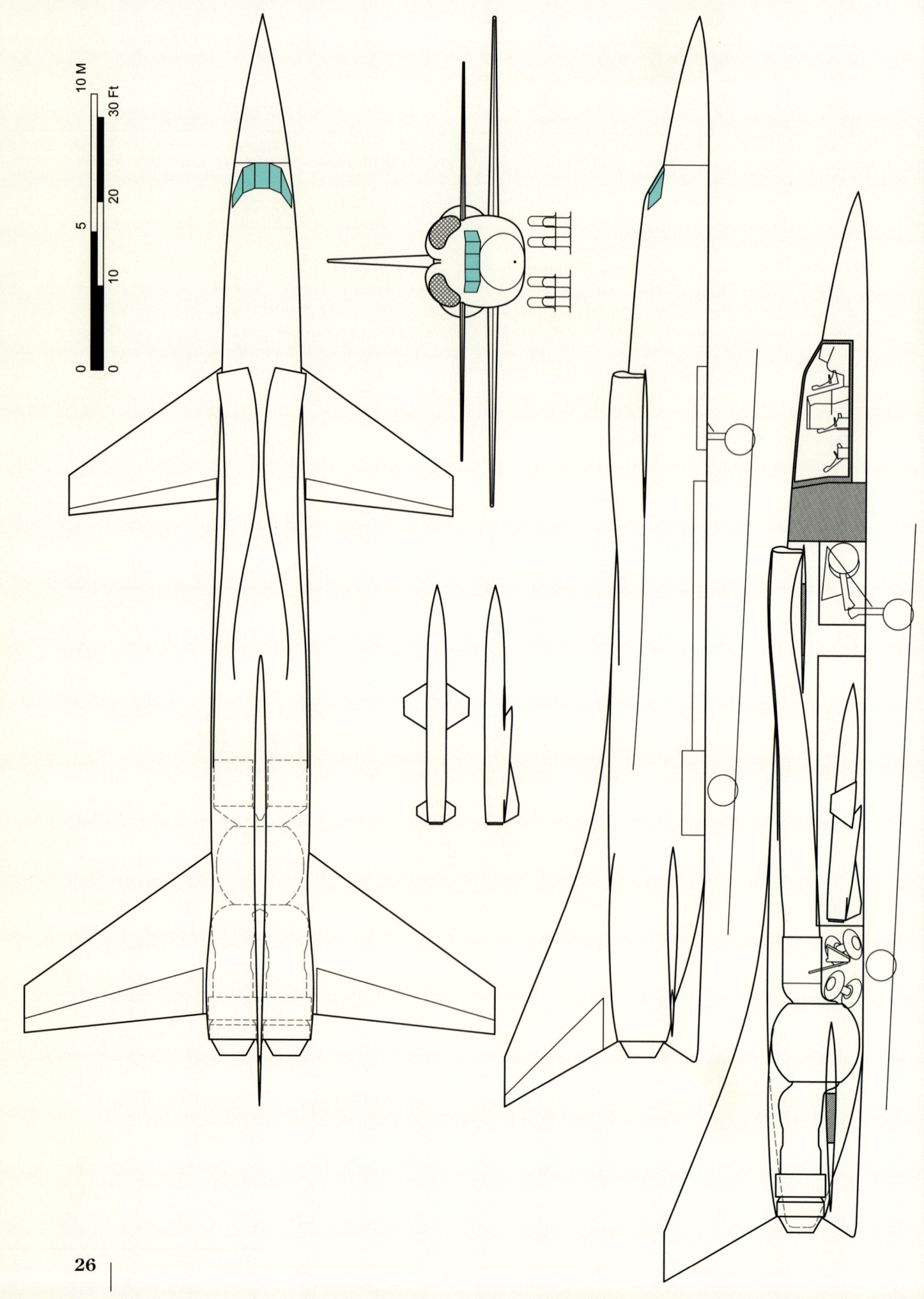

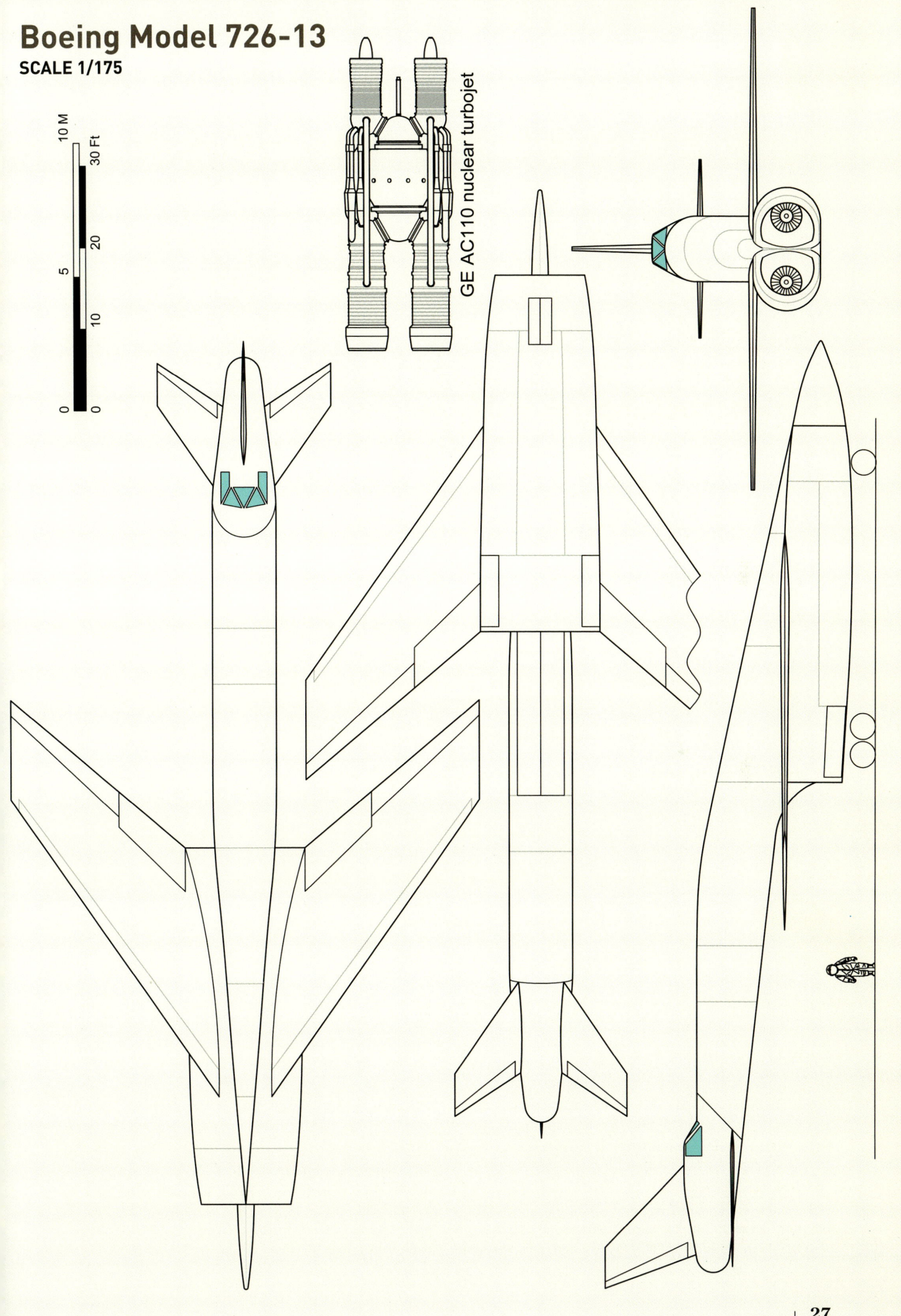

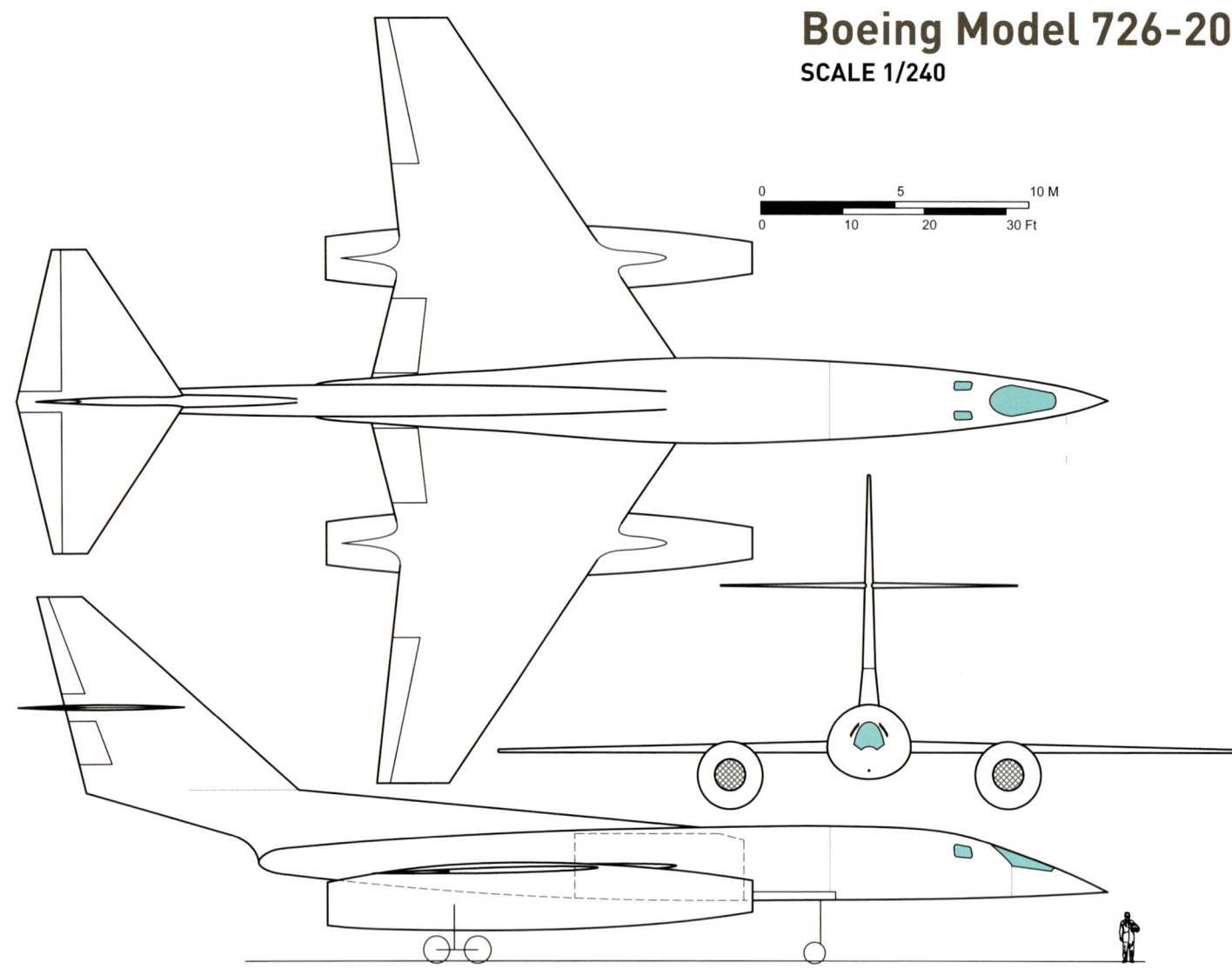

Boeing Model 726-20
SCALE 1/240

The nuclear ramjets would take over from the turbojets and cruise the bomber at Mach 3 and 62,000ft altitude… almost. This was not as high as hoped, and was in fact a little beyond what the aircraft could actually attain. At a temperature of 1,350°F, the ramjets could not quite maintain Mach 3 level flight at any altitude, though at 62,000ft it came close. It was surmised that if the reactor temperature was raised to 2,000°F, it would have more than enough performance to cruise at Mach 3 approaching 70,000ft. A single 10,000lb bomb, or the equivalent of other loads, was to be carried.

Boeing also studied a direct-cycle ramjet, but further details on this variant, apart from the fact that it was a two-stage vehicle, are not currently available.

Republic Mach 4.25

Alexander Kartvelli of Republic Aviation Corporation gave a presentation on future supersonic aircraft in 1960 which included VTOL types and orbit-capable scramjet powered vehicles. One design presented was an unusual bomber powered by nuclear ramjets. Two ramjets based on the GE AC-210-1 nuclear aircraft engines (the same proposed a few years earlier in a NACA study, described previously) would power the aircraft to a cruising altitude of 85,000ft and a cruise speed of Mach 4.25. Mission radius was 8,500 nautical miles, allowing the aircraft to operate from CONUS bases and strike pretty much anywhere. It was expected that it could be operational between 1970 and 1975.

The aircraft looked like nothing so much as two giant engines with wings, each engine being a cylindrical ramjet with an interior conical inlet that gradually necked down to a narrow throat, then expanding back up to the diameter of the hockey puck-shaped nuclear reactor. A convergent-divergent nozzle was behind each reactor. Small canards were mounted to the sides of the engines, with modest swept wings added further aft; vertical fins were atop each wing near the tips.

Boeing Model 813-1034
SCALE 1/240

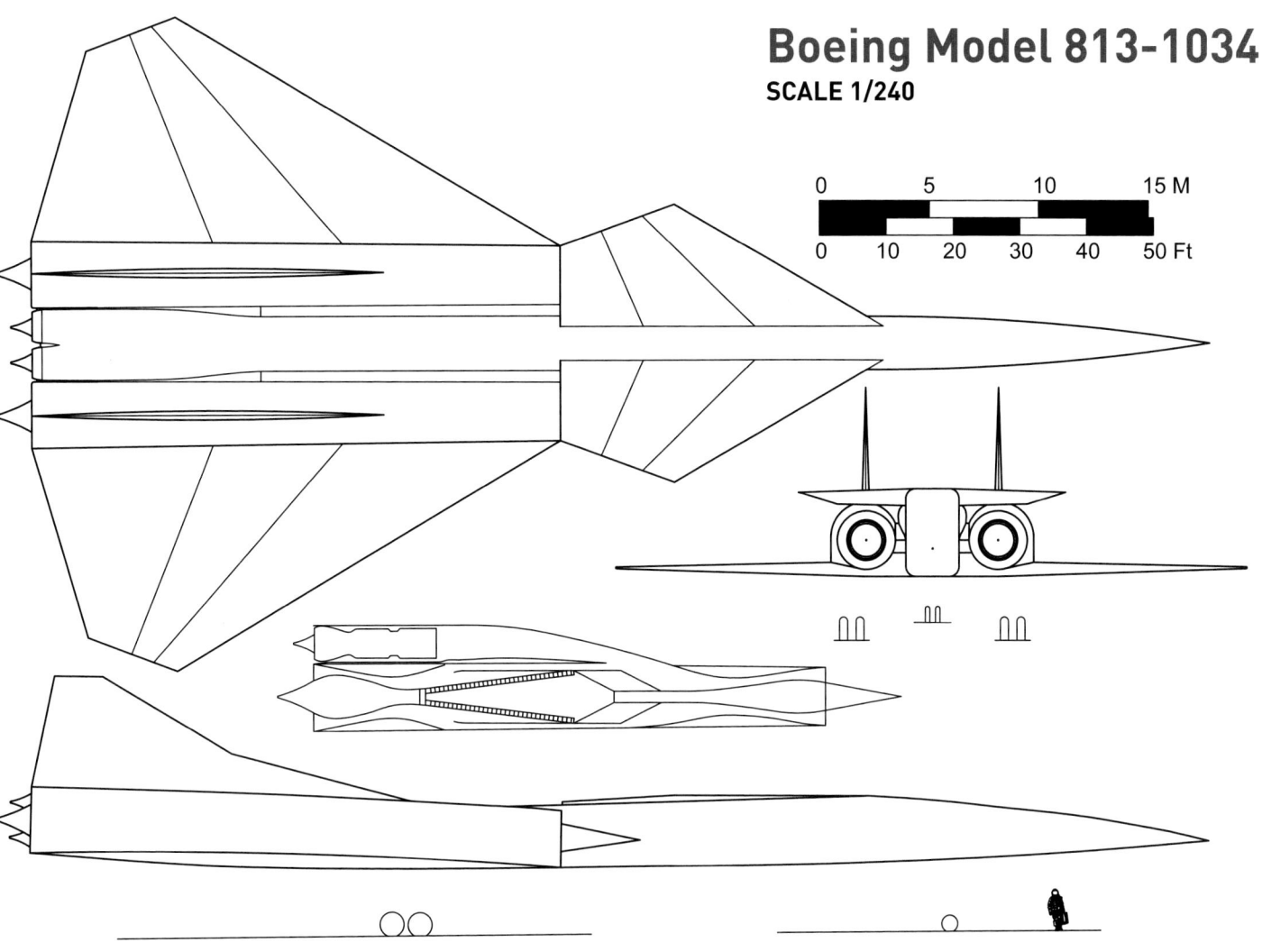

The crew of two were located in a small and massively shielded cockpit at the extreme front, in a faired-in volume between the engine cylinders. While not described, it appears as though the cockpit was a pressurized metallic container, likely lead-lined, suspended within a much larger water-filled 'bath'. The shielding was so extensive that there were no windows and thus no direct vision out of the craft. Flight would have been purely by instruments except for a single periscope used for landing. The nose gear was located directly beneath the cockpit… a necessity given how massive it would have been.

Behind and below the cockpit was the weapons bay. Available artwork depicts two different but fairly generic-looking rocket missiles of indeterminate type and capability. They are probably not representative of an actual weapon, though they might have been intended to represent some sort of air launched ballistic missile.

In order to get up to speed, four solid rocket boosters were used; two with vectorable nozzles, two with fixed nozzles. The launch process was not described, whether the plane lifted off under rocket power horizontally from a runway, or whether it was a zero-length launch off a ramp. Additionally, it's unclear how the rocket staging would have worked. Clearly the second set of boosters could not fire while the first pair were still attached, and firing in the position they are shown the second pair would roast the aft fuselage of the bomber.

The nuclear ramjets would have been useless at low speed. At the end of the mission, the craft would have been a glider… a massively heavy, rather draggy glider dropping at high speed towards a runway that the pilot would have some difficulty seeing clearly. To provide some small measure of control, a trio of J79 turbojets was provided, tucked within the rear fuselage. How air was ducted to the engines and exhausted is ill-defined at best in the available imagery.

It may be that this design was just artistic handwaving, but it should be pointed out that another design presented at the same time – the AP-100 – was the result of substantial serious engineering analysis and testing.

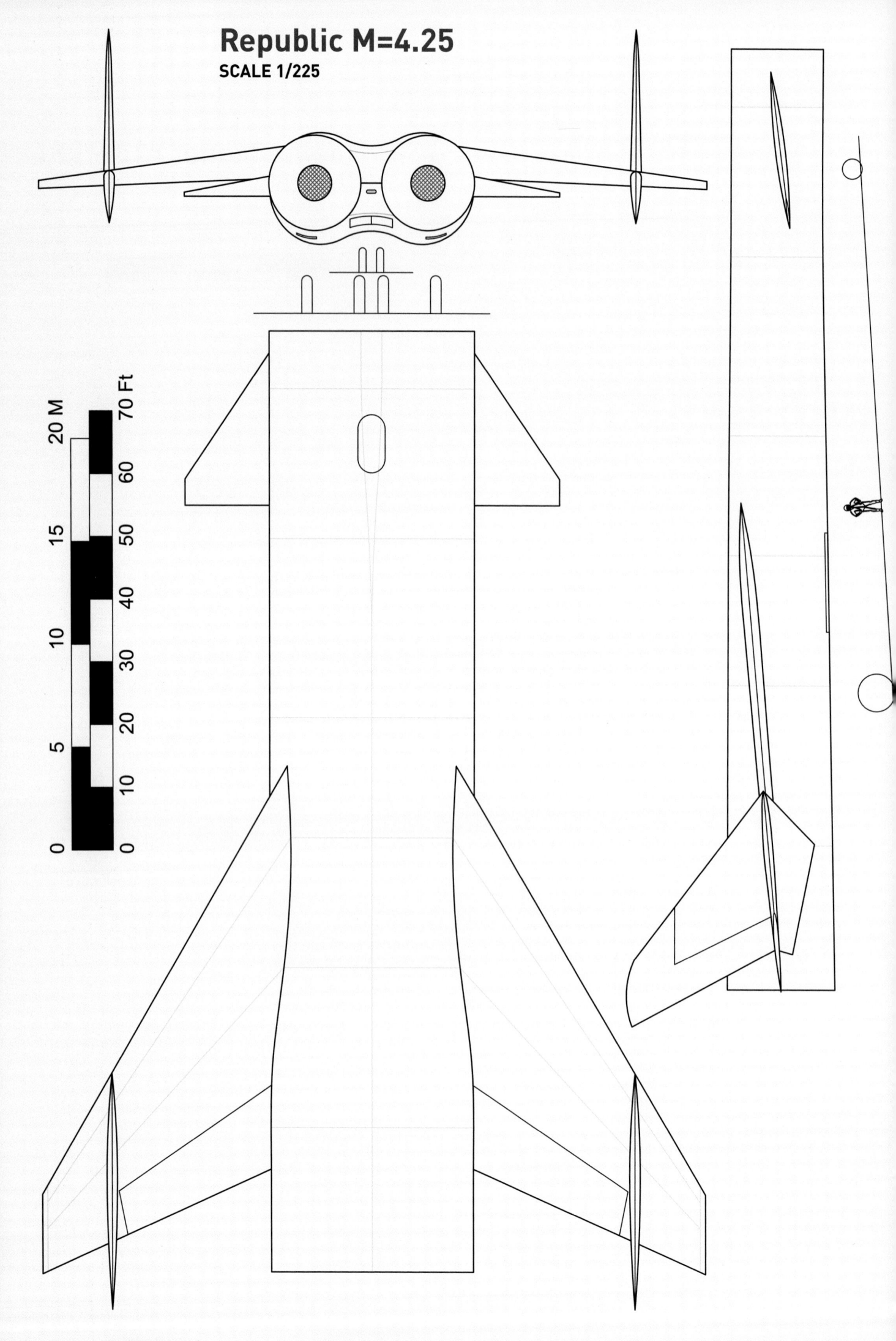

Republic M=4.25
SCALE 1/225

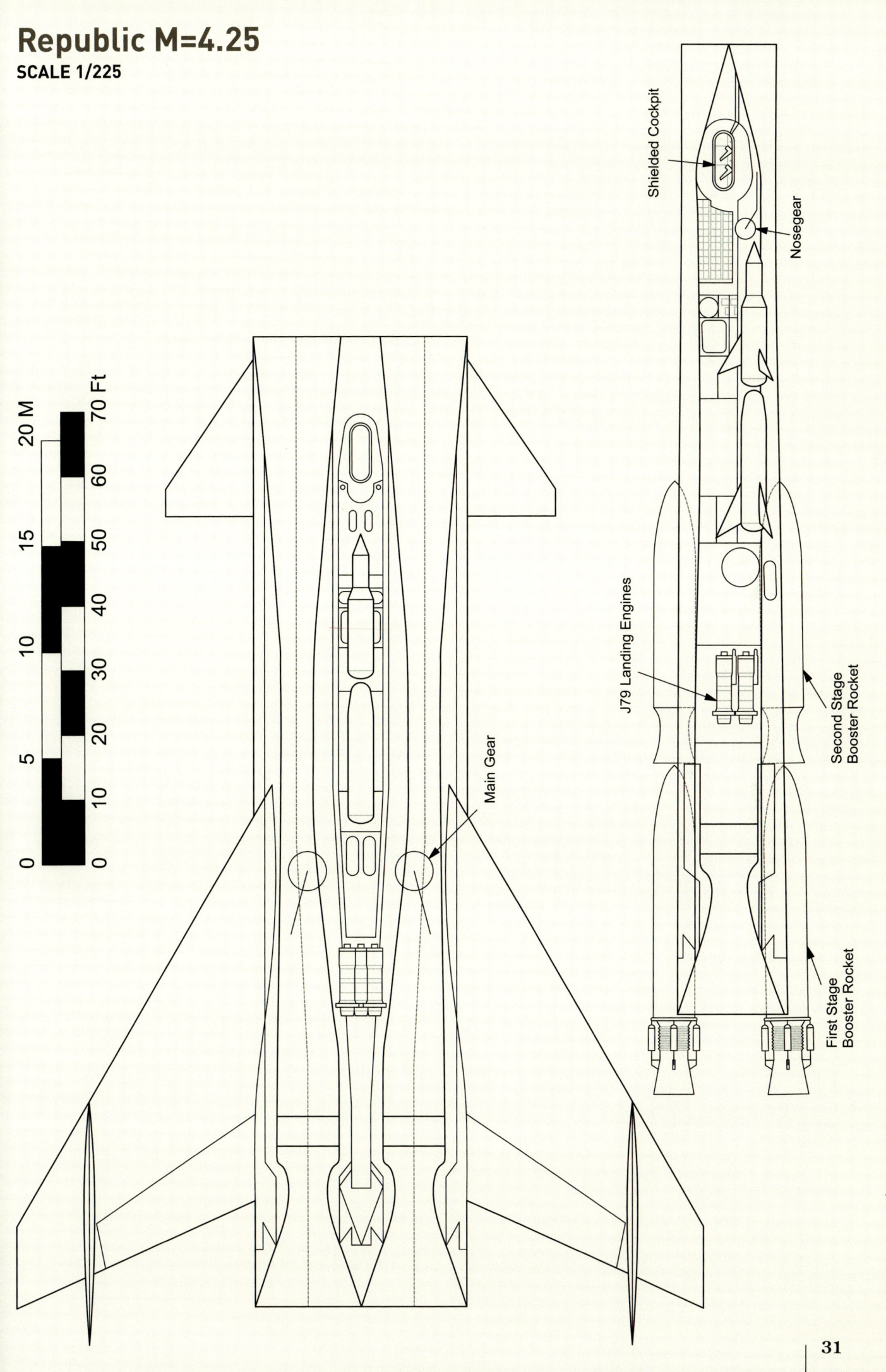

Convair Supersonic Carrier-Based Aircraft

Convair issued a report on naval applications of ANP technologies in 1961. This described a number of wildly differing vehicles... nuclear powered cargo lifter helicopters, nuclear powered airborne early warning craft, nuclear ramjet powered missiles for launch from ships and subs. Additionally, two supersonic carrier-based strike aircraft were described.

It was acknowledged that the current state of the art in nuclear turbojets did not lend themselves to supersonic flight without chemical fuel augmentation, but refinements of the Pratt & Whitney indirect cycle engine and reactor had, it was believed, led to the ability to supercruise at Mach 3 and 50,000ft. Instead of two loops of liquid metal, this design had only one... the reactor heated the metal, the metal heated the air in the engines. Columbium alloys would be needed to withstand oxidation in the higher temperature regions of the system. The reactor was a Pratt & Whitney 200 megawatt PWAR 11.

The existing Pratt & Whitney 'NJ 19' nuclear system was not capable of propelling an aircraft to Mach 3. So a composite propulsion system was planned... a nuclear turbojet (using the JTN-11, appropriately modified) for low speed to Mach 2/40,000ft, followed by a switch to a nuclear ramjet. As the aircraft accelerated, the turbojets would be gradually cut out of the loop and the ramjets would take over until by Mach 3 and 60,000ft the aircraft was propelled solely by the ramjets. A small amount of power would be used by the turbojets at these speeds to counter their base drag. The potential of flight to Mach 4 and 80,000ft on nuclear ramjets alone was foreseen. A heat exchanger would take the place of combustors in both the turbojets and the ramjets, using liquid metal for the heat transfer. The heat exchangers would, in the case of both turbojets and ramjets, create air temperatures of 2,000°F.

Due to the need for low landing speeds – a requirement of carrier duty – the wings of both designs were large. This is a problem for supersonic flight as it means high drag; consequently, triple-sonic flight would only be practical at high altitudes. But an advantage of the high cruise altitude is that in such a tenuous atmosphere, scattering of the radiation would be greatly reduced; this would reduce the amount of shielding the crew compartment would need.

Aircraft structure would be largely titanium 811 alloys, a similar solution to that chosen for the Lockheed A-12 and SR-71. The A-12 was still being developed when Convair issued its report, so the company's engineers would have been unaware of the Lockheed design and its titanium structure. The wing structure was conventional plate-stringer construction and would be 2.5% thick. With no need to contain fuel, the wing structure would be light and efficient. While the aircraft are described as being purely nuclear, they were in fact given a modest supply of JP-4 fuel. Presumably this was to be used for additional thrust at takeoff.

Convair estimated that these aircraft could enter service around 1970, and that by that point the Forrestal-class carriers would be the only ones in service that could be modified to handle them. A number of fairly serious changes would need to be wrought to these ships to safely accommodate nuclear powered aircraft. While such aircraft were on deck, the decks would have to be cleared of unarmoured personnel; special heavily shielded vehicles designed to not only tow the aircraft but re-arm them, move shielding around and, importantly, remove the reactor module from the aircraft would be needed. A new elevator rated for 150,000lb would be added to the port rear of the deck, used to lower the still-hot (both thermally and radioactively) reactor down to the new 'hot shop' area at the rear of the hangar deck.

The reactors would be removed from the aircraft as quickly as possible after each landing and transported to shielded accommodations in the hot shop. The aircraft, now stripped of the reactors, would be no more radioactive than any other aircraft and could be moved around deck and lowered down to the hangar deck like any other aircraft. The hot shop, equipped with remote manipulators and 300 tons of new shielding ranging from 0.1 to 1.3in thick, would maintain and store the reactors; for convenience – and presumably to annoy environmentalists – a large chute would be added to the extreme tail of the ship in case a reactor needed to be simply shovelled overboard.

The existing internal hangar doors would be modified to serve as additional emergency radiation shielding. The 'island' would receive considerable attention. As the bridge and primary flight control areas would of course need to continue to operate while the nuclear powered aircraft were operating on deck, the glass would be replaced with 4in thick leaded glass, and additional 2in-thick depleted uranium shielding would be added.

In wartime conditions, an aircraft might land and be re-armed without going through the bother of removing the reactor. The process would be done with as much automation as possible; the re-arming and mobile shielding vehicles being quite possibly remotely operated. The aircraft would take off again without having completely powered down the reactor. It was – perhaps optimistically – estimated that this process would take no more than 15 minutes.

In the event that an aircraft was badly damaged on deck, a new disposal area was installed on the port

Convair Carrier-Based Combined Engine
SCALE 1/160

Convair Carrier-Based Attack Recon
SCALE 1/160

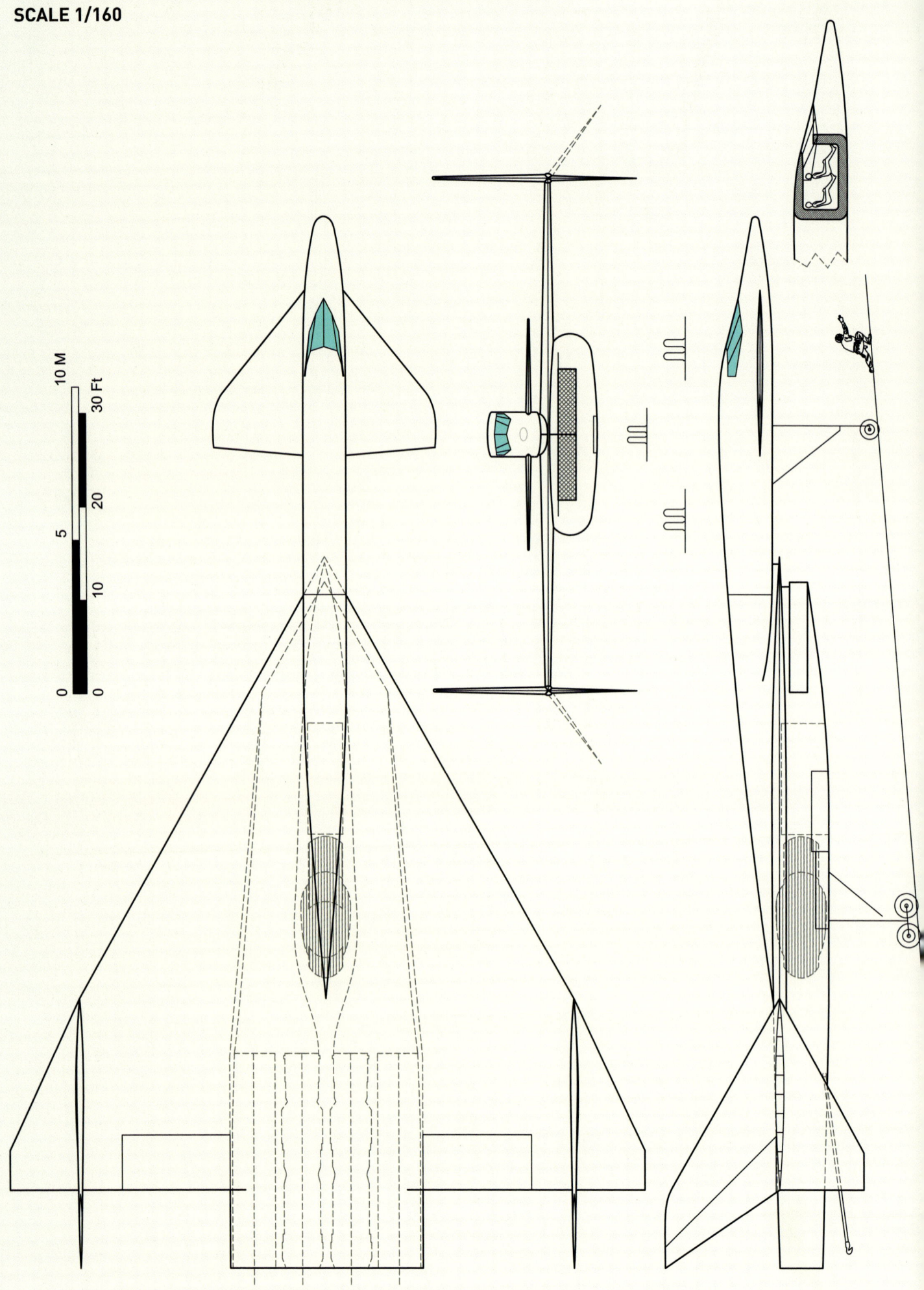

34

side of the flight deck aft of the forward elevator where a plane could be safely shoved over the side. It was estimated that in the event of reactor damage leading to a meltdown, but where the reactor shell itself was intact, the shell would maintain sufficient strength to contain the molten reactor components. At least, that is, long enough for the reactor to sink several thousand feet, whereupon the pressure of the ocean would crush the shell and spill the contents into the abyss. Thus solving the problem forever.

Convair proposed two configurations of similar size, weight and performance. Both could fly as fast and as far, carrying a 5,000lb payload (presumably a nuclear weapon). Configuration I was much like the North American XB-70 in broad strokes; a delta wing sat atop an engine module fed from a bifurcated vertical ramp inlet just below the leading vertex of the wing. A fuselage sat atop the wing and projected forward, with canards near the nose. The wing had two vertical stabilizers and two 45° downward-canted wingtips that could hinge down a further 45°. At low speed they would provide good lift; at high speed they would turn down and increase stability while reducing drag. The reactor sat in the engine module; two turbojets sat side-by-side at the rear, with one ramjet outboard of each turbojet.

Unlike the B-70, the vertical stabilizers were located directly atop the hinges for the wingtips so that at high speed the wing would be capped, top and bottom, with large fins. The lower wingtips would again fold down after landing to decrease wingspan; to further aid in fitting the craft within the hangars of Forrestal-class aircraft carriers, the forward fuselage could hinge back and the vertical stabilizers could be folded down to lay atop the wings.

The crew of two sat in tandem in a small shielded compartment, with the pilot being given a surprisingly expansive exterior view, a concession driven no doubt due to the needs of landing on an aircraft carrier. The nine hour mission would expose the crew to 0.09 REM/hour.

Configuration II was somewhat similar in layout except for a very different engine arrangement. It still had two nuclear turbojets and two nuclear ramjets, but here the turbojets were each in a cylindrical underslung nacelle, with the ramjet wrapped around them (somewhat like the configuration of the SR-71's engines). The nacelles were connected to the aircraft with two pylons: a vertical pylon connected to the underside of the wing, and an angled pylon connected to the lower side of the fuselage. This not only created a stronger and more rigid structure, it also created a shorter pathway for the superheated liquid metal to get from the reactor to the engines by way of the lower pylon. Additionally, the lower pylons served to contain the main landing gear legs when stowed.

For Configuration II, the wing was mounted at the shoulder of the straight fuselage. The wing was somewhat smaller than in the prior design, made possible by the much better low-speed flaps that were permitted by the changed wing and engine arrangement. Weight data was similar to the prior design, just slightly lighter; performance was generally the same, though the second configuration could reach a maximum of Mach 3.8 to the first design's Mach 3.7.

While the forward fuselage could hinge to the side for hangar clearance as with Configuration I, the cockpit was remarkably different. The first design had what must have been considered adequate visibility for a carrier landing, but that was clearly not the case for the second design. So for landing, the front half of the cockpit would tilt upwards, lifting the pilot and the heavy shielding above him. In doing so it would increase the size of the forward-facing canopy and much improve the pilot's forward view.

These Convair designs came at the very end of the manned nuclear aircraft programme in the United States. By 1961 the WS-110A was close to producing the B-70, but politics had changed: the Kennedy administration was less overjoyed at the prospect of manned bombers than the Eisenhower administration had been. Slashing programmes was the order of the day, and the WS-125A programme had spent well over a billion dollars in its 15-year history but didn't have a great deal to show for it. The optimism with which atomic flight had been born had largely faded; the fear of nuclear catastrophes following a crash or a meltdown was much greater. So President Kennedy ended the ANP programme in April 1961, killing off hopes for an atomic powered manned aircraft. But America was not quite done with nuclear powered bomb droppers just yet...

Project Pluto

Theoretical studies of nuclear ramjets were undertaken by North American Aviation all the way back in 1947. These involved a mathematical treatment of a generic nuclear ramjet missile of straightforward design. In overall configuration it was not notably different from other, more conventional aircraft of the time... with the exception of a total lack of fuel. It was understood early on that a nuclear ramjet would have nearly unlimited range; the structural limitations and strategic targets being the only things that limited the distance it could travel. This was refined quickly into a two-stage vehicle using a rocket first stage and a nuclear ramjet second stage, the second stage being a simple body of rotation with four identical tailfins. This earliest design could not carry an atomic bomb of its day, yet it was to have intercontinental range. While this design did not proceed much further, a spiritual descendant received a vast amount of study including component testing. It would become the American nuclear powered aircraft programme that came closest to actually being built.

Nuclear ramjets offered the promise of high speed and great range; coupled with the fact that a nuclear ramjet would be unlikely to have a long operational lifespan, a cruise missile would be the perfect platform for a nuclear ramjet.

The Department of Defense asked the Atomic Energy Commission (AEC) to assist in investigating the concept in 1955; the AEC in turn sought help from the Lawrence Radiation Laboratory in 1957. Lawrence, which was to become the Lawrence Livermore Laboratory, was to head up the reactor development programme, named Pluto. Lawrence had experience with similar reactors; for several years they had been involved with project ROVER (an early nuclear rocket), and were experienced at designing lightweight, high power reactors.

It was found that nuclear ramjets of reasonable sizes all seemed to have maximum thrust at a flight speed of about Mach 3. Also, thrust would increase drastically with an increase in engine temperature. Nuclear reactors are of course able to attain extreme core temperatures, but maintaining structural integrity while being subjected to a violent oxygen-rich environment at extreme temperatures was a daunting prospect. The reactor for project Pluto would differ from nuclear rockets in several important ways. The greatest difficulty was the change in propellants: with a nuclear rocket, the typical working fluid is hydrogen, a reducing agent; but a ramjet would use atmospheric nitrogen and oxygen... and hot oxygen would easily attack most structural materials. A coating of beryllium oxide was chosen; this also served as a good neutron moderator.

The first reactor built for the Pluto programme was the Tory II-A. This was not a flight-ready engine, but was designed to be a compact engine of the right size for a flight-ready engine. Operating temperature was 2,250°F. The Tory II-A was designed to test the materials and engineering that would be needed on a flight engine. It was too heavy and was too big in cross-sectional area; the design could not handle manoeuvre loading. The control elements were contained in external structures, while a flight engine would have internal controls. Nevertheless, the Tory II-A produced 155 megawatts, heating 708lb per second of air to 1,975°F.

The Tory II-A reactor contained approximately 100,000 fuel elements, each 4in long with a hexagonal cross section .297in across the flats. A longitudinal 0.2in diameter hole provided a channel for air flow. The fuel elements were composed of a homogeneous mixture of BeO and UO2. These ceramic rods were produced by Coors Porcelain Company (of Coors beer fame) in Golden, Colorado. Molybdenum base plates held the reactor in place during tests and took the pressure-drop loading.

The reactors were relatively safe devices to be around until they were activated for the first time; after that they were dangerously radioactive. So the reactors were built onto flatbed railcars; a short length of track (8,200ft) was laid between the testing area and the disassembly building. Remote waldos were used to manipulate the reactor and associated hardware after tests. Testing occurred at Site 401, located on the Atomic Energy Commission's Nevada Test Site.

A large quantity of air needed to be fed into the Tory II-A at high pressure to simulate flight conditions... 800lb of air per second at 1,000°F and 400psi. For most experiments that need significant volumes of high pressure air, compressors can normally do the job; however, in this case the volume required was beyond the capability of compressors to keep up. So a tank farm was set up, using high pressure oil well casing pipe to store 120,000lb of air at 3,600psi. This would provide enough air for a one-minute test of the Tory II-A reactor. Reactor tests were carried out on the Tory II-A between May and October of 1961. The reactor reached a maximum power of 168 megawatts and a maximum core temperature of 2,548°F. There was some minor cracking of several fuel elements, but otherwise the reactor held up well.

Tory II-A Parameters:

Power:	155 megawatts
Flow Rate:	708lb/sec
Max fuel element wall temperature:	2,250°F
Exit gas temperature:	1,975°F
Core Diameter:	32in
Core length:	48in
Side reflector thickness (graphite):	24in

An improved reactor was needed once the Tory II-A proved itself so the Tory II-C reactor was built as a Mach 3 low altitude flight-capable prototype powerplant. This reactor had internal control rods and 465,000 fuel rods each 3.92in long. The hexagonal fuel elements were tightly bundled together and formed 27,000 air flow channels.

The reactor was contained in a flanged tube 103in long and 47.5in in diameter. The ramjet engine would produce 280,000 (gross) pounds of thrust for 3-10 hours, and could sustain lateral manoeuvres of

Pluto General Arrangement, circa 1964
SCALE 1/90

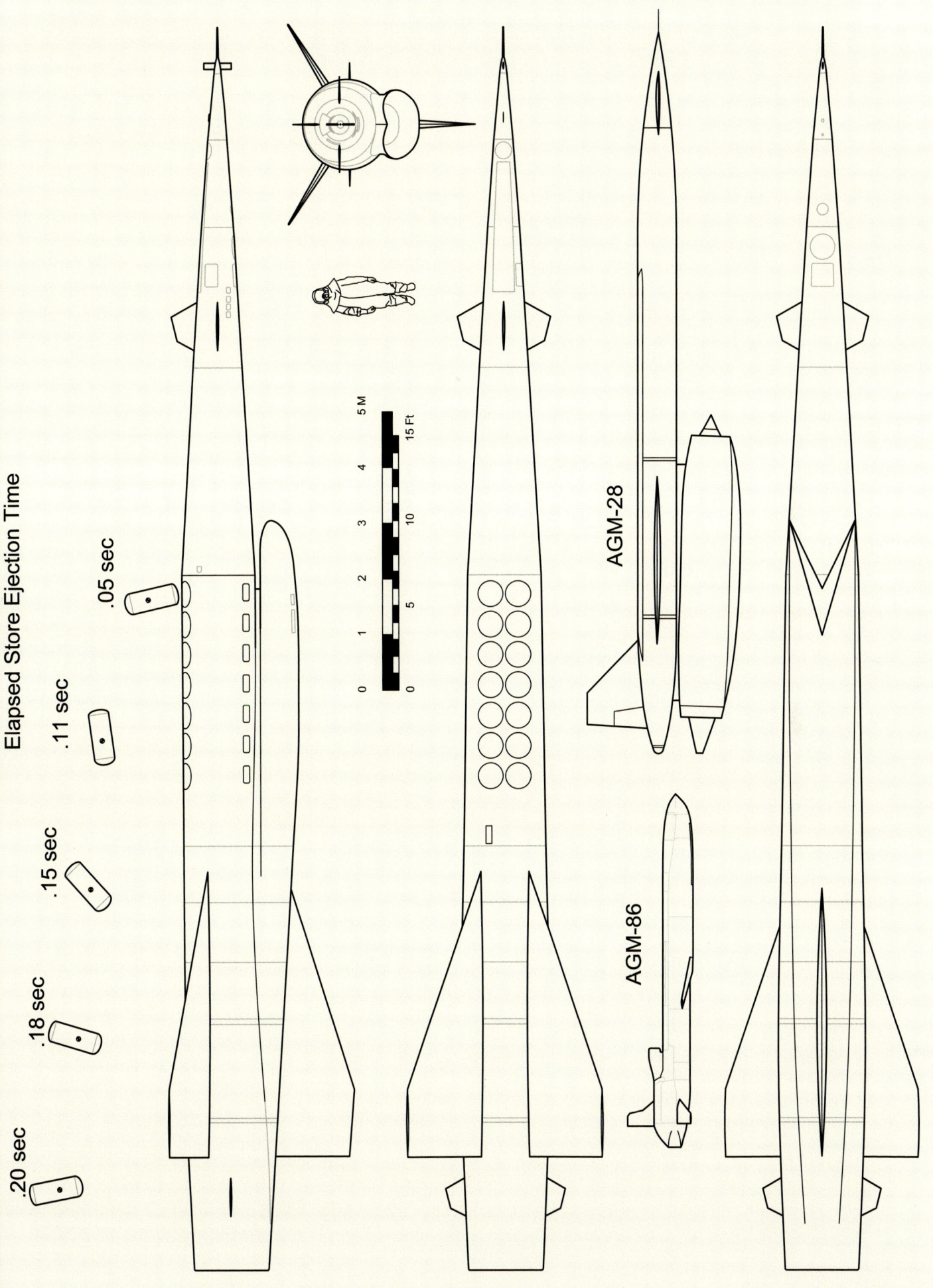

up to 4g. The test facility had to have an increase in compressed air storage in order to accommodate longer tests on this more powerful reactor so air tank capacity was increased to 1.2 million pounds by using about 25 miles of 10in oil well casing. This permitted up to five minutes of full power operation, and it took five days for the compressors to fill.

In order to bring the air up to the proper test temperature, a pebble-bed heater was used. The heater was composed of 1.2 million pounds of 1in diameter stainless steel balls. The heater would be brought to 1,200°F over a period of 30 hours by the use of a conventional oil-fired furnace blowing through the bed. The air from the tank farm, cooling down as its pressure decreased, would then be passed through the heater; the vast surface area and mass of the steel spheres would assure reasonably constant high air temperature for the duration of the test.

The Tory II-C reactor was tested at full power twice. On May 20, 1964, the Tory II-C reached a maximum power of 523 megawatts on startup, and maintained 484 megawatts for five minutes. Fuel elements reached a temperature of 2,590°F during this test, which was performed at the design conditions of Mach 2.8 at sea level. Net thrust was 37,950lb. While the gross thrust was 280,000lb, drag on the reactor – which was not designed to be aerodynamic, nor could it really be – was vast.

An improved Tory II-C, known as the Tory II-C/AF, was under study at the cancellation of the programme. The Tory II-C/AF was simpler than the Tory II-C, with a simplified side structure, no vernier or safety rods, and fewer tie rods. The core used higher fuel element porosity, an increased uranium loading and a 2in increase in diameter to increase thrust by 24% over that of the Tory II-C. Weight was reduced by 420lb. The Tory II-C/AF never reached the hardware stage, but was considered to be a promising reactor concept which would noticeably improve the performance of nuclear ramjet vehicles.

While the Tory II-C demonstrated a flight-type reactor, further development on more advanced reactors was foreseen. The Tory III reactor was a proposed design that eliminated internal metal supports by installing a ceramic base dome to support the 250,000lb drag load. Also, improved materials were expected to allow for a fuel element temperature of 3,000°F. Metals, while adequate, suffered from numerous deficiencies, including neutron absorption and a requirement for cooling in the most extreme temperature environments. With the Tory III, all metal would be removed from within the reactor. The reactor would still be contained within a corrugated steel 'girdle' providing axial support. The girdle would be cooled with air bled off from the inlet, amounting to about 2% of the total air flow.

An all-ceramic reactor would weigh less and operate hotter than one with metal supports, thus producing greater thrust. The aft dome, which was to be perforated to allow air flow and divided into seven segments, would be made from either silicon carbide or silicon nitride. Testing was performed on subscale plaster models; the models were loaded up to 210psi on their forward surfaces and allowed to crack; even with substantial cracks, the domes continued to hold. It was only after unloading and disassembly that the domes were shown to have been badly damaged.

In 1963, Ling-Temco-Vought, Inc. was selected as the prime contractor to develop the airframe for a nuclear ramjet missile, while Marquardt was chosen as prime contractor on the propulsion system. The weapons system was called the Supersonic Low Altitude Missile (SLAM) and was to be based at either fixed or mobile launch sites. The SLAM missile was a slim, low-drag wingless design. At the flight conditions SLAM was to fly at (Mach 2.8 at 1,000ft altitude or below), wings were not needed; the lift generated by the fuselage would be more than adequate to keep the vehicle airborne. While it doesn't look like the typical lifting body, that is exactly what it was.

A single underslung inlet fed air to the reactor. Different images show either a bifurcated inlet, or an axisymmetric inlet with a shock cone. The former inlet appears to be the later concept. Fixed stabilizers were located well aft, with a fixed underslung vertical stabilizer. Aerodynamic control was by means of two small all-moving canards and a small all-moving vertical stabilizer mounted on the nose, as well as two surprisingly small ailerons at the tail.

The design was still being studied when the SLAM programme was cancelled in 1964, leading to some variance in the available data. Vehicle lengths ranged from 67-112ft, and cruise altitudes ranged from 1,000-30,000ft. Mach numbers were also variable. Hard numbers that can be nailed with certainty to a specific design are so far hard to come by, with surprisingly little being made readily available in a declassified form.

But regardless of detail variances, the basic concept remained the same. The SLAM was a surprisingly simple missile, due to the complete lack of fuel. The vehicle was to fly at above Mach 2 at essentially tree-top level; the heating and aerodynamic loads it would have experienced would have been far greater than those experienced by any other vehicle ever built. To counter this, the structure was built extremely ruggedly, leading to the nickname 'the flying crowbar'. Primary structure for the forward section of the missile was to be made from PH 15-7 Mo stainless steel, while for the aft section – roughly from the reactor aft – was to be made from Rene 41 nickel alloy, and the nozzle from columbium.

Aerothermal heating, including the effects of constantly shifting shock interactions, would be sufficiently severe that local hot spots were expected to form that could damage the skin. The solution was to bring a government spending metaphor to life: the SLAM would be literally gold-plated. Gold's high thermal conductivity, coupled with its chemically inert nature, meant that it would make a satisfactory thermal 'equalizer', taking heat from the hot spots and distributing it to cooler areas. A golden missile would hardly be the most subtle of systems, but the emissivity of gold would help to somewhat reduce the IR signature of the missile. Not that there was likely to be an interception system that could chase down a Pluto, but concentrated anti-aircraft artillery might have had some small chance, given sufficient warning.

An air conditioning system was installed to cool the electronics and control systems. The radiation emitted by the reactor would have been enough to fry the electronics of the time, so thick shielding was installed to protect them from damage.

Had the SLAM missile been built, it would have been equipped with, for the time, very advanced guidance and control systems. The use of a forward mounted vertical stabilizer meant that the vehicle would have been unstable in yaw; without active computer control, the slightest deflection of the rudder would have caused the vehicle to go into an unrecoverable spin. Also, the SLAM missile was to be self-guiding, using Terrain Contour Matching (TERCOM) to locate itself. This system, essentially the same as used in modern cruise missiles until GPS gained dominance, compares a radar map of the terrain below with stored radar map data. This was expected to produce a weapons delivery accuracy of a few hundred feet. The system was reportedly built and flown over 33 different areas with 282 separate radar fixes.

The mission profile of a SLAM missile would have started with the missile being launched within the continental United States. It would then boost to 35,000ft and cruise at Mach 3.5 at that altitude to a loiter area (also known as a 'Failsafe Point'). The missile would orbit there until either ordered recalled, at which point it would splash down into the ocean, or until ordered to proceed to target.

If called upon to continue to the target, the SLAM would cruise at 35,000ft until just outside the enemy's air defence detection system. It would then drop down to below radar detection altitude and penetrate enemy territory using TERCOM to adjust its course as needed. It's at this point that the SLAM earns its place in a book on bombers. The SLAM was indeed a cruise missile, a single-use expendable unmanned vehicle. This would seem to move it outside the definition of a 'bomber'. However... while the very earliest North American Aviation nuclear ramjet missile carried – and died with – a single warhead, SLAM was different.

The SLAM missile could attack a multitude of targets, unlike single-warhead ICBMs and conventional cruise missiles. The SLAM would go on a 'grand tour' of targets, carrying up to 26 separate weapons. The yield of these bombs was highly variable, and correlated with the number of bombs. According to one source, a single Pluto could carry a 5,500lb payload which could be broken down like this:

Number of weapons	Yield
1	26 megatons
5	1.3 megatons
9	1.1 megatons
14	750 kilotons
16	200 kilotons
36	50 kilotons
42	5 kilotons

The weapons bay of the SLAM missile was located in the middle of the vehicle. The bombs were stowed vertically and were ejected out of the top of the vehicle, which prevented them from interfering with the ramjet inlet or the ventral fin.

Patent drawings assigned to the USAF are available which show the weapons ejection system in some detail. While it is not certain that these drawings depict an official configuration for the SLAM weapons bay, it is interesting to note that the SLAM configuration is clearly shown, while in the text of the patent it is referred to vaguely as a turbojet powered missile.

The bombs would be stowed in two parallel rows. Circular hatches covered the ejection ports; these hatches were to be hinged so that when open they presented as little area as possible to the airstream. The bombs would be ejected by an explosive charge and left to fall to the target. From 1,000ft up, the minimum possible fall time was about eight seconds; in that time, the SLAM would have proceeded about 1.7 miles away... far enough and fast enough to probably escape harm from the nuclear explosion. If the bombs were equipped with aerodynamic decelerators such as flaps or parachutes, the Pluto could have been well beyond the horizon by the time the bombs went off.

Pluto Booster Rockets
SCALE 1/100

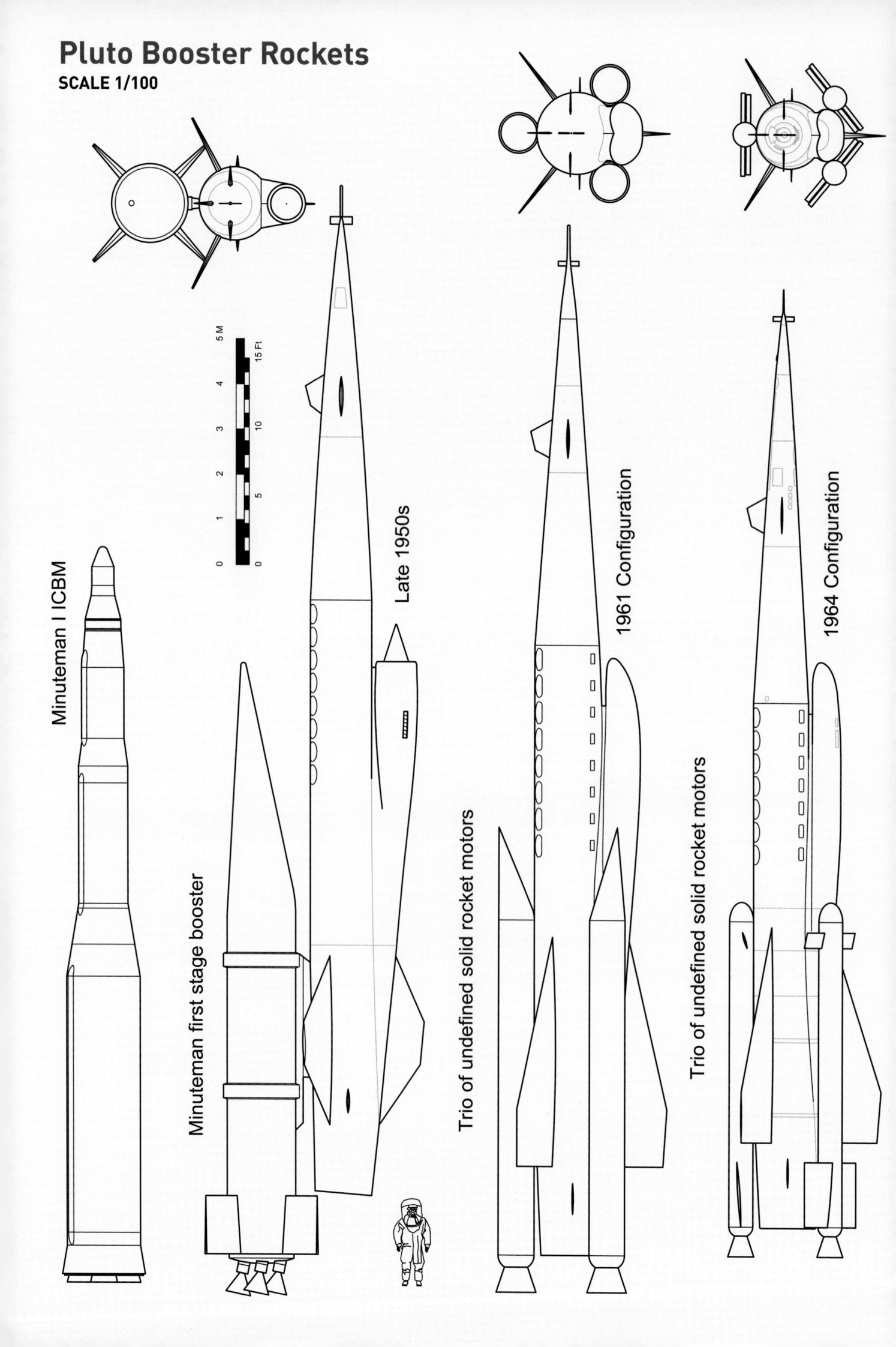

Minuteman I ICBM

Minuteman first stage booster

Late 1950s

Trio of undefined solid rocket motors — 1961 Configuration

Trio of undefined solid rocket motors — 1964 Configuration

The small bombs might have been W33 nuclear artillery shells, the Y4 variant of which could produce five kilotons yield. The W33 weighed about 240lb, while 42 bombs in 5,500lb payload capability works out to 130lb per bomb. Similarly, the single 26 megaton bomb sounds like the 25 megaton B-41 bomb… which weighed in at nearly 10,700lb. It's unclear if the numbers given for Pluto assumed weapons improvements that were projected, or simply hoped-for.

The SLAM had one more weapon besides the nuclear bombs: itself. A 100ft long vehicle flying at Mach 2.8 less than 1,000ft up would produce a profound sonic boom. The Soviet Union is known to have called for the design of aircraft whose specific role was to fly at supersonic speeds low over enemy troop formations; by proper shaping of the aircraft, sonic booms would be sufficiently powerful that exposed humans would be killed or injured and softer structures destroyed. While SLAM was not designed with that in mind, but instead merely to provide the most efficient aerodynamic form, the potential for a damaging sonic boom would remain.

The thermal radiation from the engine and from the aerodynamic heating would likely have started a few fires. Fields of dry tinder, as well as thin-skinned fuel tanks easily burst by the sonic boom, would be particularly vulnerable.

Worse yet, the Pluto engine development team was never able to completely eliminate the problem of dust-to-sand-grain sized bits of fuel breaking loose; the SLAM would have left a noticeably radioactive trail wherever it went. This was the primary reason why such direct-cycle nuclear engines were not favoured for other nuclear powered aircraft… they'd leave a trail of radioactive ruin wherever they went. For a nuclear powered cargo plane, or a nuclear powered bomber meant to be kept constantly on the alert in peacetime, these issues would obviously be unacceptable. But for SLAM, this was not necessarily a problem, so long as the trail of radiation was deposited on enemy territory.

As a final insult to the enemy, at the end of its mission the SLAM would have impacted the ground in enemy territory at full speed, destroying not only itself but anything nearby… and leaving a broken, dirty reactor core either buried in the ground or exploded into bits, covering the surroundings in radioactive contamination.

The SLAM missile could have been stored and launched in a number of ways. All involved the use of solid rocket boosters to get it to high speed; like any ramjet, it produced no thrust until it was in motion. Several variations on the solid rocket motor theme are known, but so far no documentation on them has been seen by this author. The number of booster rockets varied from one to three, but specifics on type and performance are lacking.

One method was to launch it from aircraft; but an aircraft big enough to carry a SLAM missile would have been as big as a bomber… in essence, removing one bomber from the potential inventory to permit another to be launched. Another concept was the 'Armadillo', a mobile vehicle similar to the larger truck-launched ICBMs so favoured by the former Soviet Union. The SLAM could have been launched from movable hangars, similar to how early cruise missiles (such as the Snark) were to have been based. But these would be fixed emplacements, easily seen and fairly vulnerable to attack. Silos were more expensive than hangars, but they were far less vulnerable to attack. Most of the available documentation seems to suggest that the hangar approach was preferred.

As of 1963, funding for the Pluto/SLAM programme was to be split between the Atomic Energy Commission ($325,000,000 total) and the United States Air Force ($853,000,000 total). Ling-Temco-Vought in 1964 estimated that the per-missile production cost, including reactors but not warheads, would be between $41,000,000 and $59,000,000 for a total production of 50 missiles. Test flights would have begun in 1966-1967, with operational capability beginning in 1969.

One of the great concerns for the Pluto team was how to go about flight testing. It was clear that ground tests of engines could continue at the Nevada testing area, but flights test would be needed and clearly SLAM was not something that lent itself to being environmentally friendly to the testing area. So the proposal was to test the SLAM missile over the Pacific: lots of room to roam, and at the end of the test it would be directed to power dive into the ocean where it would quickly sink to the bottom. Launches would take place at Eniwetok, where a simulated operational launch base would be set up; splashdown would occur in the area of the Marianas Trench with the missile and its reactor plunging into the abyss where, it was assumed, the wreckage could be safely ignored.

Not described in the available documentation was how the TERCOM system would be tested. Obviously radar checking of local terrain would be impossible while flying over the ocean; but equally obviously using a nuclear ramjet over friendly terrain was a non-starter. The TERCOM system would need to find some system that would fly it for at least a little while at Mach 3 and treetop level over, say, North Dakota. What exactly that system was intended to be remains unknown.

Optimised characteristics of SLAM missiles

Parameter	Early Tech (Tory II-C)	Advanced Tech (Tory III)
Payload compartment Dia. (in.)	55	58
Payload compartment Len. (in.)	213	300
Total Vehicle Length (ft.)	84	88
Hot reactor dia. (in.)	57	46
Hot day design Mach number:		
1,000 ft. above sea level	3.2	3.5
30,000 ft. above sea level	3.9	4.2
Reactor wall temperature (°F)	2,500	3,000
Max. Number of warheads	18-24	26
Payload weight (lb)	14,000	15,000
Missile weight (lb)	55,800	60,779
Booster weight (lb)	61,380	67,465
Expected missile range (nm):		
1,000 ft. above sea level	9,450	11,500
30,000 ft. above sea level	72,400	98,300

Maximum range for the most advanced version was nearly 100,000 miles, meaning that the vehicle would stay in the air for around 31 hours.

The programme was cancelled by the Department of Defense in July 1964. When it began, it had been seen as just about the only unmanned vehicle that could reach deep into the Soviet Union with large nuclear weapons; but by the time of cancellation the Atlas and Titan ICBMs had proved themselves while Pluto/SLAM was still some years away from doing so.

Proving and fielding the system would involve numerous environmentally catastrophic test programmes; simply flying the vehicle over enemy territory could potentially be a war crime, never mind disposing of the vehicle by crashing it into a city or military complex and turning it into a radioactive waste dump. Unlike a conventional bomber or an ICBM, the flight path of the SLAM could not pass over friendly territory without the friendlies becoming quite unfriendly. The whole concept had just become politically untenable.

Since 1964, the notion has come up again repeatedly and received cursory study; but the radioactive nature of the exhaust has always proved a hindrance to reviving the project. As a consequence of the numerous extravagant problems, Pluto has become something of a punchline... any list of 'Top Ten Craziest/Most Evil/Most Unwise Weapons systems' will almost certainly have Pluto at or near the top. Nobody has been damnfool enough to seriously suggest the idea since.

That is... until the Russian 9M730 Buresvestnik ('Petrel') was partially revealed in 2019. The 9M730 – NATO reporting name SSC-X-9 'Skyfall' – was involved in some sort of disaster. A radiation release was reported at the naval testing range in Nyonoksa in northern Russia, with five deaths. It later transpired that a nuclear-powered cruise missile crashed and scattered radioactive material. Little of real value has been released about the 9M730... it has been reported as having a nuclear thermal rocket but this is incredibly unlikely. It has also been speculated to have a nuclear ramjet or a nuclear turbojet. A video and a few largely unenlightening photos of what is purported to be the 9M730 were released that showed a vehicle which appears to be of broadly conventional 'cruise missile' layout, seemingly subsonic. If it is indeed subsonic, then the likelihood of a nuclear ramjet is vanishingly low. A nuclear turbojet is more likely, though a nuclear turbojet sized for a cruise missile seems remarkably technologically aggressive. The possibility exists that the 9M370 is not nuclear powered at all; it may be a ruse or a hoax. As of this writing, Russian military policy has not been giving the world a warm fuzzy feeling about either sanity or stability, so hardly any explanation would be unreasonable.

CHAPTER 2
Seaplanes

As most of the planet is covered in water, it makes sense that from time to time the United States has looked at bombers that could operate from the surface of the sea. A key advantage would be the ability, theoretically, to operate from a huge variety of different locations without the possibility of their runways being taken out by enemy bombardment.

There are also a number of problems with the concept. Water, especially salt water, does most metallic structures no good whatsoever. Everything from waves to corrosion introduces problems that landplanes don't have. And while it's useful being able to land on any large enough, deep enough and calm enough stretch of water, that doesn't mean that the aircraft can be serviced there. Permanent facilities in the middle of the ocean are difficult at best; temporary ones, such as logistics ships or submarines, are inconvenient and expensive.

So far, and very likely going forward into the future, the negatives have outweighed the positives regarding seaplane bombers. Even so, over the years a wide variety of water-based bombers have been designed for the Unites States Air Force and Navy, and among those designs have been a number of supersonic configurations.

Convair Betta I

The earliest known US designs for supersonic seaplane bombers arose from US Navy specifications issued in August of 1948. As described in *US Supersonic Bomber Projects Volume 1*, Convair's primary response to Outline Specification 115 (OS-115) was a delta-winged composite aircraft with a manned stage and an unmanned expendable 'pod' containing a multitude of additional jet engines, fuel and a bomb bay. This aircraft was designed to operate from the deck of future 'supercarriers', and used conventional landing gear. But Convair also pondered the notion of a seaplane concept. Only artwork seems to exist of this, depicting a different delta winged composite aircraft with both stages having seaplane hulls. Top speed was to be Mach 1.2.

More work was devoted to two other aircraft concepts that arose in 1949. The first, named 'Cudda', was a conventionally configured subsonic aircraft, looking much like the later Martin P6M SeaMaster. The second was named 'Betta' and was designed for supersonic flight. The Cudda and the Betta were entirely different designs but shared an important conceptual similarity: both relied on large deployable hydroskis for takeoff and landing. At the time, water tunnel testing had showed that the concept held great promise; as the aircraft accelerated it would quickly rise out of the water, riding on the skis. This would reduce drag, thus shortening takeoff runs; and it would reduce the mighty walloping that seaplanes tend to get when taking off and ramming at high speed into waves. The shock absorbers on the deployable hydroskis would dampen those impacts, reducing stress on airframe and crew. At least, that was the theory; the experience that Convair would have with the F2Y SeaDart a few years later would demonstrate that the idea was not quite the miracle solution that had been hoped.

The Betta was, like the original OS-115 submission, a delta winged vehicle. But unlike that cruder concept, the Betta was studied in greater depth and was a single integrated aircraft. The fuselage was long, reasonably slim and blended with the engines, the vertical tail and to some degree the wings. The aircraft had three non-afterburning GE J53 jet engines side-by-side on its back fed from a single narrow arc of an inlet, an arrangement that resulted in the vertical stabilizer being directly in line with the middle engines exhaust. In contrast, the cockpit was offset to port, making the forward fuselage distinctly asymmetric.

Two rectangular hydroplanes were integrated into the lower fuselage under the wings. The bomb bay, designed for an undefined 10,000lb payload – which, conveniently, is the approximate weight of the early Mark 4 atomic bomb which happens to fit quite comfortably within that bay – was positioned in the aft fuselage. This is an unusual place for a bomb bay; typically they are placed as close as possible to the centre of gravity so that when the heavy payload is suddenly dropped the aircraft does not pitch up or down. But as the hydroskis occupied that position, the aft fuselage had to suffice. The aircraft would almost certainly have had to have had some substantial automatic pitch controls to deal with the result of dropping the bomb.

A similar Betta design, dating from the same time, kept the overall configuration but moved the vertical

43

Convair Betta I
SCALE 1/175

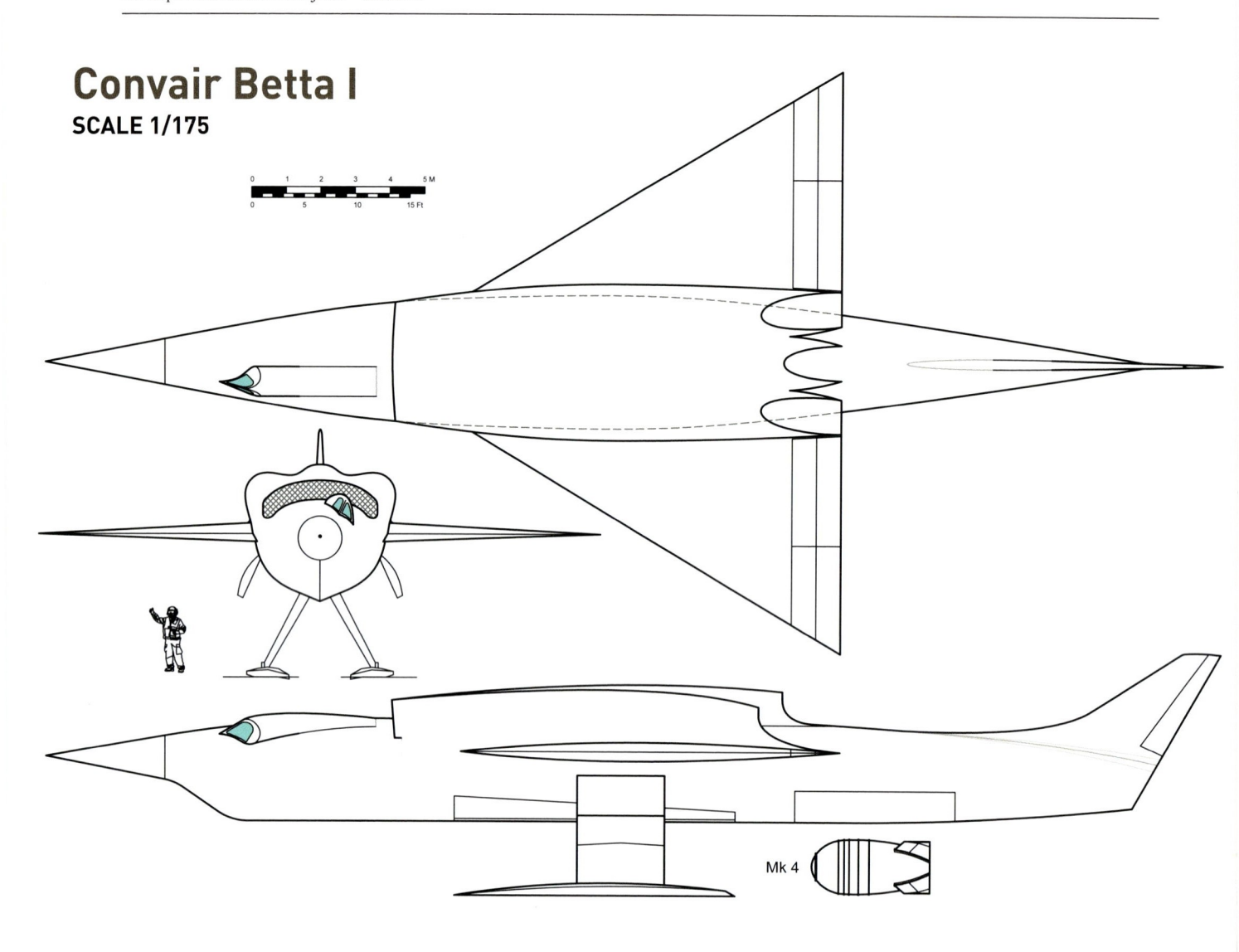

stabilizer forward, atop the engine module. This had the advantage of removing it from the exhaust of the central engine, but since the moment arm was so much less effective, the stabilizer grew substantially in size.

Martin M-275

The development of the Martin P6M SeaMaster is currently not available in great detail, but some of the early designs are somewhat known. Designed under the M-275 designation, most of the known concepts leading to the final P6M configuration were fairly conventional, being much like the final design except for variations in the location of the turbojet engines. One design, however, was quite unusual. Dating from around 1952, details on it are currently frustratingly vague; fortunately, in 1954-early 1955, the NACA ran a series of wind tunnel tests on the configuration. By this time the P6M design was already completed, with the first airframe officially rolled out in late December of 1954.

The P6M was a subsonic aircraft, though a very fast subsonic aircraft, and ideas were floated to use more powerful engines to push it through the transonic into the low supersonic. The NACA study from 1955 described the design as transonic and shows that it was tested at up to Mach 1.13. As 'supersonic' designs go that barely qualifies… but qualify it does. It was a four-engined configuration with very clean lines, utilizing afterburning Curtiss-Wright J67s (proposed, but never put into production, licence-built versions of the British Rolls-Royce Olympus engine that powered the Avro Vulcan and Concorde). The engines were located within the fuselage, leaving the highly swept wings clean except for small wingtip stabilizing floats. The engines were fed air from a single roughly elliptical inlet just above and behind the very pointed nose. Two of the engines were beside the tandem cockpit, exhausting underneath the wing roots; two more in the extreme tail. This would have meant an extraordinarily long inlet duct for the tail engines.

The wind tunnel model does not include details such as control surfaces (the diagrams do however show the control surfaces for the horizontal stabilizers), bomb bay or cockpit canopy frames. However, a bomb load of 30,000lb was assumed, contained in a rotary bomb bay. The bombs would be delivered after a subsonic cruise and a supersonic dash.

Martin M-275

SCALE 1/250

Control Surface Arrangement Unknown

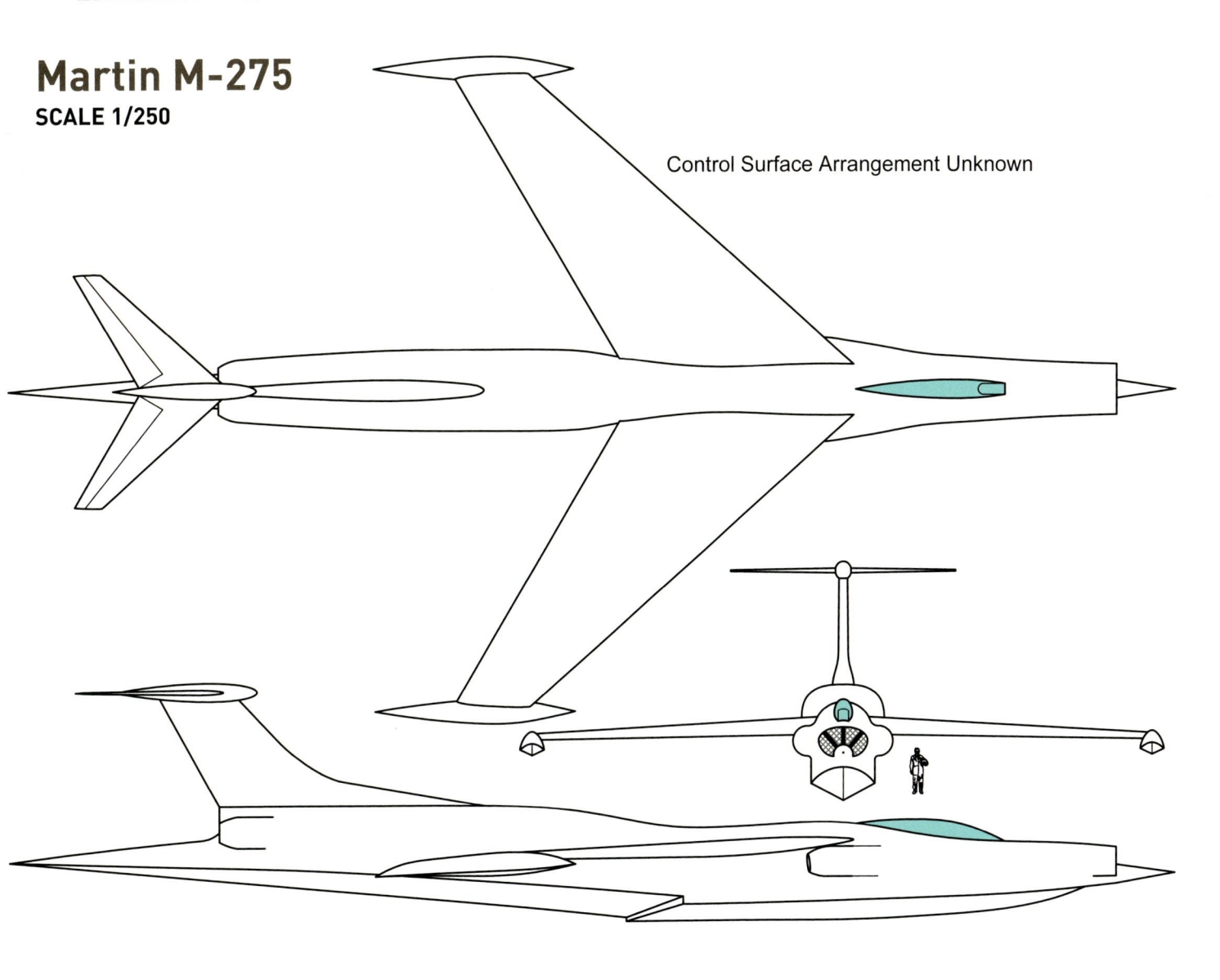

An alternative configuration was considered. Using much the same fuselage and tail unit, the engine and wings were very different. Two engines were installed in each of two upward-angled wing-root nacelles; the wings projected upwards from the nacelles before angling back down towards the water. It's unclear if this second configuration is also a Martin design, or a NACA-Langley concept for a modification. The common fuselages had a high fineness ratio for aerodynamic performance and a stepped planing hull for hydrodynamic performance. Both configurations shaped their inlets and nacelles with the area ruling principle in mind.

Martin Model 316

The Martin Model 316, apparently dubbed the 'Skipper', dates from December 1954. Compared to the previous Martin design is was quite conventional in appearance, but the planned Mach number (1.35) was a little bit higher.

Sadly, most of the information on this design again comes from a NACA wind and water tunnel test report, so many design details are lacking. Again it was designed with four Curtiss-Wright afterburning J67 engines, but they were mounted one in each wing root and two side-by-side over the rear fuselage, fed by an inlet over the central fuselage. As with the aforementioned M-275, Model 316 had a high fineness ratio fuselage with a planing hull, but this time with a cockpit with side-by-side seating.

Curiously, photos of the NACA water tank model show a prominent '326' on the tail… not '316'. And frustratingly, a list of known Martin projected Model numbers lists both the 316 and 326… and neither are seaplanes.

Martin Model 329 C-1 and C-2

The Martin P6M SeaMaster proved that high-speed turbojet aircraft could make functional seaplanes. While the P6M failed to enter service, largely for political reasons rather than technical failings of the design, Martin nevertheless studied more advanced seaplane concepts for the US Navy. Before the

Martin Model 316
SCALE 1/250

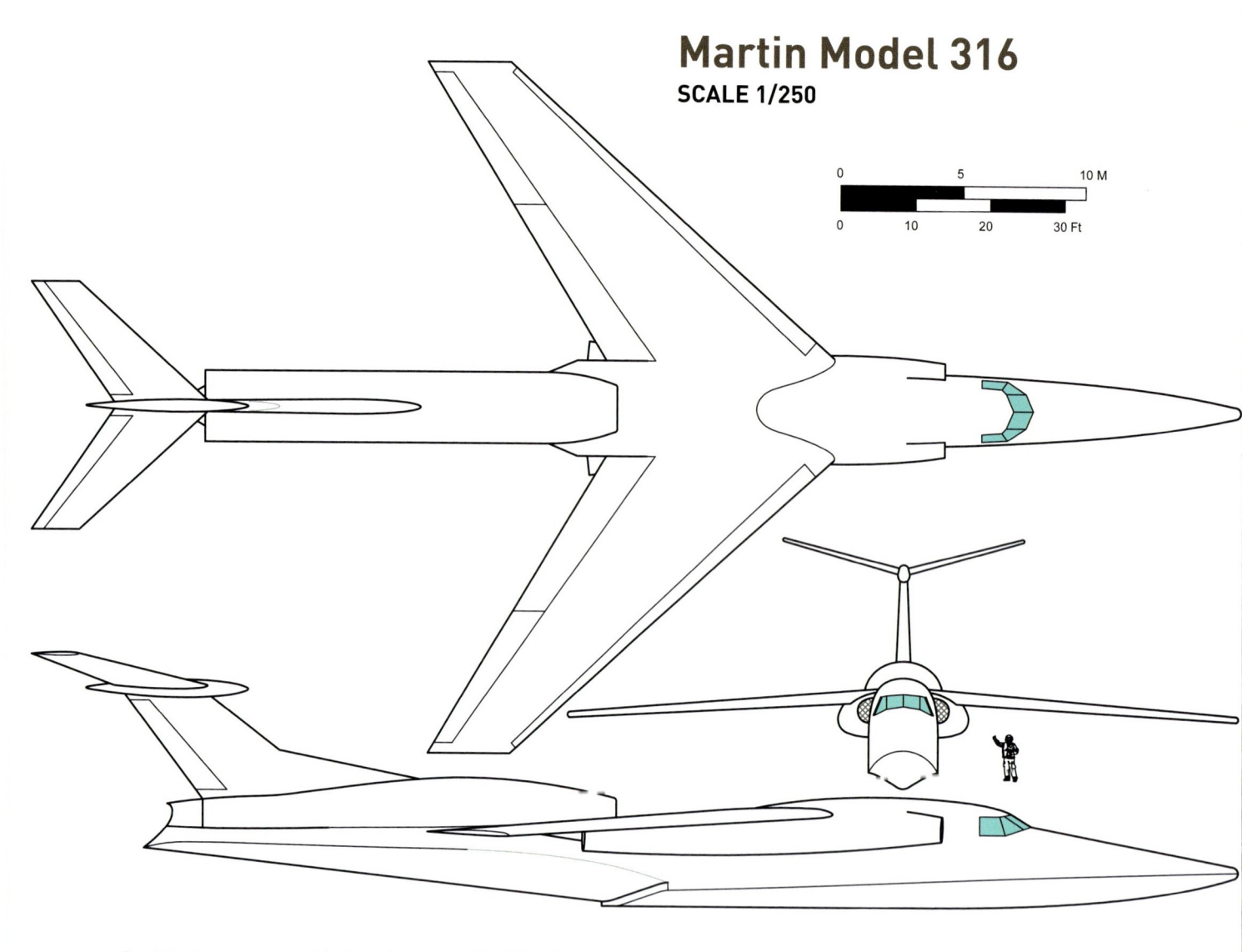

SeaMaster was cancelled in August of 1959, Martin – aided by NACA – devoted considerable time and effort to Model 329, an all-new seaplane bomber design capable of supersonic speeds.

Starting in 1954, the Model 329 programme studied a wide variety of designs, with top speeds ranging from as low as Mach 1.4 all the way to Mach 3. The Model 329 A-series took the P6M and made it modestly supersonic (Mach 1.4) by lengthening and area-ruling the fuselage. Radius was intended to be 1,500 nautical miles. The A-1 and A-2 designs were both powered by four afterburning J67 engines, two on the aft fuselage and two on the wings. The A-1 mounted the engines above the wings, while the A-2 mounted the engines below the wings. Variations continued up to A-12A, including using the Orenda PS-13 engine and the use of boron-based 'zip fuel' for dash speeds up to Mach 2.

The Model 329 B-series increased speed to Mach 2 and range to 1,900 nautical miles. The B-series was influenced by Martin work done on the Air Force WS-302 tactical bomber, and included six afterburning engines. The most unique configuration for the B-series was Model 329 B-6D, which used a detachable sled for takeoff.

The Model 329 C-series from 1956 were studied under a Patrol Attack Seaplane contract from the Navy. Compared to A and B, the C designs were studied in greater detail, including hydrodynamic testing at the Martin plant in Baltimore with considerable assistance from NACA (in the form of hydrodynamic and wind tunnel testing at NACA Langley). The C-1 and C-2 versions were the primary variants studied. Both had six non-afterburning Curtis-Wright TJ-36 engines (licensed US-produced version of the Canadian Orenda Engines Iroquis turbojet), two in a single nacelle on the aft fuselage, the other four atop the wings in individual nacelles.

C-1 and C-2 differed largely in having different fuselages; C-1 had a conventional flying boat planing hull similar to that of the P6M, while C-2 had a smoothly rounded lower fuselage with a retractable hydroski. While more complex than the planing hull and providing less internal volume due to the retraction mechanisms, the hydroski had the advantage that, once retracted and

Martin Model 329 C-1
SCALE 1/175

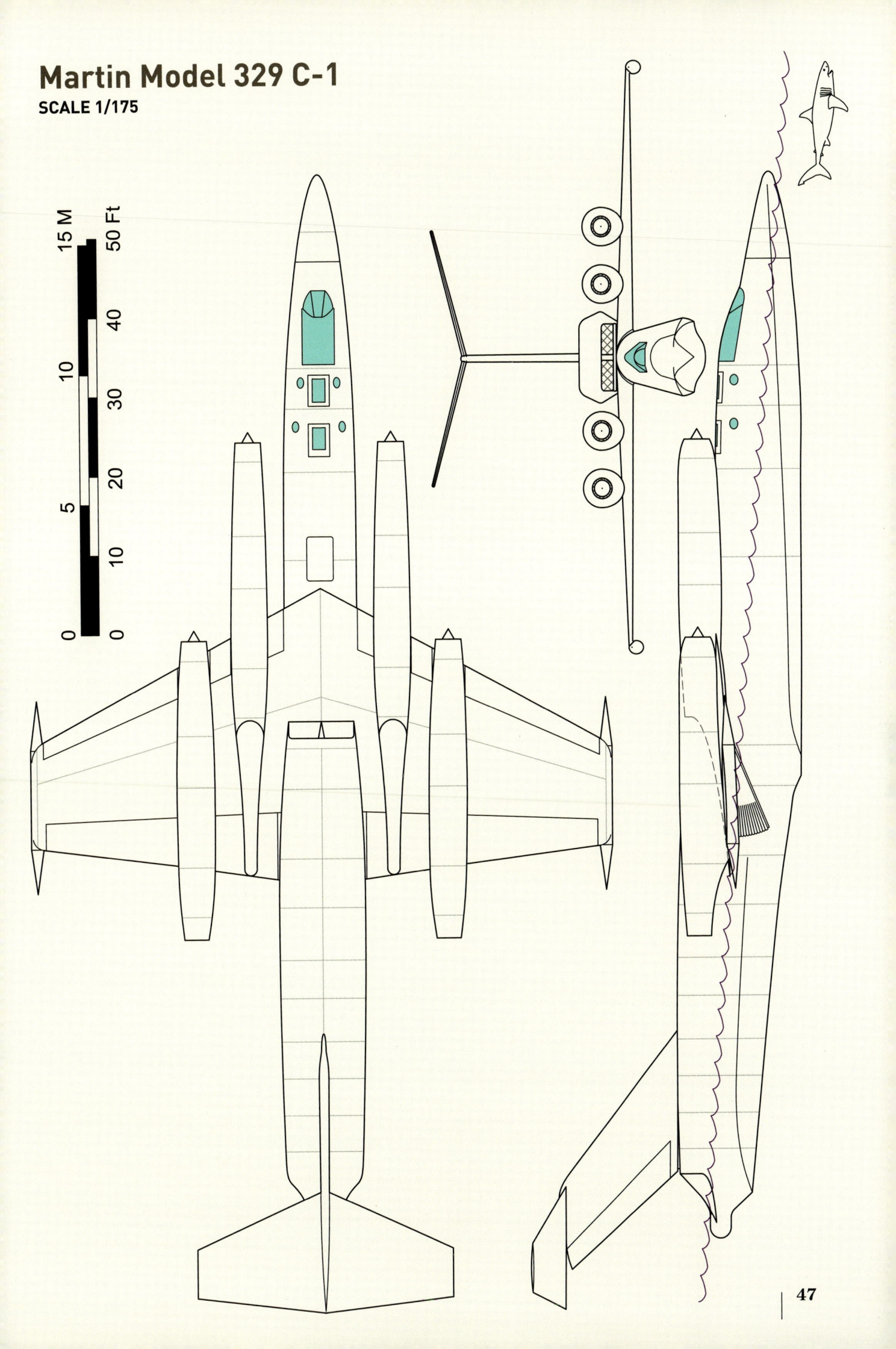

15 M / 50 Ft
10 / 30
5 / 20
0 / 0

faired in, the fuselage would be as aerodynamic as that of any supersonic land-based aircraft. Additionally, the hydroski-equipped Model 329 C-2 was found to have superior hydrodynamic qualities, including less trouble with water spray entering the outboard engines and impacting on the aft fuselage. It was concluded that for the 329 C-1 alternate inlets would likely be required for the outboard engines, but these were not designed when the reports were published.

The 329 C aircraft utilized essentially straight wings with a 28° leading edge sweep. The shift of aerodynamic centre during the subsonic to supersonic transition required a substantial horizontal stabilizer at the end of the vertical stabilizer, mounted high to avoid water spray and aerodynamic interference from the wing at high angles of attack. Swept and delta wings were rejected early on in the design process due to the straight wings' superior stability characteristics.

The Model 329 C designs both had wingtip stabilizing floats with small secondary deployable hydroskis in each float. The skis pulled down a skirt which formed a sort of vertical fin. This would provide stability as the aircraft began to rise out of the water.

Model 329 C was designed to dash at Mach 2 at altitude and cruise at Mach 0.95 at sea level, with a total range of 1,500 nautical miles. Weapons load could be 16,000lb worth of conventional bombs, but the primary intended load was a single 6,400lb 'special weapon' (an undefined nuclear device). The basic mission called for a high-altitude cruise, dash and nuclear weapons deployment; the structure was stressed for low-altitude missions (with 16,000lb of conventional stores, from bombs to sea mines) as well, but only as a secondary concern. Aircraft size and weight were constrained to roughly those of the P6M to facilitate easier handling with existing equipment and facilities.

In light of modern stealth design, Model 329 does not appear to be a particularly stealthy aircraft but both C-models were designed to use contour breaks in their fuselages to reduce radar reflectivity.

The forward portion of the fuselage for both C-models contained the pressurized crew compartment, the radar systems and electronic equipment; the centre section contained the fuel and the bomb chute. The bomb was loaded through a hatch in the upper fuselage forward of the wing. Defensive systems, including radar, chaff, jamming systems and three rearward-firing missiles, were located in the aft fuselage.

Range could be increased up to 50% by switching to more exotic fuels such as ethyldecaborane. As energetic and promising a fuel as that may have been, practical experience showed that boron-based fuels were logistical and safety nightmares; working with the stuff on a flying boat being battered by waves would bring a whole new meaning to 'exciting'. At a takeoff weight of 220,000lb, the Model 329 C-1 would require a takeoff run of 4,150ft. The crew members were to be equipped with B-58-style individual escape capsules.

The basic engine configuration of six non-afterburning turbojets was compared to a configuration with four afterburning versions of the same engines, with the inboard wing engines removed. The four-engine version of the 329 C-1 was found to have somewhat greater range than the six-engine version. The six-engine 329 C-2 would have greater range than either version of the C-1, while a somewhat smaller four-engined C-2 would likely be the optimum design. It was proposed that the conversion from six engines to four could be carried out to the basic configuration without great difficulty.

Martin Water-Based Attack Aircraft

The Glenn L. Martin company reported to the US Navy's Office of Naval Research on a study of water-based transport and attack aircraft in 1955. The attack aircraft was assumed to be based on 1955-1960 level technology (present day to near future) and utilized retractable planing hydroskis for takeoff and landings.

The attack aircraft was the size of a fighter and meant for tactical strikes against the likes of ships, bridges, rail yards, trucks, troop concentrations, fuel dumps, other aircraft and airfields. It was planned for use in numerous widely dispersed bases around Europe to defend against a Soviet incursion. By water-basing the attack aircraft, runways would not need to be built. A standard base would include 90 aircraft, while a Small Airhead Base would have 30 aircraft.

The attack aircraft designed by Martin was a fairly conventional design with a shoulder-mounted swept wing. A single turbojet engine occupied the rear fuselage, fed by an inlet located on the upper fuselage near the trailing wing root (well away from water spray). The wing had notable anhedral, with wingtips that would have dipped into the water while floating. The fuselage was largely landplane-conventional, with few 'seaplane' design aspects.

In order to get the plane smoothly off the water (and to safely land on the water), the fuselage was fitted with a large extendable hydroplaning ski near the front. Additional hydroskis would extend from the wingtips. With a little forward motion, these skis would pick the plane up, eventually 'unsticking' it from the water and allowing it to lift off reasonably smoothly. Aerodynamically the plane was nearly as clean as a landplane; the hydroskis were expected to weigh less than equivalent landplane landing gear. Thus, theoretically, this attack aircraft might be superior to an equivalent landplane.

The skis would allow for takeoffs and landings from non-water surfaces as well. Runways made of wetted wood planks, for example, or dirt, mud, sod,

Martin Model 329 C-2
SCALE 1/175

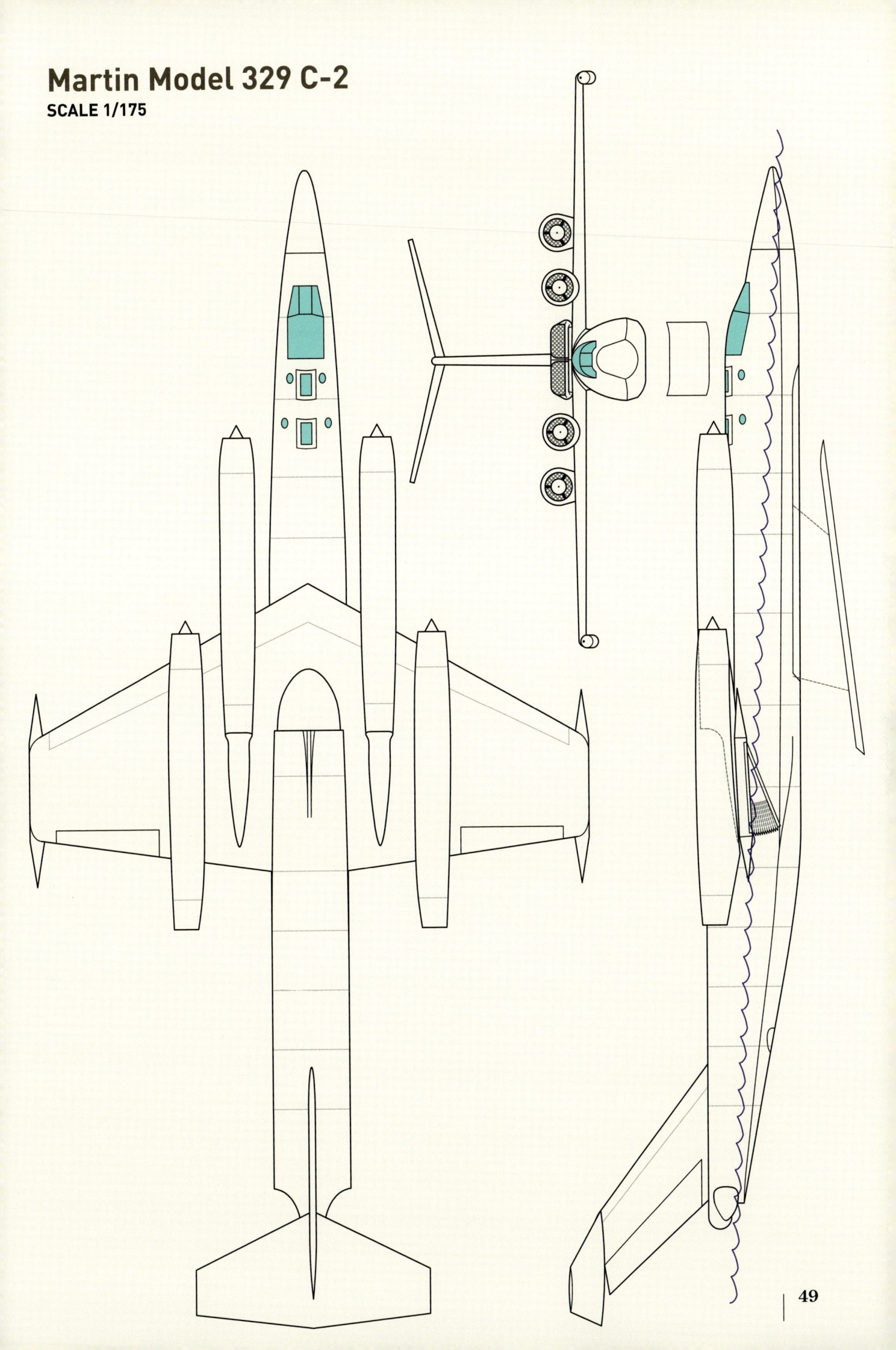

49

Martin Water-Based Attack Aircraft
SCALE 1/100

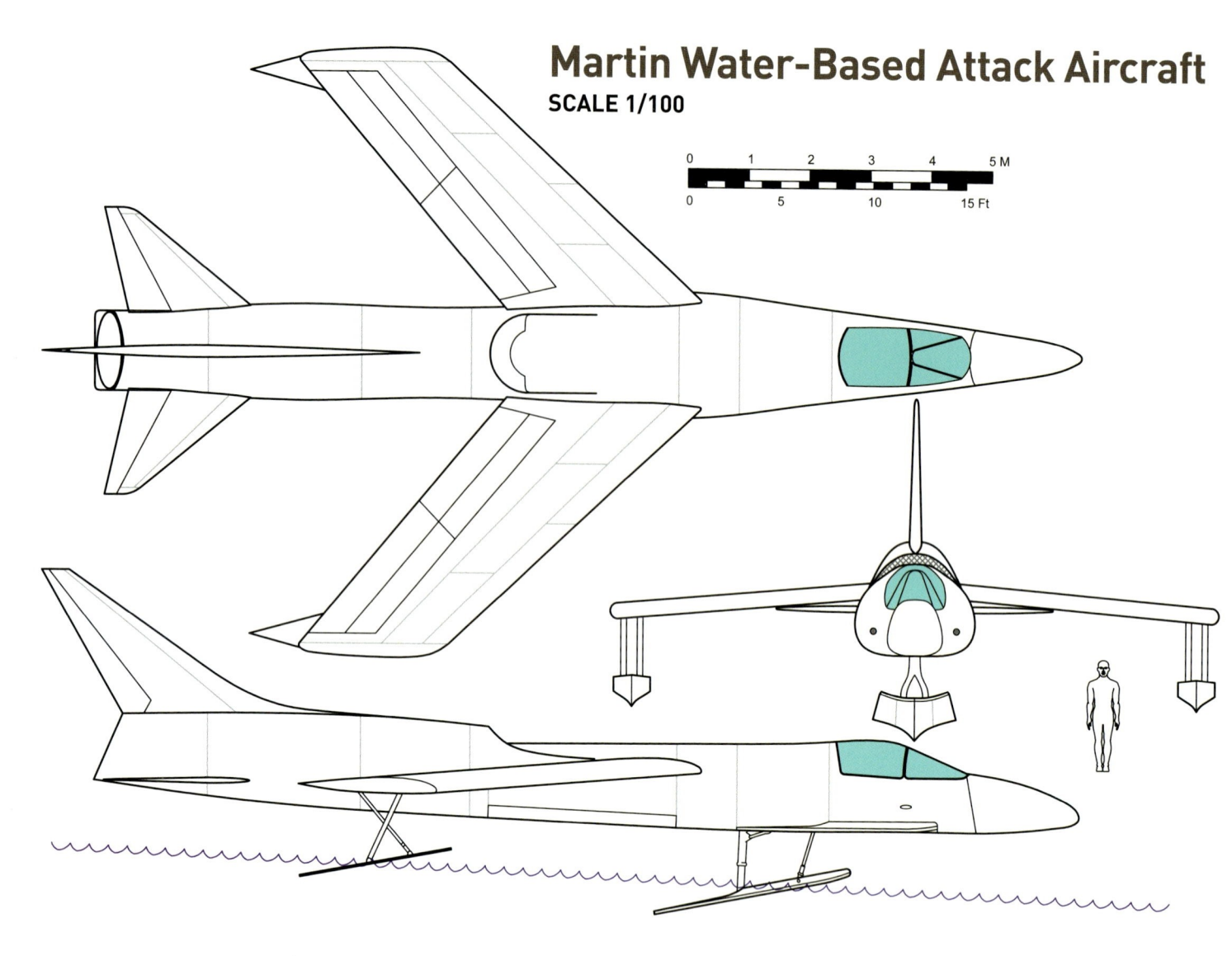

snow or even steel aircraft carrier decks. A difficulty in the design was the fact that at static conditions the aircraft would rest rather deeply in the water, allowing water to enter the exhaust, and making forward motion difficult because the nose would be under the surface. The aircraft would thus most likely start from a beach and hit the water at a minimum of 30 knots; at this speed it would ride high enough on the hydroskis to prevent water stall. Takeoff speed would be 140 knots, taking about 3,500ft for the run. The attack aircraft could operate from open ocean water, but additional infrastructure, such as rafts the plane could dock with to raise it out of the water, would be needed.

Aft of the fuselage hydroski was a rotary bomb bay. A weapons load of 2,072lb could be carried. Two 30mm guns would also be carried for strafing and dogfighting. The aircraft was capable of top speeds in the just barely supersonic, reaching about Mach 1.12.

Convair Combat Seaplane Designs

In 1955 Convair was contracted by the Navy to design a seaplane that could be used for both fighter and attack missions. This aircraft was to be a substantial advance over the state of the art, with a top speed in the area of Mach 3. A number of designs were produced, most single engined, a few twin-engined. The single-engine designs were to use the Allison 700 B-3 (J89) engine, an advanced engine that would be considered for the Lockheed Blackbird programme. Like the ultimately successful Pratt & Whitney J58 engine, the J89 would have had bypass ducts outside of the core leading from the compressor stage to the afterburner; this would have allowed it to operate as a turboramjet in order to attain the proposed high airspeeds.

Three main configurations are known from this study. One used a single J89 in a configuration with delta wings, a T-tail and a deployable hydroski for takeoff and landing. The inlets were rectangular and located at the wing roots; this would put them in position to ingest seawater however, so secondary inlets were located aft of those atop the fuselage. These would be used to get the aircraft moving fast enough to rise up onto the hydroski, at which point the main inlets could be safely opened.

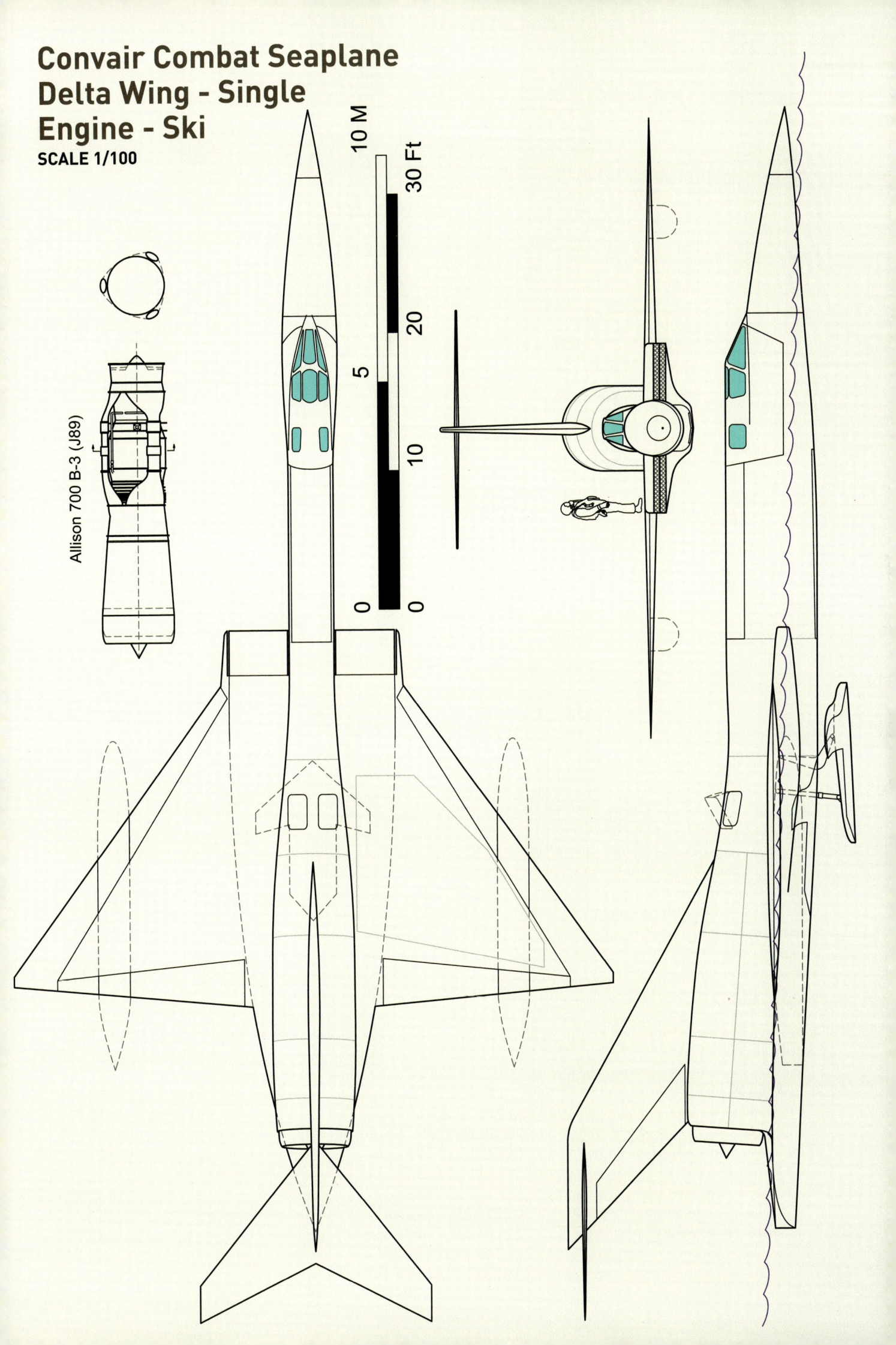

Convair Combat Seaplane
Delta Wing - Single Engine - Ski
SCALE 1/100

Allison 700 B-3 (J89)

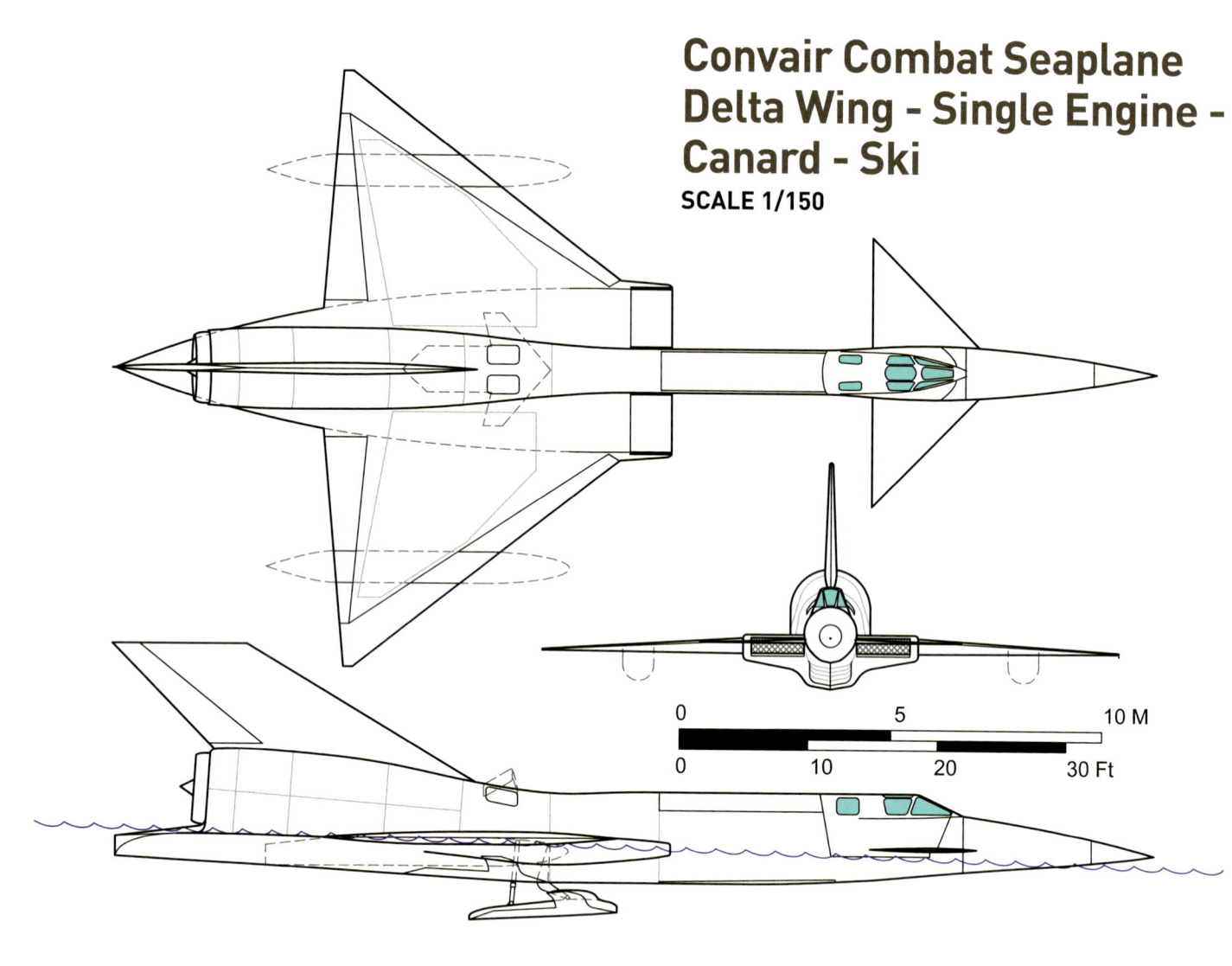

Convair Combat Seaplane Delta Wing - Single Engine - Canard - Ski
SCALE 1/150

The second design was much the same as the first, but utilized two General Electric X-275A turbojets. These were early designs for what would become the GE YJ93 engines used on the North American XB-70. Other than the engines and a reshaping of the inlets, the design was little changed.

The third design was essentially the first, but with the horizontal stabilizers removed and replaced with delta canards. The vertical stabilizer was a bit shorter. The first three designs used essentially the same fuselage, one that displayed considerable complex contouring in line with the area rule principle. Additionally, the fuselage was not a traditional one for a seaplane, with a distinct keel only developing aft of the wing. The nose ahead of the cockpit was noticeably wider than the fuselage aft of the cockpit; this would have resulted in a large diameter nosecone perfect for the installation of a large radar system. This would have been less useful for the attack mission than for the fighter mission. While air-to-air armament is not well defined, it certainly would have been made up of guided missiles, likely long range missiles such as the AIM-47 Falcon as demonstrated on the Lockheed YF-12.

The final design replaced the delta wings with straight wings, and recontoured the fuselage. It used the same J89 engine as the first design and in the same position, but the rest of the aircraft was different to one degree or another. The hull was much more boat-like, with a sharp keel running almost to the nose, and without the sudden thinning of the fuselage aft of the cockpit. A retractable step was used to aid in lifting off from the water rather than a ski; the straight wings were given variable incidence to both increase low speed lift and to raise the inlets well above the waterline… though it can be guessed that the ducting would be something of a challenge. To aid in that, it wasn't simply the wing that tilted up, but a section of the fuselage as well, providing a large flat vertical plane that contained both sides of the inlet ducting. A single large door was provided at the top of the fuselage for the secondary inlet.

All of the designs used a jettisonable escape capsule rather than ejector seats. This was doubtless in response to the Mach 3 top speed. All also included jettisonable external fuel tanks; the delta winged designs mounted the tanks (each containing 7,084lb of fuel) at about ⅔ span while the straight winged design mounted them to

**Convair Combat Seaplane
Delta Wing -
Twin Engine - Ski**
SCALE 1/100

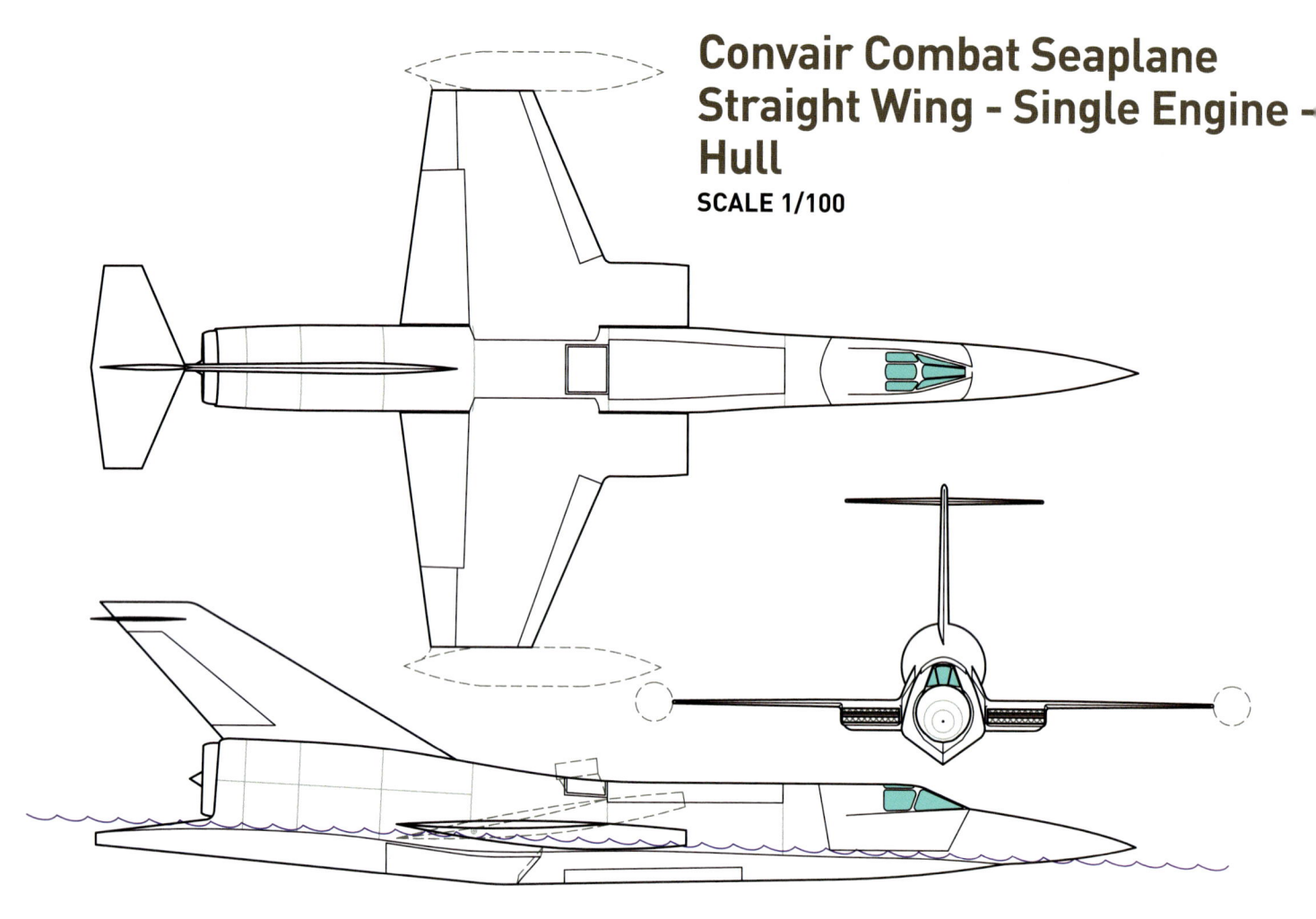

Convair Combat Seaplane Straight Wing - Single Engine - Hull
SCALE 1/100

the wingtips. The straight-winged aircraft external tanks differed in more than their location; they held only 3,500lb of fuel each, but also contained "jettisonable stores".

All of the designs had a single missile bay, 158in long by 32in wide (barely large enough for the AIM-47), just behind the cockpit module. The bays had doors on both the top and bottom of the fuselage; the bottom doors were used to launch the missile, while the top doors were used to access and load the missile bay while floating on the water. Seemingly to make up for the smaller fuel load of the external tanks, the wider forward fuselage of the straight-winged design located sizable fuel tanks to either side of the missile bay.

Convair Supersonic Attack Airplane
Convair-San Diego (specifically a team led by German aeronautical engineer Hans Amtmann) conducted several studies of a "supersonic attack airplane" for the US Navy in 1955 and 1956, producing a number of different, but related, designs. The concept called for a water-based bomber capable of carrying a 3,000lb nuclear weapon on a low-level mission with a cruise speed of Mach 0.9, a radius of 1,700 nautical miles and a maximum speed of Mach 1.25 at 35,000ft. Most of the designs look like stretched versions of the F2Y Sea Dart, with a sleek V-bottomed 'boat hull' and low-set delta wings.

Most designs had four engines, though some had two and others six. Some designs featured B-58-like engine nacelles hanging below and ahead of the wing; to keep them out of the water, the pylons were hinged at the base to tilt the engine upwards. A few designs, though, featured swept wings and horizontal stabilizers on the wings; some of these designs bore more than a slight resemblance to the Model 23 nuclear seaplanes described in the following chapter.

The design illustrated here dates from April 1955 and utilized six G.E. J79 turbojets all located on the upper fuselage. Two were well forward, installed in nacelles that organically grew from the shoulders of the fuselage right behind (and above) the cockpit. Four more were located well aft, fed from a single duct that connected to an inlet between and above the forward engines. The fuselage was a hybrid, with a V-bottom 'boat hull' at the nose and again at the tail, with a rounded lower surface amidships. It was there that the capacious bomb bay contained a single sizable 'special' munition in the form of a presumably generic bomb-shape.

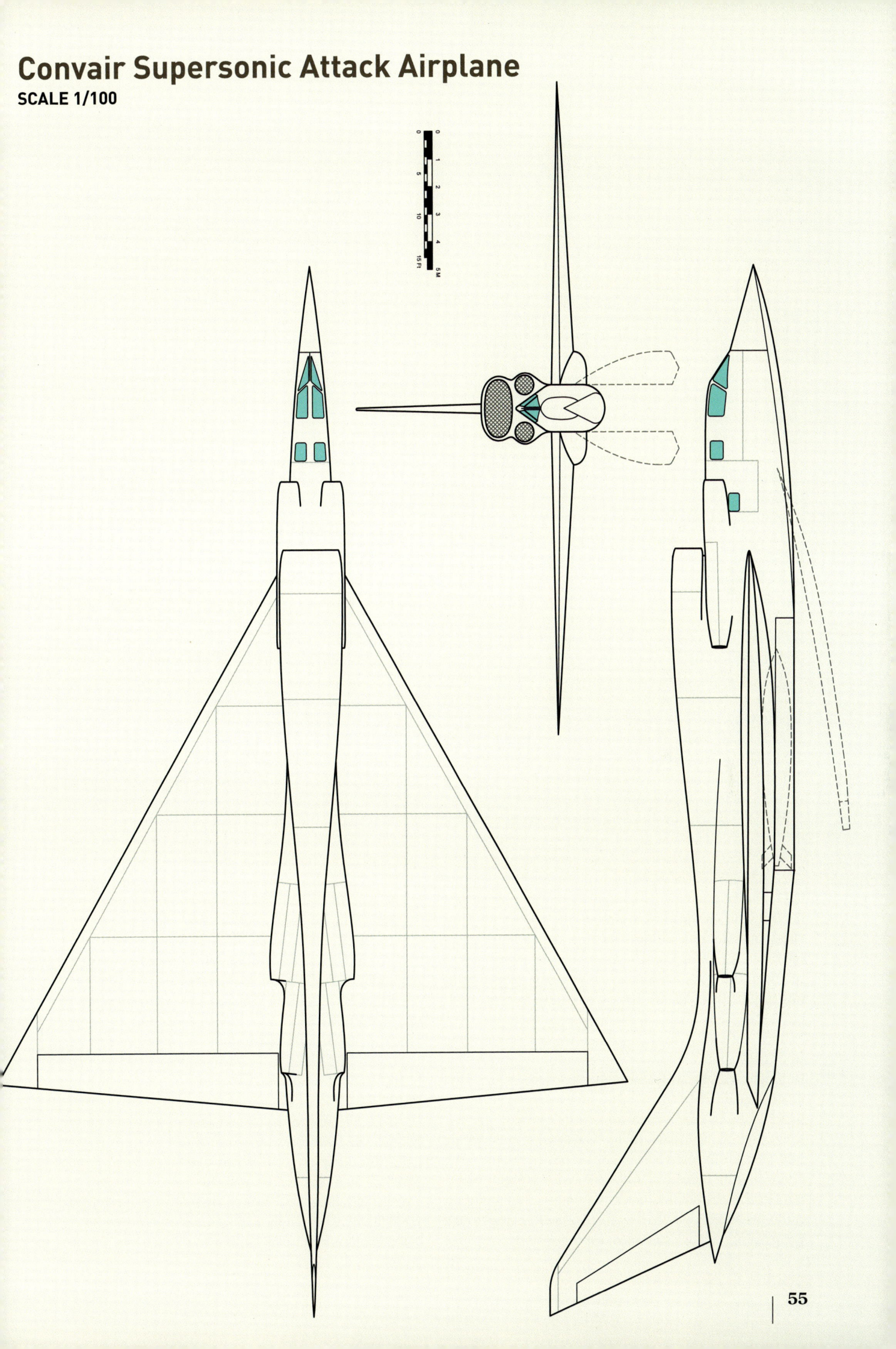

Convair Supersonic Attack Airplane
SCALE 1/100

Landing gear was provided in the form of a pair of hydroskis. These would deploy from fairings along the wing roots and would project well below the aircraft and give it a distinctly nose-up attitude while accelerating.

Convair Water-Based B-58

In 1956 Convair-San Diego issued a report on the feasibility of seaplanes as strategic bombers (see *US Supersonic Bomber Projects Volume 1* for discussion of this regarding Weapon System 110A). Included here was the idea of creating a water-based version of the B-58 to use as a medium-range, medium-payload strike system for the Strategic Air Command.

Modifying the B-58 to operate from the water was not as simple as just bolting on a couple of floats. Instead, virtually the entire aircraft needed to be redesigned, to the point where the result only vaguely resembles the original B-58. For starters the engines needed to be relocated, moving from below the wings to two of them mounted above the wings and two more in a single nacelle above the rear fuselage. The wing engines used pylons that could hinge upwards to move the inlets further still from the water… 45° upwards for water taxi and runup, 30° for the actual takeoff run and horizontal for flight.

The landing gear was removed, with the main landing gear replaced with two hydroskis. The wing aspect ratio was increased by reducing leading edge sweep to 50°, and it appears that the leading edge camber was removed. The vertical stabilizer was redesigned and given a horizontal stabilizer at the tip to improve takeoff performance. The crew was reduced to two, the defensive systems operator being declared irrelevant as there was no longer a gun in the tail.

The main weapon of the water-based B-58 remained a pod located under the centreline. Unlike the conventional B-58, though, here the pod would need to be designed so that the weapon could be safely submerged for extended periods of time. The basic weapon was a single large missile with a range of 300 miles. An internal weapons bay was also to be provided, along with the provision to carry two underwing jettisonable fuel tanks.

Two alternate configurations were studied. The first exchanged the two underwing hydroskis for a single larger fuselage-mounted hydroski. This change negated the possibility of the large centreline weapons/fuel pod, so a single solid propellant air-to-surface missile would be carried in a weapons bay in the forward fuselage. A more radical still configuration change was considered… a V-bottomed boat hull with swept wings rather than delta; the wing turbojets were installed in fixed nacelles above the wing tailing edges. The inlets for the fuselage engines were extended much further forward; the internal weapons bay was much smaller.

Along with longer fuselages for all configurations, the 'water based B-58s' ended up not having a whole lot in common with the standard B-58. In actual practice these would be very different aircraft, just with some similarities in appearance, a few systems in common and a similar mission… apart from the small detail of where they were based. Operationally, Convair suggested that there be 28 wings of these new water-based medium bombers in the "Advance Base Force". Each wing would be composed of three squadrons, with 15 bombers per squadron: 1,260 bombers in total. The squadrons would be split into three flights of five aircraft, dispersed for safety reasons.

The Advance Base Force would be split into non-war-ready components safely in continental US bases, and war-ready components in numerous theatre bases. These latter bases would be split into rear-area support complexes and forward area bases. The rear area bases would be semi-permanent with a main base and satellite bases, and would be capable of carrying out maintenance of the aircraft as well as staging tankers for in-flight refuelling of the bombers. The rear-area bases would be close enough to the enemy to launch strikes, though in-flight refuelling would be a must.

The forward bases would be generally temporary, though a fixed position within the waters of friendly powers would be considered. Logistics for the water-based bombers would be carried out either entirely via other aircraft, including flying boat cargo and fuel transports, or through the use of submarine logistics. The latter concept would include the emplacement of submerged and hidden fuel tanks and submerged caches of ordnance. All of these bases would be near to shore, with inflatable ramps used to haul the bombers onto beaches for basic maintenance, servicing, refuelling and reloading. Other facilities would be similarly austere.

One-third of the actively deployed bombers would be in the forward bases, with the rest in the rear area bases. Locations for forward area bases included Britain, Japan, the Philippines, the western Mediterranean, the Middle East and many locations in the western Pacific… and many others. Politics would be one of the deciding factors.

Convair Hydro-Ski Supersonic Attack Airplane

Around 1956, Convair-San Diego proposed to the US Navy a supersonic water-based attack aircraft derived from the company's F2Y Sea Dart and substantially smaller than the very slightly earlier "Supersonic Attack Airplane". It was a two-seat delta winged seaplane using a single centreline hydroski; while the basic configuration was similar to the Sea Dart, F-102

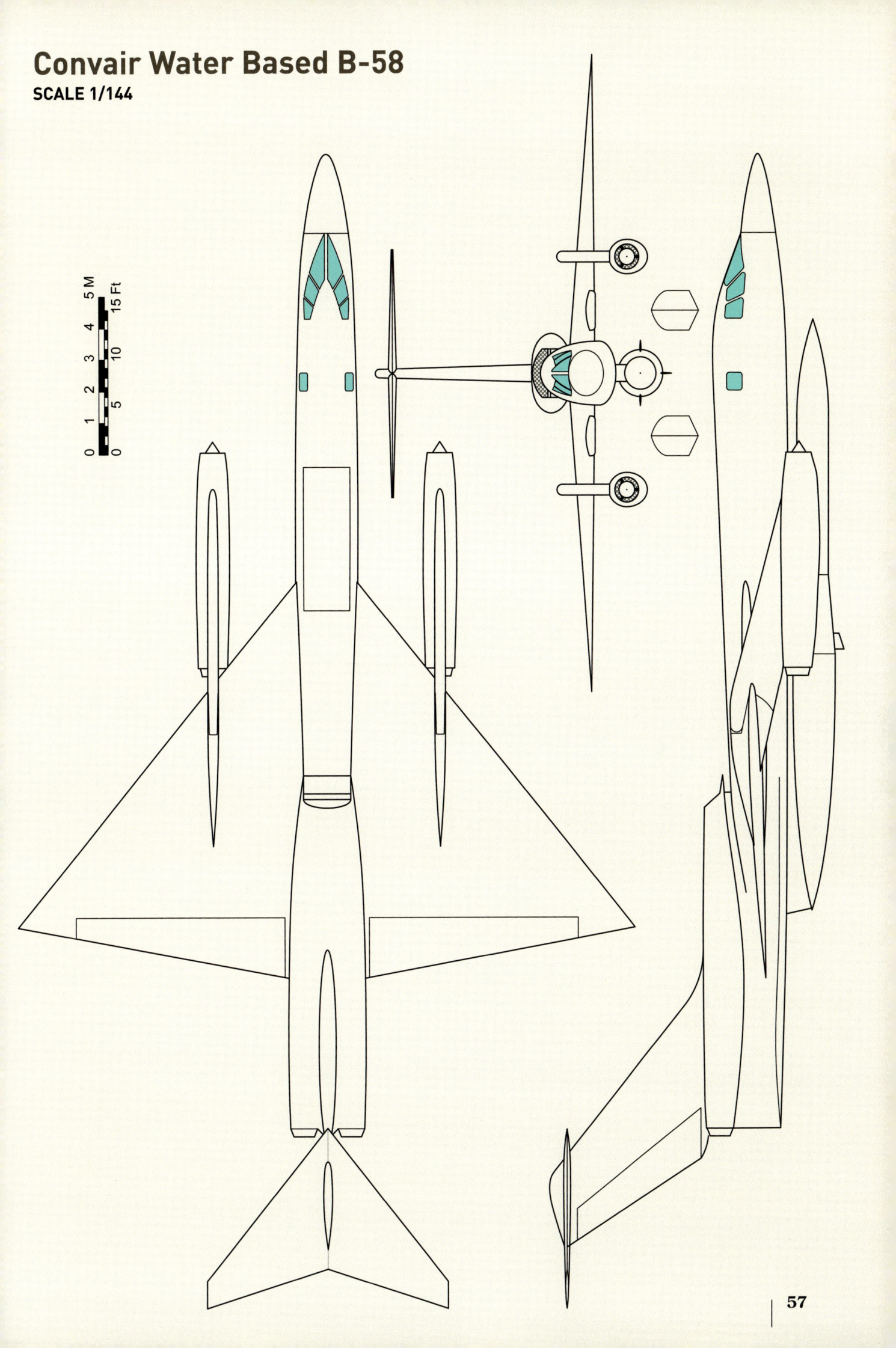

Convair Water Based B-58
SCALE 1/144

Convair Water Based B-58
SCALE 1/144

experience informed the design, in particular the use of the area rule principle.

Two General Electric J79 turbojets would be used to power the aircraft to a maximum speed of Mach 1.49. More advanced versions of the J79 would be installed as made available. An attack speed of Mach 1.4 at 40,000ft was considered sufficiently fast to be able to evade enemy defences... a point of view that would not last long.

A single bomb bay was located aft of the hydroski, with capacity for a single "special" (i.e. nuclear) weapon. The crew of two was composed of the pilot and the radar operator/bombardier. For high altitude level bombardment missions radar would be used for aiming; for low level missions, a mix of radar and visual aiming would be used for a 'toss' of the bomb. The bomb shape shown was hypothetical, but assumed to be as large as any the aircraft might need to carry at 30in in diameter, 140in long and 2,000lb in weight. A small number of conventional bombs could be carried instead of the nuke... four 500lb bombs, two 1,000lb bombs, two 750lb bombs or a single 2,000lb bomb.

In addition to the hydroski, the aircraft had deployable beaching gear. These would be useful for pulling the aircraft up ramps onto ships or shore, but would not be useful as actual landing gear. Four feet of each wingtip could fold up to reduce the span for storage in ships and hangars. This mechanism would be integral to the aircraft, allowing the feature to function while floating in the water.

A deployable refuelling probe was installed along the fuselage's upper surface aft of the cockpit and on the centreline. Along with using conventional tanker aircraft, a 'buddy' system would allow a pair of the aircraft to fly an extended range mission to deliver a single weapon, with one of the aircraft serving as a tanker. Where the normal unrefuelled mission radius was 800 nautical miles, in the buddy system the radius bumped up to 1,250 nautical miles.

Convair proposed modifying several classes of vessel to serve as tenders for the attack airplane. These were not true 'aircraft carriers' as the aircraft did not take off from the decks; instead, they would be removed from the vessel to float in the water, using their buoyancy and hydroskis to lift off from the ocean's surface. One such class was the CVE 55 Anzio class escort carrier, which would be modified into a seaplane tender capable of handling a dozen attack aircraft and up to four helicopters.

The aft half of the flight deck would be removed and a deployable ramp added to the tail. The ramp would have a small hydrofoil attached to it for control while the vessel was underway. The remaining forward section of the flight deck would serve as a storage area for up to eight of the attack aircraft; four more could be held on the lower hangar deck. A crane would be used to lower planes from the flight deck to the hangar deck, and another crane to lower planes from the hangar deck down to the ramp. Numerous other modifications would be made to the ships.

Another class of vessel considered for the role of tender was the Baltimore class cruiser. A hangar deck and 'aviation' deck would be added to the rear of the vessel; an elevator would be installed to move planes from one deck to another and a crane would be used to lower planes into the water. The main weapons – 8in and 5in turreted cannon – would be removed; the armament at the front of the ship would be replaced with two twin Terrier surface-to-air missile mounts. Radar and associated control systems for the missiles and aircraft would be added. Eight attack aircraft could be accommodated, six on the aviation deck, two on the hangar deck.

A third class of tender would be based on the submarine USS *Guavina*, AGSS 362. The *Guavina* was a Gato-class submarine launched in 1943. After spending the war years in the Pacific theatre, it was modified and recommissioned into an oiler in early 1950 and spent the better part of the following decade demonstrating the ability to refuel seaplanes at sea, using a flight deck built on the aft of the sub to service the aircraft.

Convair designers had the notion of further modifying the *Guavina* (and subsequently other submarines of the class). Modifications planned included raising the hull superstructure 2ft and widening it to 26ft; the addition of a hydrofoil-equipped ramp; adding a turntable to aid aircraft servicing; turning the forward torpedo room into quarters for aviation personnel; additional radar on the conning tower, connected to a new Combat Information Center; plus two watertight tanks added to the topside, just below the new deck, each containing six nuclear weapons. These containers and the weapons within would be accessible from the interior of the submarine while submerged.

Unlike the surface vessels, the submarine would be incapable of carrying the aircraft; instead, the aircraft would rendezvous with it at some preselected sheltered bay for refuelling and rearming. Two aircraft could be serviced on deck at a time. In the event that more aircraft needed servicing at a time, two boats would be supplied that would allow floating aircraft to be started and crews exchanged.

Convair Mach 4 Configurations

The Pratt & Whitney JT11D-20 turbojet – better known as the J58 – is well known as the engine that powered the SR-71 to in excess of Mach 3. As it turned out, the Blackbird series of aircraft are the only ones to have been powered by the J58, but early on in its

Convair Hydro-Ski Supersonic Attack Airplane
SCALE 1/110

Convair Hydro-Ski Supersonic Attack Airplane Support Vessels
SCALE 1/1200

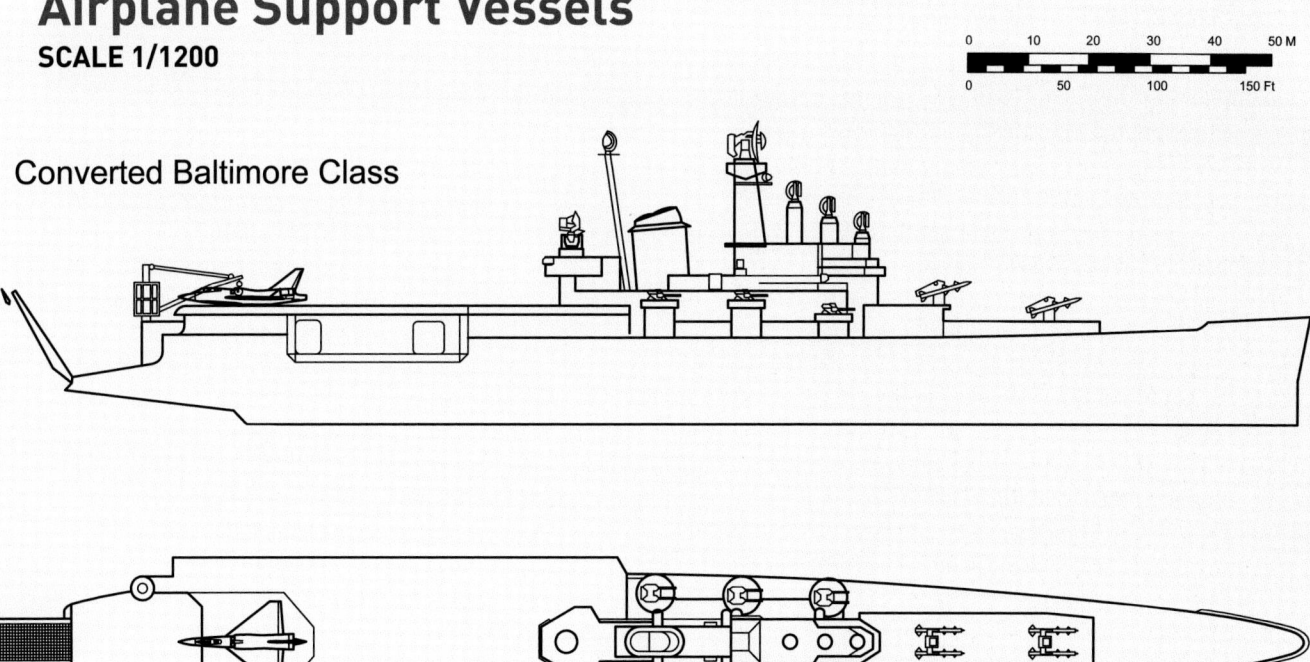

Converted Baltimore Class

Converted USS *Guavina*, Gato Class

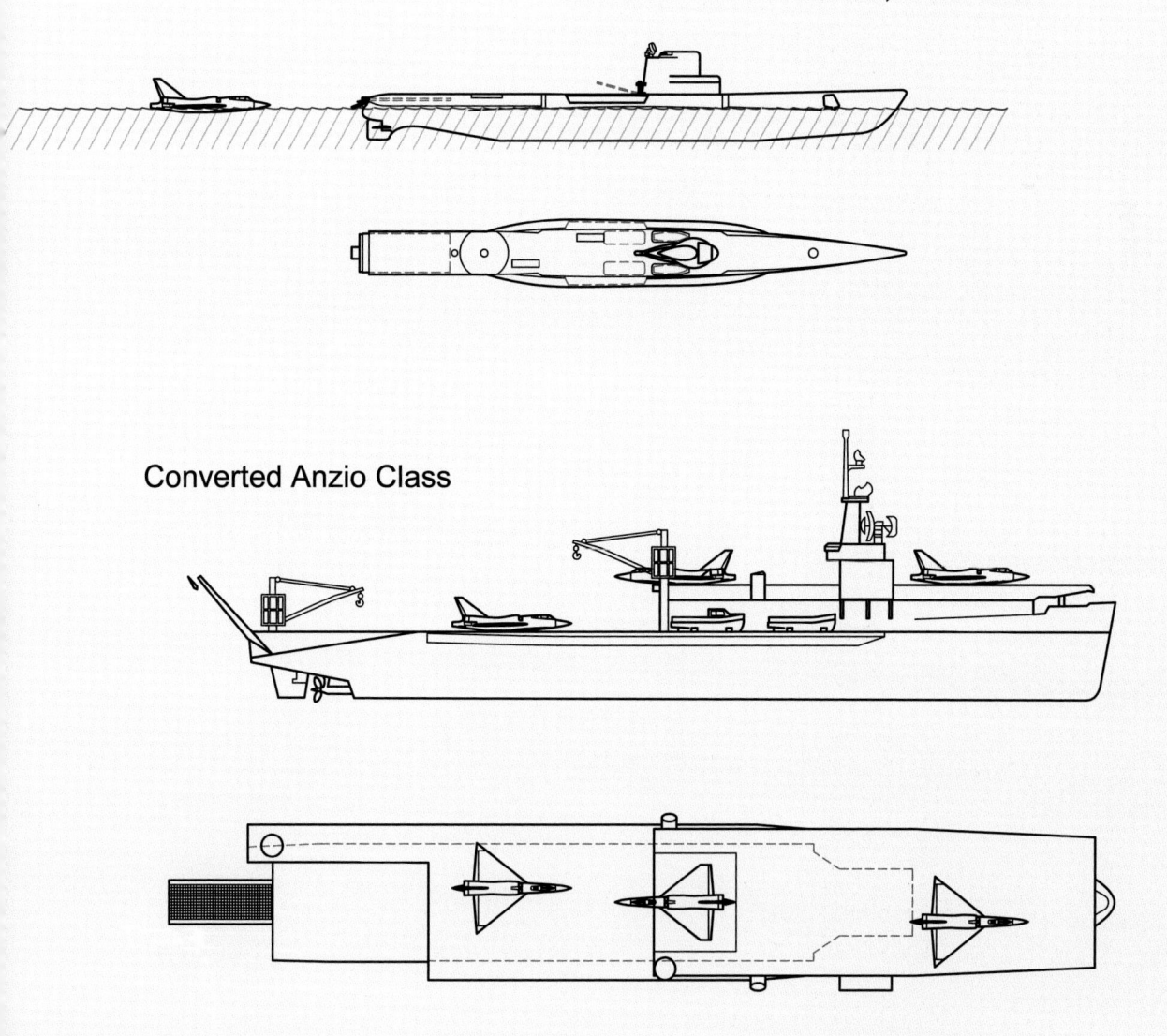

Converted Anzio Class

development there were plans for incorporating it into a wide variety of aircraft, including subsonic designs. But it was seen early in development as being capable of very high speeds… faster, indeed, than the SR-71 would end up going. In 1958 the US Navy Bureau of Aeronautics, which had invested a great deal in the development of the J58, contracted with Convair to study applications of the engine. In response, in July 1958 Convair produced a report on the use of the engine in supersonic attack seaplanes.

In Convair's analysis, the Mach 3 speed the Navy was interested in was not an optimal use of the engine. They concluded that the most efficient flight condition for the J58 was Mach 4 at 80,000ft. Three aircraft were designed, all somewhat similar in configuration and all using three of the engines in airframes made largely of stainless steel. It was projected that the aircraft could enter service around 1967-69. The weapons load for all configurations was given as 6,000lb, but not otherwise described. Takeoff and landing – no sea-state was described here, so presumably "calm" – was expected to take 40 seconds and about 7,000ft.

Configuration I featured a pointed fuselage with stubby clipped delta-like wings. The three engines were side by side on the upper surface, fed by a large inlet featuring a central wedge. Small canards maintained pitch control while large and highly swept wingtip fins provided yaw stability; all wings and fins had blunt trailing edges. A hydroski similar to that used on the Convair Sea Dart would aid in water takeoffs and landings. The cockpit was fully recessed, with no indication given of an external view for the crew. Takeoffs and landings must have been aided by way of periscopes or TV.

Configuration II was laid out much like the first design, but it was designed to fly 'upside down' compared to the landing orientation. This put the large engine inlets, which for reasons of pressure recovery should be on the underside of the aircraft, on the top of the plane while on or near the surface of the water. This configuration may well have also generated substantial 'compression lift', with shockwaves from the inlet pushing against

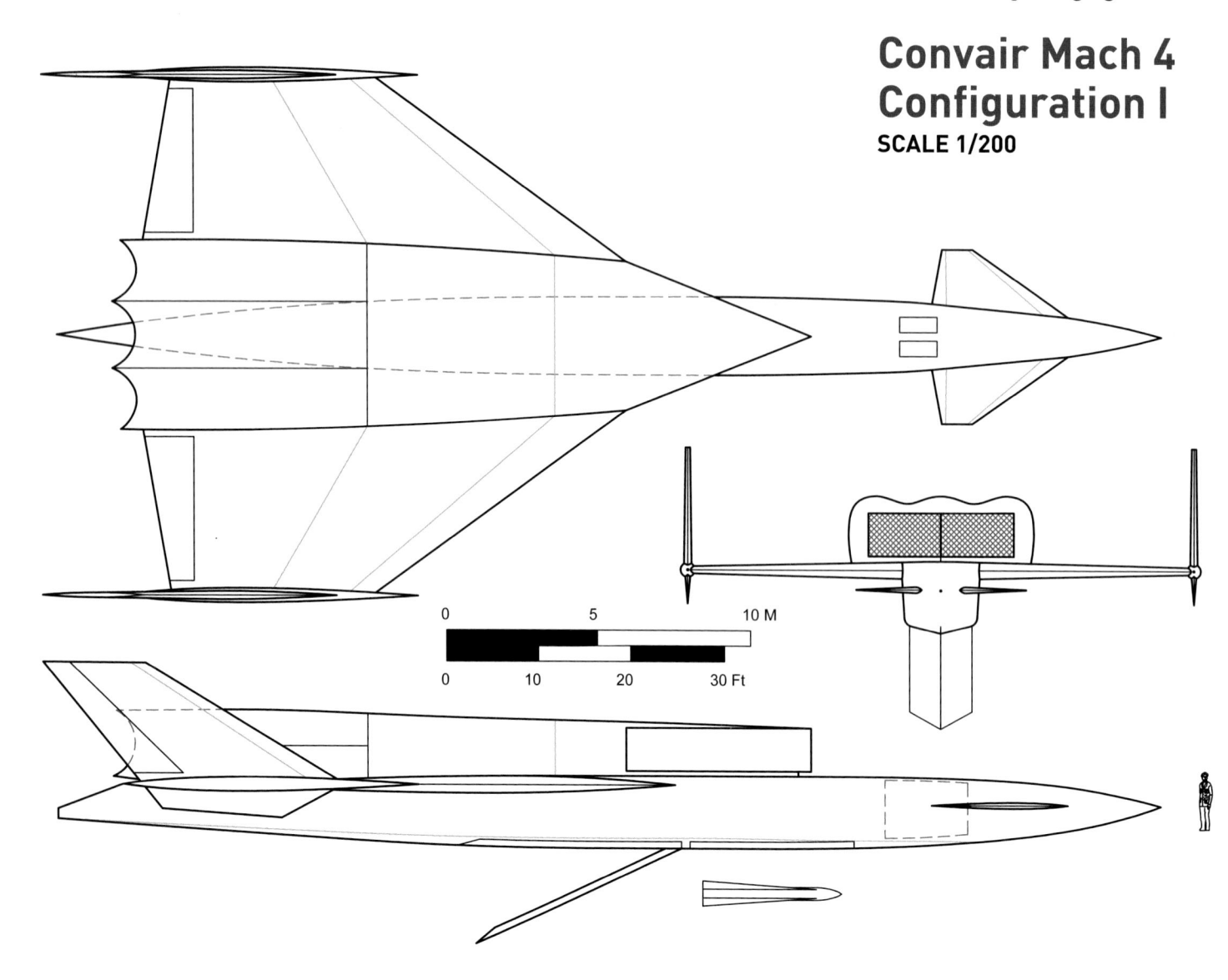

Convair Mach 4 Configuration I
SCALE 1/200

Convair Mach 4
Configuration II
SCALE 1/144

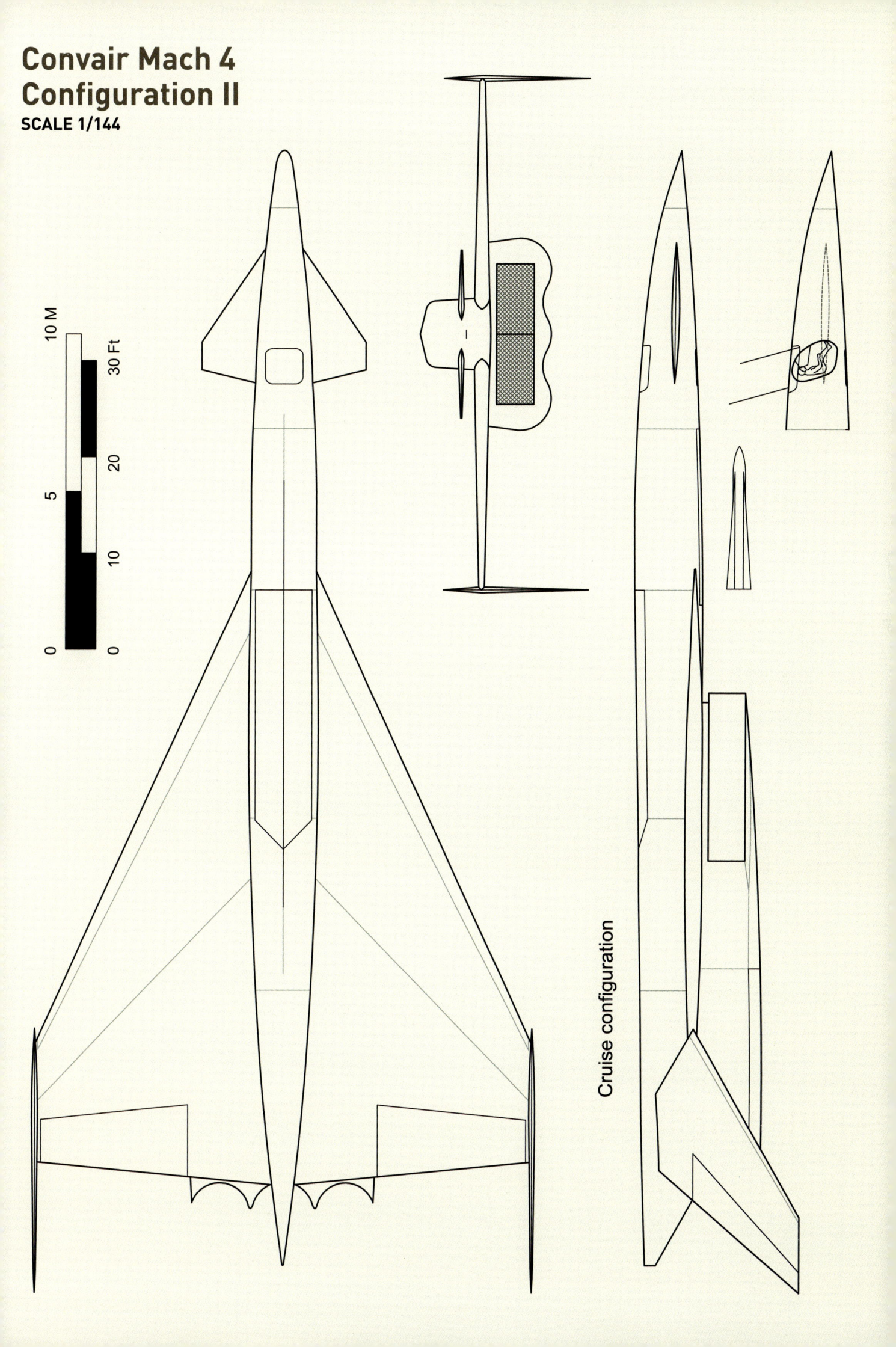

10 M / 30 Ft

Cruise configuration

Convair Mach 4 Configuration II
SCALE 1/144

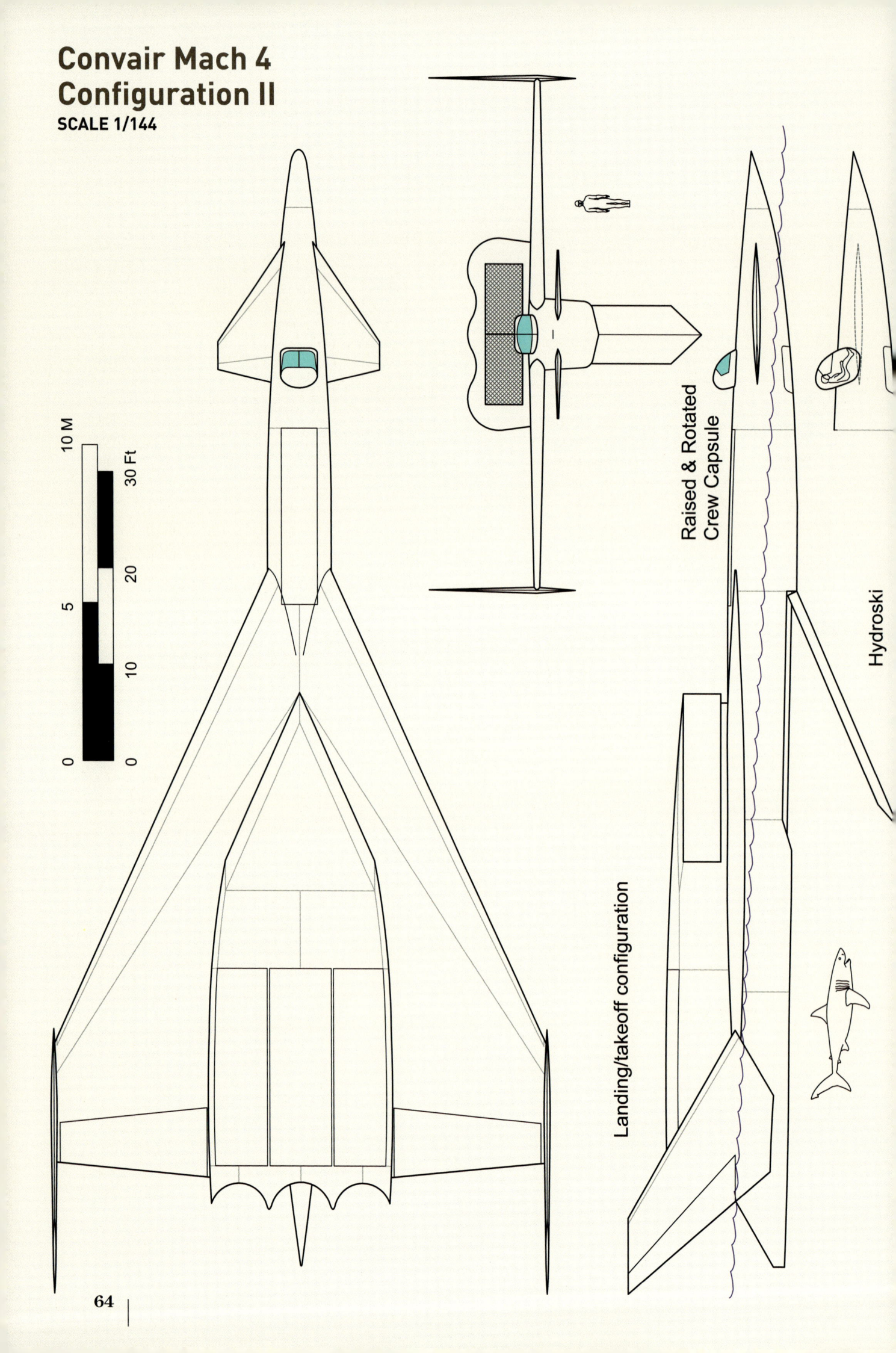

Raised & Rotated Crew Capsule

Hydroski

Landing/takeoff configuration

64

the underside of the wing in much the same way the North American B-70 did (see *US Supersonic Bomber Projects Volume 1*). Convair likely was not aware of North American's findings at that time, though it's curious that the inlets for Configuration II were moved back substantially compared to those of Configuration I, placing the leaded edge of the inlet in much the same place relative to the main wing as on the B-70.

The "rollover" feature also put the weapons bay and vertical stabilizers safely out of the water, while orienting the bomb bay on the underside during horizontal flight and also creating large ventral wingtip fins… again useful for generating lift and stability at high speed. The weapons bay was located directly ahead of the engine inlet, a fact likely to cause issues. The aircraft was quite a bit smaller than the B-70, despite being substantially faster at Mach 4+.

The difficulty of course is that pilots, like most people, don't work so well upside down. To prevent pilots from having to fly or land upside down, they were put in a single ejectable capsule that would roll 180° within the fuselage to stay upright. Additionally, for takeoff and landing the capsule would project above the upper surface of the aircraft to give the crew a better view, using sizable forward-facing windows.

Configuration III was much like Configuration I, but with the inlet moved much further forward. Here at last a clear and definite canopy was on display, immediately ahead of a large arc-shaped inlet. The pointed conical nose of the aircraft would serve as an inlet spike; the forward portion of the inlet would translate back and forth adjusting for Mach number.

Even though the inlet duct was much longer than on Configuration I, it was expected that wind tunnel testing would show lower overall drag, due in part to a lack of interference on the inlet from the canard. The canards from Configuration I were enlarged and moved upwards from the sides of the forward fuselage proper to the sides of the inlet.

Convair Mach 4 Attack/Reconnaissance Seaplane

This design from 1959 does a fantastic job of fitting the 'bizarre' category. While in normal flight it was a

Convair Mach 4 Configuration III
SCALE 1/200

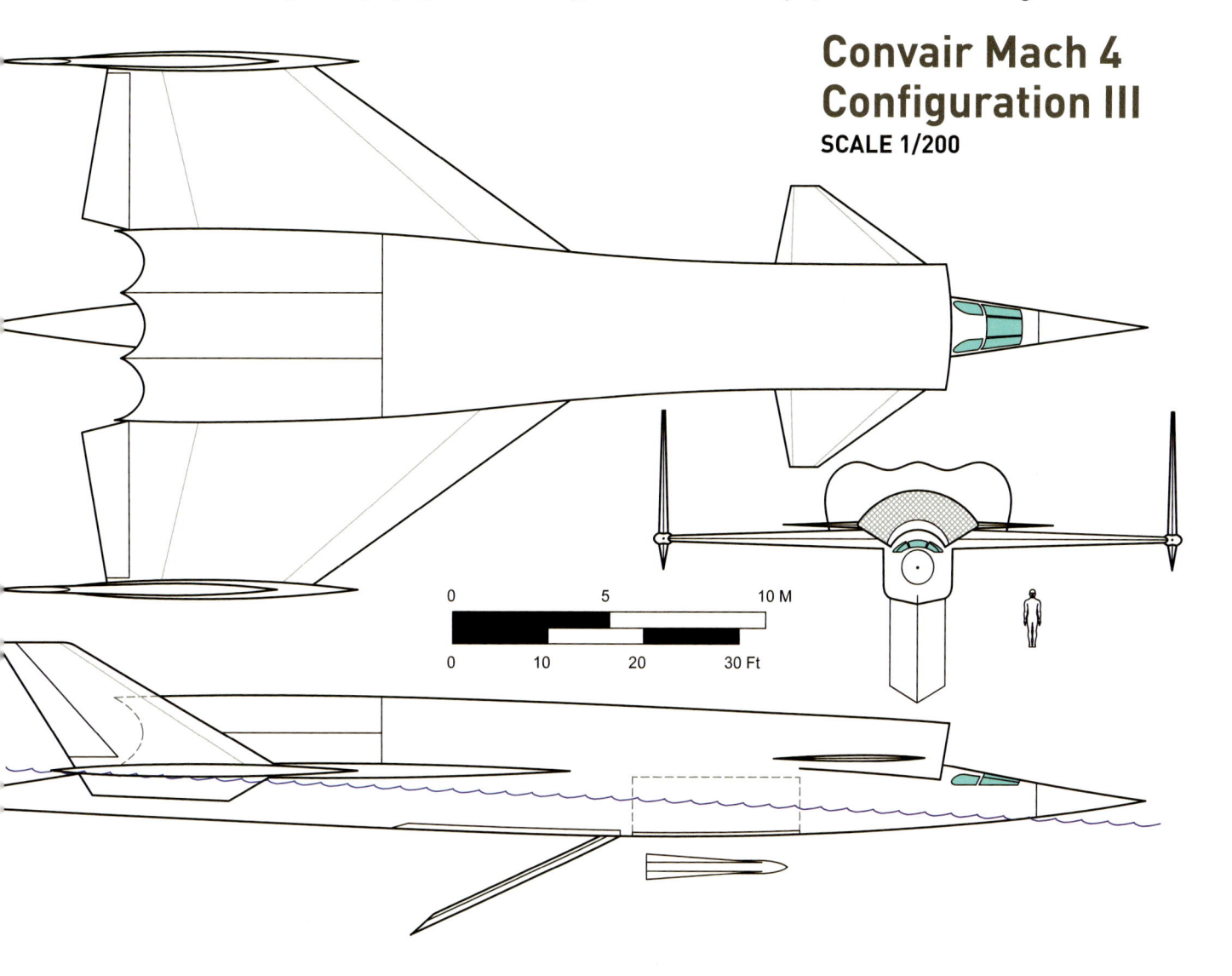

Convair Mach 4 Attack Recon Seaplane
SCALE 1/200

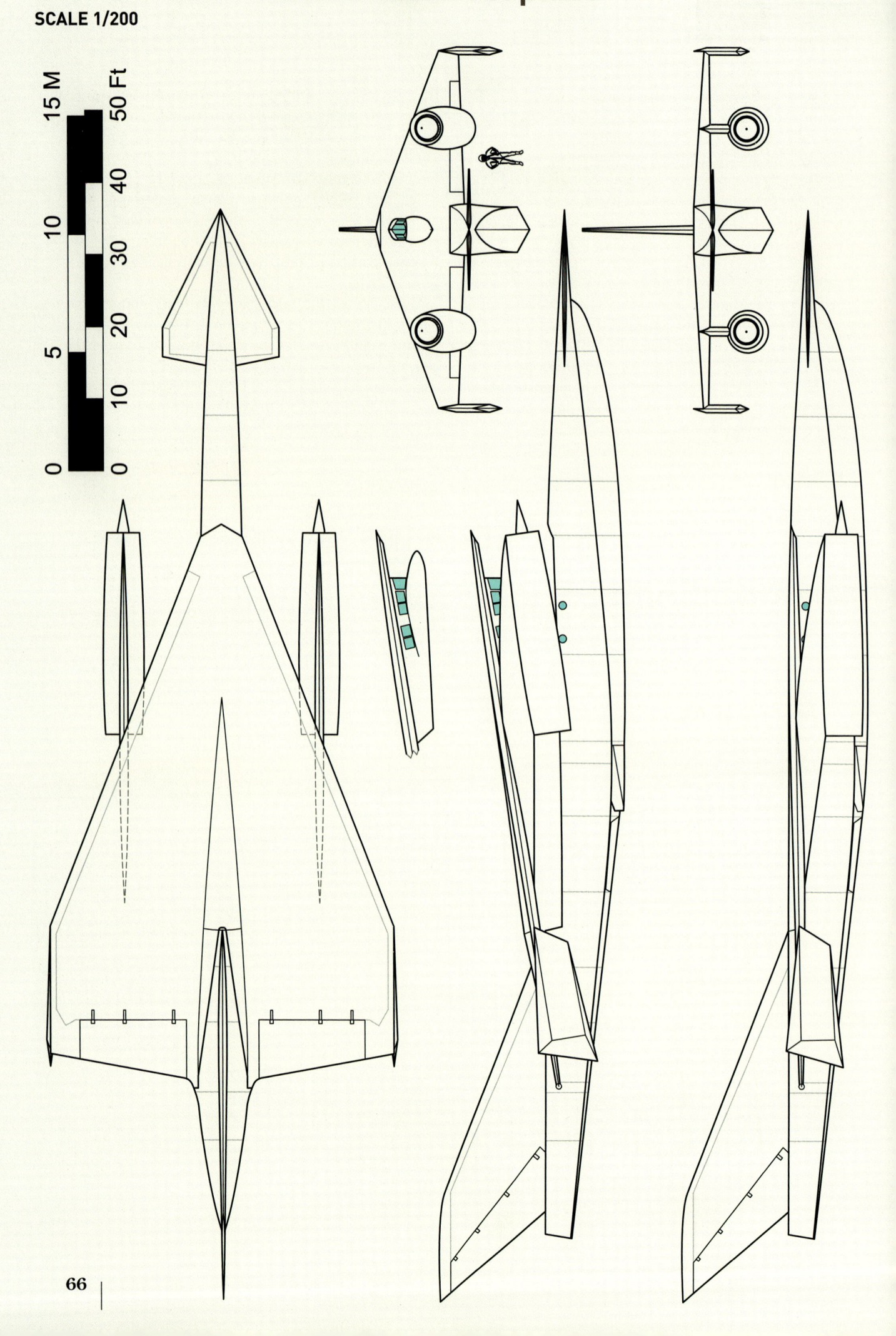

more or less conventional supersonic configuration, with a long, slim fuselage, severely swept delta wings with small tip-fins, a swept vertical stabilizer, canards and two podded engines suspended below and in front of the wings in much the same manner as the inboard engines of the B-58, it was in low speed flight that the aircraft showed its strange side.

In order to both increase lift and get the underslung engines out of the water, the wing was hinged most of the way back to tilt upwards ten degrees. This was not a unique feature for jet seaplane designs, but the wing also took the cockpit with it. With the wing lifted upwards the pilot could get a decent view of the surroundings, useful for landing safely. But as the wing lowered back into position for high speed flight, the cockpit was dropped into a hole in the fuselage. Once in place, the only exterior view the two crewmen had was through two small, circular ports in the side of the fuselage; it seems likely that all they could really see would be the engines. But at least that small view would help with the claustrophobic surroundings.

With the cockpit dropped into the fuselage, no canopy was present to create drag or thermal hot spots. The cockpit being separated from the airstream would also aid in keeping it cool at high speed. The wingtip fins would serve as stabilizing floats while on the water, and a retractable step would help the boat-shaped fuselage break loose from the water on takeoff. The bomb bay was relatively small and was located just aft of the step. The only performance number known is the Mach 4 top speed; altitude and range are unavailable.

NASA TM X-191

The NACA, and then NASA, was tasked with aiding the American aviation industry develop and advance the technological state of the art. This included all areas of aviation technology, from materials to propulsion to aerodynamics. A big part of what the NACA/NASA did for industry was wind tunnel testing of configurations developed by various corporations; while this aided the company by providing essentially free work and data, it meant that others would have access to the same information.

Thus wind tunnel test reports were issued that showed new and innovative aircraft configurations and the results of aerodynamic testing. What these reports often did not do, unfortunately, was state clearly who the work was for, or what the company designation of the aircraft was. So there are a number of supersonic seaplane bomber concepts revealed in these aerodynamic studies, but their identities are often a mystery.

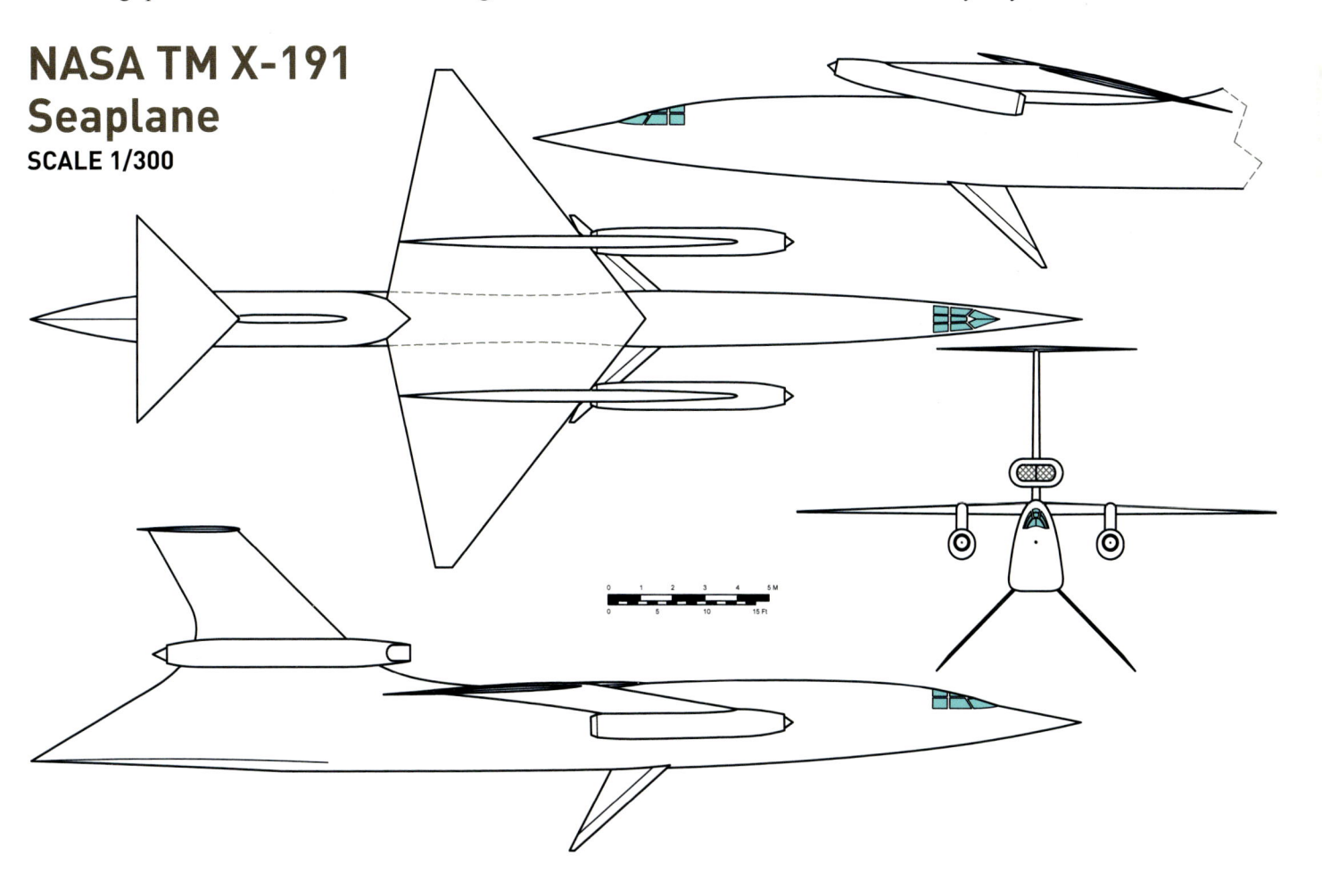

NASA TM X-191
Seaplane
SCALE 1/300

One such aircraft was shown in NACA and later NASA reports. The design originates from no later than 1957, when work was done at the NACA's Langley Field. It has the appearance of a Convair design, but it could easily be a Martin concept, or, less probably, Boeing, Republic, Grumman, Lockheed... anybody. Vague allusions are given to the design being an in-house Langley configuration, based on Navy and industry requirements; this could mean a clean-sheet design or a modification of an industry design. In any event, the work originated with requirements from the US Navy's Bureau of Aeronautics and called for a subsonic cruise, Mach 2 dash attack aircraft with a combat radius of 1,500 nautical miles.

The aircraft bore a distinct similarity to a number of Convair designs, with a shoulder mounted near-delta wing, two podded engines (afterburning Orenda Iroquois FS-13s) suspended below and ahead of the wings and two additional engines in a nacelle at the base of the vertical tail. The wings were variable incidence, tilting upwards 10° to increase low speed lift as well as raise the engines well above the water. The fuselage was very slim and pointed, the forward half was aerodynamically clean and did not have much of a boat hull shape, while the aft third or so had a V-bottomed planing surface.

This unboatlike fuselage was made possible due to one of several proposed lifting systems... initially a hydroski, later hydrofoils. The 215sq ft hydroski, dating from 1957, was similar to hydroskis used on the Convair Sea Dart and was located just forward of the middle of the fuselage. The 38.7ft long slab (nominally 67in wide, it had deployable side-flaps to decrease width and area to increase beam loading and reduce landing impacts) fit cleanly into the relatively flat underside of the hull, and deployed nearly 12ft down for takeoff and landing, tipping nose-up by only 2°.

Wind tunnel testing showed the design to have substantial transonic drag rise, which came as no surprise; water tank testing showed that the hydroski worked well to raise the aircraft on takeoff and keep water spray from the engines. Takeoff speed with the wings tilted up was estimated at 200 knots.

In 1959 wind tunnel and water tank testing were carried out at the recently renamed NASA Langley Research Center on the bomber model refitted with supercavitating hydrofoils. These were blade-like winglets that projected below the fuselage in an inverted V-configuration. Unlike the hydroski, the hydrofoils seem to have been intended to be permanently deployed; while this would simplify some things and clear up internal volume for other purposes, it also raised drag and would have other practical concerns (for example, beaching would be virtually impossible).

Another modification to the configuration occurred at the end of 1959 and dispensed with the advanced lifting systems and utilized a conventional V-hull all along the underside. A fixed step was used to help it lift off from the water. Small external tank-like stabilizers were added to the undersides of the wings. Low speed and landing/takeoff performance were approximately as good as the earlier iterations, but unsurprisingly high speed drag was higher.

CHAPTER 3
Nuclear Powered Seaplane Supersonic Bombers

The history of American aviation has not been as full of supersonic bombers as people – from laymen to military pilots to aeronautical engineers to policy planners – probably expected in the 1950s. There have, in fact, been shockingly few, and fewer still that entered service. So with such a small number of aircraft of this class actually developed, one might be forgiven for thinking that finer subdivisions of the category of 'supersonic bomber', such as 'Seaplane Supersonic Bombers' and 'Nuclear Powered Supersonic Bombers', get real thin real fast.

And one could be especially forgiven for thinking that a finer still division such as 'Nuclear Powered Seaplane Supersonic Bombers' would be so lean on designs that it wouldn't be worth discussing. But life is weird and you've read the chapter title and, well, here we are.

There were no great programmes specifically to develop nuclear powered seaplane supersonic bombers. Instead, a few manufacturers – apparently restricted to Martin and especially Convair – decided that the idea had sufficient merit that they studied and proposed the idea themselves. There may well have been more studies than the included designs indicate, and more companies proposing designs… but so far, only Martin and Convair designs have come to light.

Martin Model 331-B3

The only company other than Convair that seemed to devote much effort to nuclear powered supersonic seaplane bombers – at least the only such company whose data on that subject has been made public – was the Martin Company. This is appropriate given that Martin was the builder of a number of successful flying boats… including the only jet-powered flying boat bomber the United States ever built, the P6M SeaMaster.

After the cancellation of the US Navy's supercarrier USS *United States* in 1950, brought low due to budget cuts and the US Air Force exerting dominance in the field of nuclear weapons delivery via the B-36, the US Navy issued a requirement in April 1951 for a seaplane bomber to fulfill the role of a "Seaplane Striking Force" capable of delivery a strategic nuclear strike against the Soviet Union. Martin won the contract for an aircraft with a top speed of Mach 0.9 with the design that became the SeaMaster.

The first flight of the SeaMaster occurred in July 1955. Including prototype YP6M-1s, P6M-1s and P6M-2s, a total of 16 SeaMasters were built. The aircraft was technologically advanced and in many ways very impressive, but it was plagued with technical issues, several were lost in testing and the Polaris sea launched ballistic missile promised to be a more reliable way for the US Navy to deliver a nuclear beatdown unto the Soviets.

Even before the first flight of the SeaMaster, in May 1955 Martin looked at a more advanced version. Under the direction of the US Navy's Bureau of Aeronautics and Office of Naval Research, Martin studied nuclear conversions of the P6M as Models 331-1 and 331-2. The former would have a circulating fuel reactor within the fuselage providing superheated liquid metal to two Pratt & Whitney JT-9 turbojets; the latter would have two General Electric AC-107-2 engines each with its own reactor. The two designs were visually little different from the standard P6M design of the time. There were two distinguishing features:

1) Small hydrofoils would deploy from the bottom of the forward fuselage near the nose to aid water run performance.
2) Where the conventional P6M had two turbojets and exhausts above and behind each wing root, the Model 331-1 and –2 had only one, somewhat larger-diameter, turbojet in those positions. The reactor powering each engine would be located within the fuselage, requiring no changes to the external configuration. Diagrams show that the cockpit would even look much the same, though doubtless it would have had a more cramped, heavily shielded compartment behind vastly thicker windows.

While externally Models 331-1 and –2 would have appeared much like the P6M, internal structural modifications would have had to be extensive. Martin expanded its studies throughout 1956, moving away from 'simple' modifications of the SeaMaster. Model 331-6 stretched the fuselage and moved the nuclear engines to the topside of the rear fuselage, straddling the vertical tail, but it remained a firmly subsonic design.

Martin Model 331-B3
SCALE 1/300

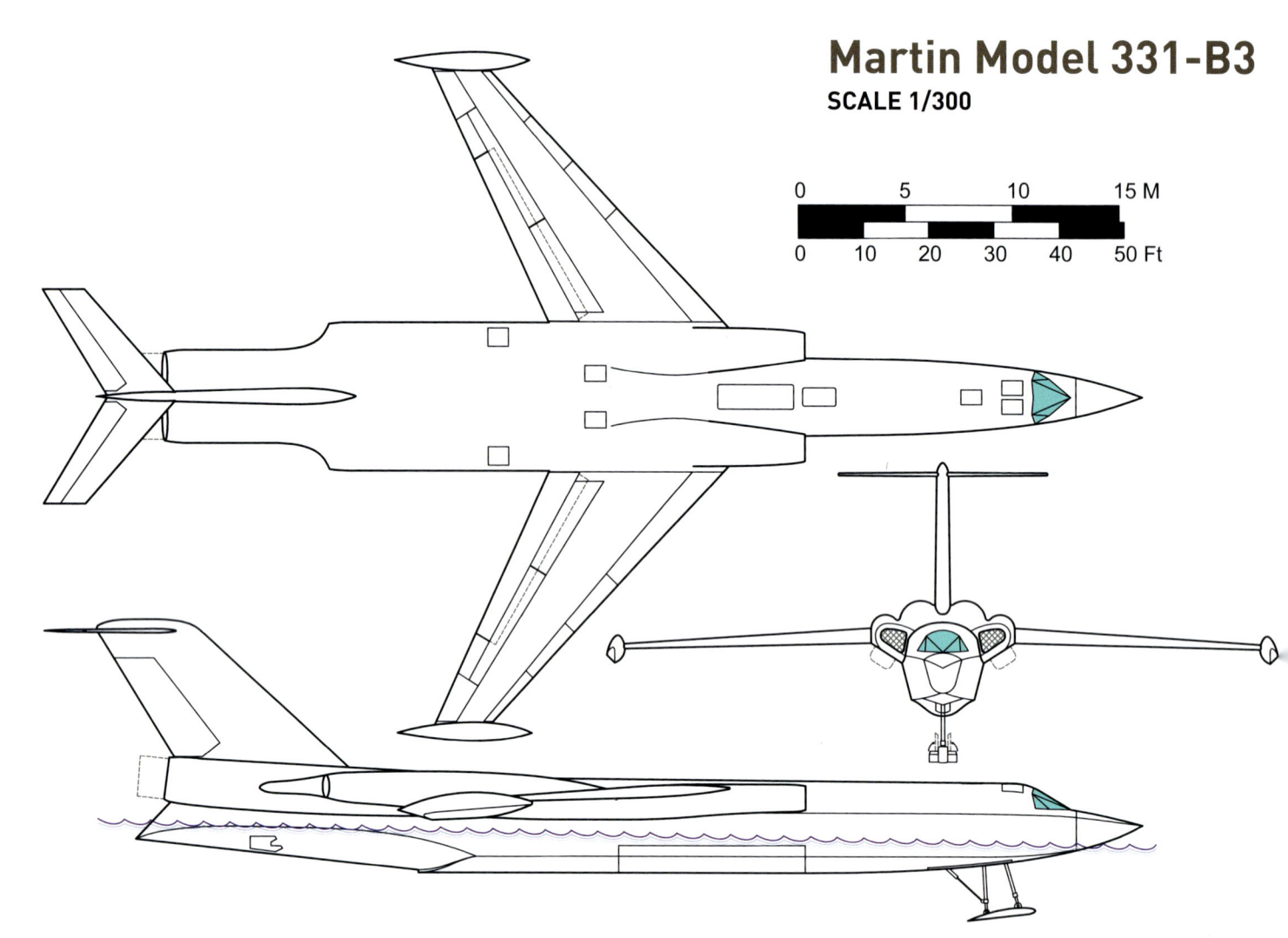

The Model 331-10 series, however was unrelated to the P6M airframe and was capable of supersonic flight. A number of Model 331 designs were produced, all more or less similar. The Model 331-B3, shown here, was a fair representation of the breed: a planing hull seaplane with shoulder mounted swept wings, T-tail and engines and inlets in the wing roots. The most unconventional aspect to the design at first glance was the inclusion of a single small deployable hydrofoil under the forward fuselage.

While other designs in the Model 331-10 series used a pair of chemically-fueled J75 (or GE 276B) engines alongside a General Electric AC-110 nuclear engine, Model 331-B3 used two non-afterburning Orenda PS13s. The nuclear engine was located within the fuselage, the reactor just behind the wing root trailing edge; long ducts took the exhaust to nozzles at the end of the fuselage. The chemical engines were located just outboard of the nuclear engine's turbines, but had no exhaust extensions.

A basic mission would see the aircraft lift off using the chemical engines for assist, then climbing and cruising at around 28,500ft and between Mach 0.85 and Mach 0.93 on purely nuclear power, or with chemical assist. Pure nuclear power allowed a cruise radius of 7,850 nautical miles, but using the chemical engines lowered that to 3,500 nautical miles. If the final dash phase was at sea level, the maximum speed would be Mach 0.97 on purely nuclear power, or Mach 1.15 if using afterburners and chemical engines. At 35,000ft the maximum speed at full power was Mach 1.5.

The Model 331 designs were predicated on the notion that they would be able to fly in 1962. But this presupposed the existence of both nuclear turbojets and the P6M SeaMaster. Unfortunately, the SeaMaster was cancelled in August 1959 and nuclear turbojets proved more difficult and expensive to produce than expected. The Model 331 and related Model 337 nuclear powered supersonic seaplanes faded away.

Convair Designs

In 1954 Convair-San Diego established a group to study the practicality of converting an existing aircraft to nuclear power. They focused on the XP5Y-1 and R3Y-1 Tradewind, a four-engine turboprop cargo transporting flying boat of which 11 were built. The Chief of Naval Operations issued a directive in May 1955 to study operational nuclear powered seaplanes.

Building on its prior efforts, Convair began work on a series of nuclear powered aircraft concepts, including "Nuclear Powered Attack Seaplanes". Three dash speeds were examined: Mach 0.9, Mach 1.1 to 1.3, and Mach 2. The high speeds required swept wing planing hulls or delta-winged craft with hydroskis. Both circulating fuel (indirect) nuclear systems as well as direct systems were examined; it was found that the crew shielding weight requirements for the direct systems were about three and a half times greater than for the indirect systems.

Due to the requirements of propulsion systems and shielding, these nuclear powered supersonic attack aircraft had to be large and heavy, reaching 475,000lb. Convair also studied offshore basing of the nuclear seaplanes, using ships and other seaplanes – including nuclear turboprop designs – for logistics and to serve as tenders.

Convair 6-Engine Nuclear Powered Attack Seaplane

Convair studied a series of "Nuclear Powered Attack Seaplanes" of varied designs, engine types and engine numbers in February 1956. One of the largest of these NPAS concepts, all of which seem to have been supersonic, was simply called the "6-Engined Nuclear Powered Attack Seaplane". It used six afterburning Pratt & Whitney NJ-2 turbojets with a single fuselage-embedded nuclear reactor. Data on this design is limited to a few diagrams. This was a large aircraft, with six outward-canted turbojets clustered around the reactor aft of the shoulder-mounted swept wing. All were fed from a pair of triangular wing-root inlets.

The crew of five were carried within a single heavily shielded cockpit quite near the nose. Unusually, windows were provided on the sides of the crew compartment, as well as large canopies ahead of the pilot and co-pilot. Presumably the sheer size of the vehicle assured sufficient shielding so that windows could be provided without compromising safety requirements. Several shielded cockpit variants were studied including unusual designs where the pilots sat behind the other crew on elevated platforms. In all cases, the nose containing the crew module would be jettisoned in the event of an emergency; once free of the stricken aircraft, the aerodynamic shell about the shielded compartment would be blown off and the cockpit would parachute out of the sky.

The Nuclear Powered Attack Seaplane was provided with two locations to carry ordnance. The first was a bomb bay on the underside of the planing hull; this was illustrated as fitting a single rather generic looking rocket missile, although it could also be built to serve a minelayer role where the bomb bay was split into left and right compartments. The bomb bay doors did not hinge outwards along the outer edge, but rotated at roughly their longitudinal midpoints. The relatively small bombs or mines would be attached to the interior surfaces of the doors and would be thus exposed and could drop without interference.

The second weapons position was atop the forward fuselage, meant specifically to carry the air-to-surface missile designed by Convair-Fort Worth for the WS-125A programme. This missile had an underslung turbojet, a design feature that would be problematic given that it was recessed deeply into the upper surface of the fuselage. One solution was to have air ducts leading from openable scoops to the missile's turbojet, and an upwards sloping exhaust duct aft of the missile, allowing the engine of the missile to be run up while still embedded within the carrier aircraft. Other solutions included raising the missile above the aircraft before engine runup.

Convair continued to work on the basic concept and produced a surprising number of designs, some carried out to high levels of detail. The Model 23 designation was used for a range of related designs included both supersonic (Model 23A and 23B) and subsonic designs (Model 23C and 23D). While the sizes of the Model 23 designs varied, they did not reach the scale of the slightly earlier NPAS.

Convair Model 23A

Model 23A of summer 1956 was a delta-winged configuration with a T-tail with an all-moving horizontal stabilizer at the tip. The delta wing was mid-mounted and cambered, with 50° sweep on the leading edge and a 10° 25' forward sweep on the trailing edge. It was also fitted with a pair of fences to control spanward airflow. Like other supersonic seaplanes designed by Convair at the time, Model 23A had a single large hydroski to aid in takeoff and to absorb landing shock.

As Model 23A was designed to be a minimum nuclear powered supersonic seaplane, it had only a single General Electric AC-110 nuclear turbojet: a direct air cycle system utilizing a single reactor with two compressors and two turbines and the smallest nuclear propulsion system at that level of development. This engine sat atop the rear fuselage; the engine was modified somewhat from the normal depiction by angling the turbines and exhausts outwards in order to clear the vertical tail. Each compressor was fed air via a long duct leading to an inlet on the shoulder of the fuselage ahead of the wing. Chemical fuel would be stored in the wings and in a single large tank in the lower fuselage just aft of the hydroski. Another smaller tank of jet fuel was positioned just above the front of the hydroski; this was a shadow shield to aid in protecting the crew, and would be the last chemical fuel consumed.

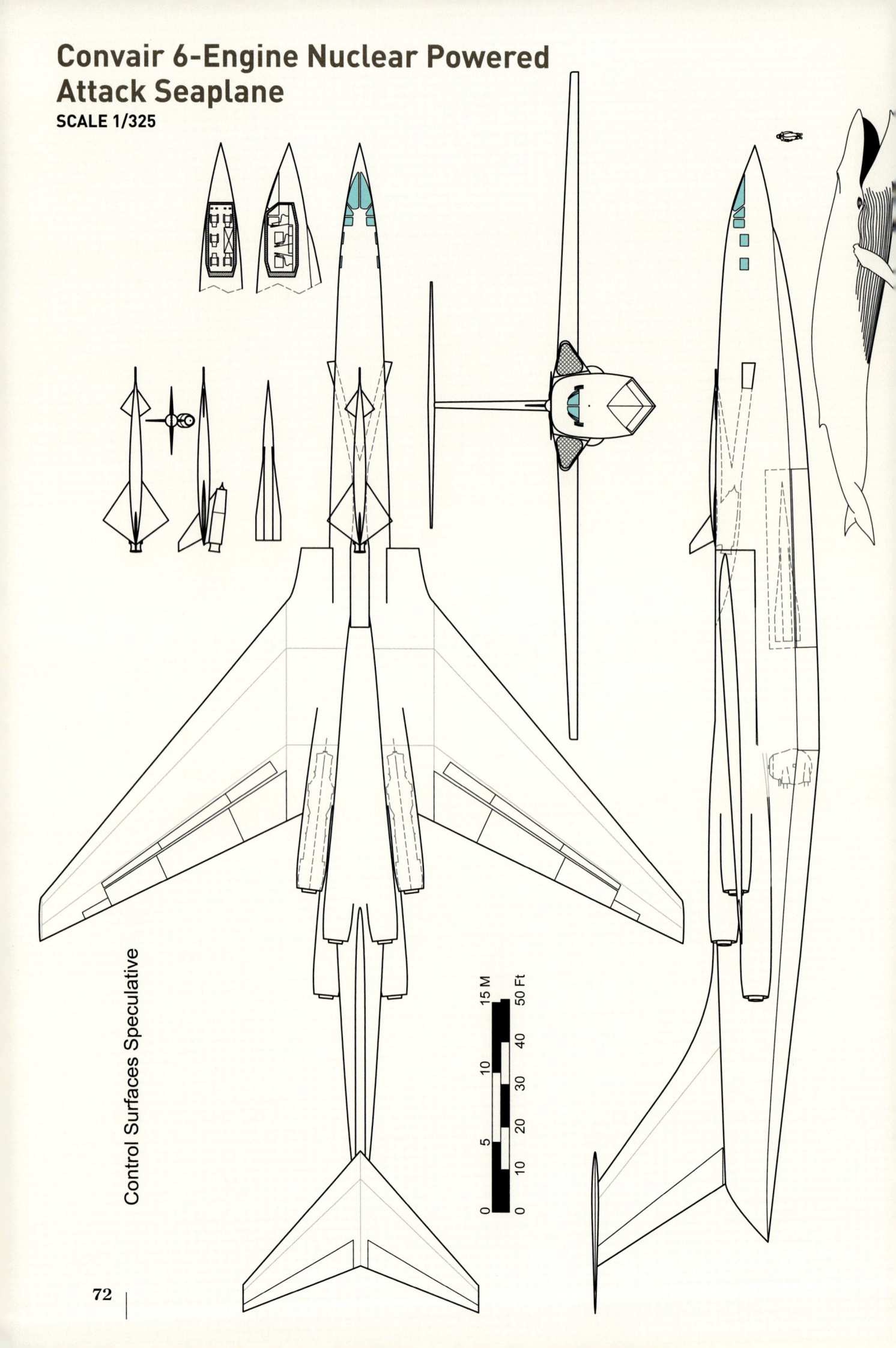

Convair 6-Engine Nuclear Powered Attack Seaplane
SCALE 1/325

Control Surfaces Speculative

72

Convair Model 23A
SCALE 1/200

73

The crew of three – pilot, co-pilot and bombardier/navigator – sat together in a single well shielded compartment near the nose. Entry and exit was via a single hatch on the port side of the fuselage. The weapons bay occupied the space between the rear of the cockpit and the front of the hydro-ski; diagrams show the bay populated with sea mines, though other weapons could of course be carried. These included special large solid rocket boosted air-to-surface missiles weighing up to 10,420lb, with a range up to 600 nautical miles; fifteen 1,000lb mines or conventional bombs (for a total of 16,000lb including associated hardware); two nuclear gravity bombs totalling 13,600lb; or ten 2,000lb mines or bombs totalling 20,000lb. The 1,000 and 2,000lb bombs would not only be carried in racks within the bomb but also would be held to – and released from – the inner surface of the bomb bay doors.

Another diagram shows a variant concept where the inlets are moved slightly outboard, downwards and aft; this increased the available real estate atop the aircraft so that a single large air-to-surface missile could be carried semi-submerged in the upper fuselage. The same diagram also depicted the weapons bay fitted with three generic GAR-X missiles… what would become the AIM-47 Falcons carried by the YF-12A. This indicates that an interceptor role was envisioned for this supersonic nuclear powered seaplane. The ability to spend extended periods flying far from base would be useful for a long-range interceptor of Soviet bomber formations.

For assistance with takeoff the aircraft had a single 60,000lb thrust Reaction Motors Inc. liquid rocket engine in the tail, just above the waterline. The engine specifics are not given, but it was provided with a single tank of hydrogen peroxide and no plumbing to the jet fuel tanks is in evidence. Consequently, this was likely a monopropellant system. It was about the same thrust level as the Reaction Motors XLR-99 that powered the X-15, but that engine was fuelled with ammonia with liquid oxygen.

The hydroski was needed to overcome issues with water launching a delta wing; the rocket engine was needed to overcome the high drag associated with the hydroski. Studies were made of the use of additional chemically fuelled turbojets to increase thrust. Two Pratt & Whitney JT-4B turbojets could be buried in the aft fuselage and would exhaust through a pair of nozzles in the truncated tail, replacing the rocket engine; the inlets would be shoulder-mounted half-circles just ahead of the trailing edge of the delta wing. Alternatively they could be located above the nuclear engine exhausts, which would be extended aft to the trailing edge of the vertical stabilizer; the inlets for the auxiliary chemical engines would be above the nuclear nacelle and would have close-off doors that would serve as aerodynamic fairings while in nuclear flight. That position could also use General Electric J79 turbojets.

J79s could be stored in deployable nacelles; one could deploy from either side of the forward fuselage. While this would be complex and heavy and would necessitate the moving of the nuclear engine inlets upwards to the top of the fuselages, once stowed within the fuselage behind the shielded cockpit the aircraft would be aerodynamically clean. Quite a number of alternative auxiliary turbojet concepts were examined, including the use of below-wing nacelles that would tilt upwards (as Convair had proposed on a number of non-nuclear supersonic seaplane concepts) and the use of Allison J89 and Pratt & Whitney JT-9 turbojets.

Further, the idea was drawn up for replacing the General Electric AC-110 nuclear engine with a pair of Pratt & Whitney "Lithium powerplants" which installed a reactor in the fuselage and fed superheated liquid metal to two separate turbojet engines in much the same position as the AC-110.

The Model 23A-1 design was essentially the same aircraft but with the nuclear engines replaced by a pair of purely chemically fuelled Pratt & Whitney JT-9 turbojets. This could serve as a prototype for the Model 23A.

The Model 23A was designed to a fairly high level of detail with diagrams detailing the structure of the wing and fuselage.

Convair Model 23A-3

The Model 23A-3 was much like the Model 23A, but with the delta wings replaced by swept wings. It was not a simple swap of the wings however; while the rest of the configuration was much like that of the Model 23A, virtually everything was changed to one degree or another.

The inlets were moved to the top of the fuselage into a single unified structure; the underside of the fuselage was turned into a conventional planing hull with no hydroski. With no hydroski, the need for the booster rocket engine went away. The wings had 2° of anhedral; in perfect conditions they would ride just a few feet above the water, but in practical conditions the aircraft would, when resting, tip to one side or the other, dipping a wingtip into the ocean. On takeoff and landing any waves would likely impact the wingtips.

Convair Model 23B

Convair designed the larger Model 23B in May 1956 around four liquid metal recirculating Pratt & Whitney NJ-2B turbojets using a single 330 megawatt reactor in a liquid metal cycle powerplant. Fitted with chemical interburning and afterburners, the various iterations of Model 23B could attain supersonic speeds in a dash, as

Convair Model 23A-3
SCALE 1/250

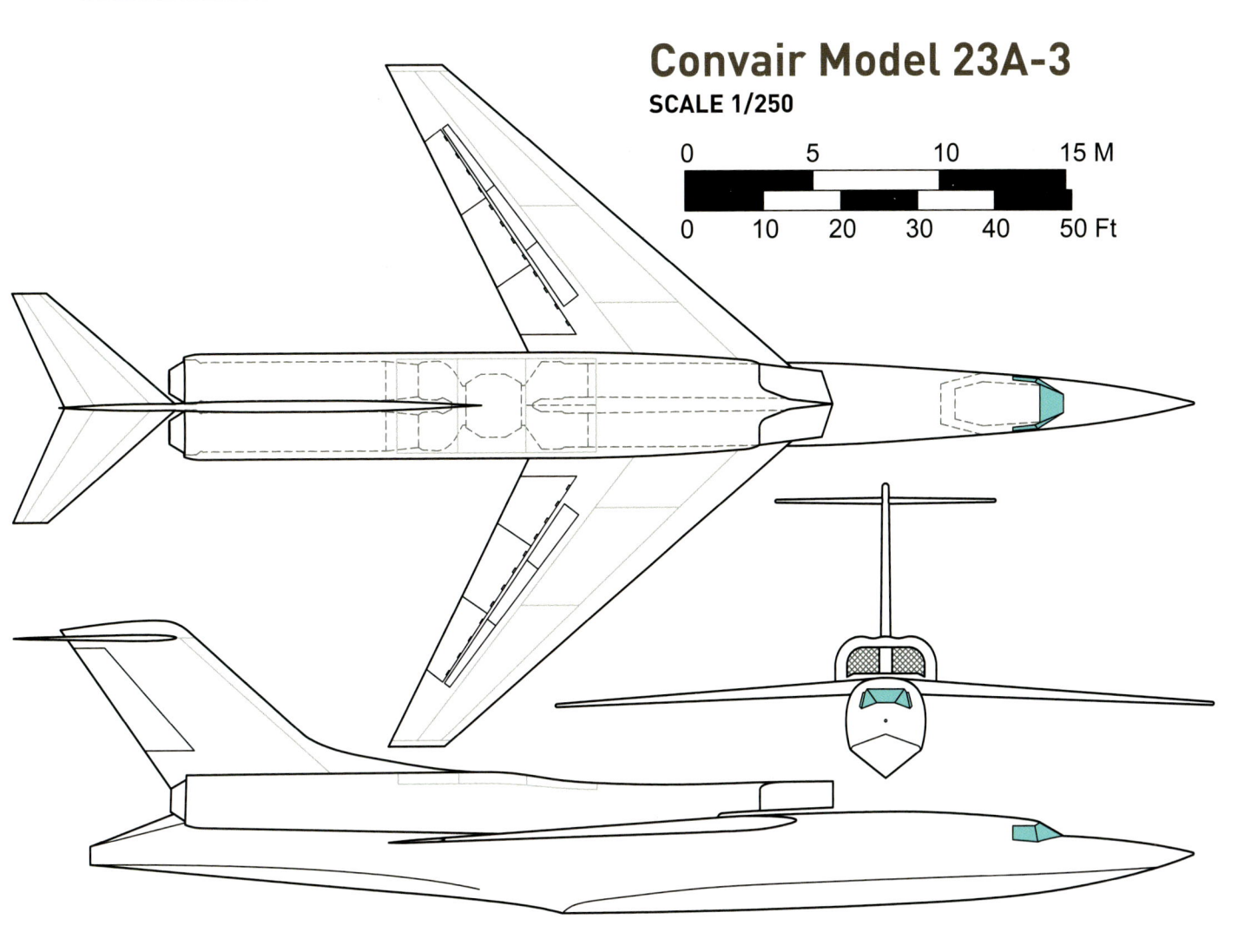

well as use chemical fuel to assist in takeoff. For a high subsonic dash, chemical fuel would be 'interburned', burned within the turbojets to increase power to the turbines. For supersonic dash, interburning would be supplemented with chemical fuel afterburning.

Model 23B was a high-swept wing of generally conventional configuration. The 45° swept wings contained the chemical fuel and used spoilers, ailerons and flaps with boundary layer control. The fuselage had a standard flying boat planing hull, devoid of the hydroskis that Convair was so often fond of; the wingtips held small stabilizing floats with relatively tiny deployable skis for takeoff use. The horizontal stabilizer at the tip of the vertical stabilizer was swept and all-moving.

The reactor was located in the fuselage under the wings; the main inlet just above the fuselage well behind the leading edge of the wing roots. The 324.5in long weapons bay was located ahead of the reactor and provided with sizable doors on the underside of the planing hull; small loading doors (110.6in long) were located above the weapons bay, indicating that larger weapons such as standoff missiles would require more substantial facilities for loading.

Chemical fuel was carried primarily within the wings, though a tank containing 10,000lb of fuel was wedged between the reactor and the armament bay to serve as a shadow shield and to provide emergency fuel. Use of that fuel, while handy for higher speeds to escape the enemy, would reduce the radiation shielding for the crew.

An alternative weapons location was the upper fuselage. A single cruise missile of the kind designed for WS-125A could be carried semi-submerged in the upper fuselage, then raised clear of the upper surface for launch. This option would require that the topside inlets be move down to wing root positions.

The heavily shielded crew compartment had five crew stations and windows only for the pilot and co-pilot. Unusually for the time, the pilots would be given joystick controllers attached to the armrests and connected to an all-electric ('fly by wire') control system. This was to aid in fatigue for the expected long duration missions. The seats, which were non-ejectable, were well padded and reclinable for comfort.

Alternatives to the four Pratt & Whitney NJ-2 turbojets with their single reactor included two GE AC-110 units.

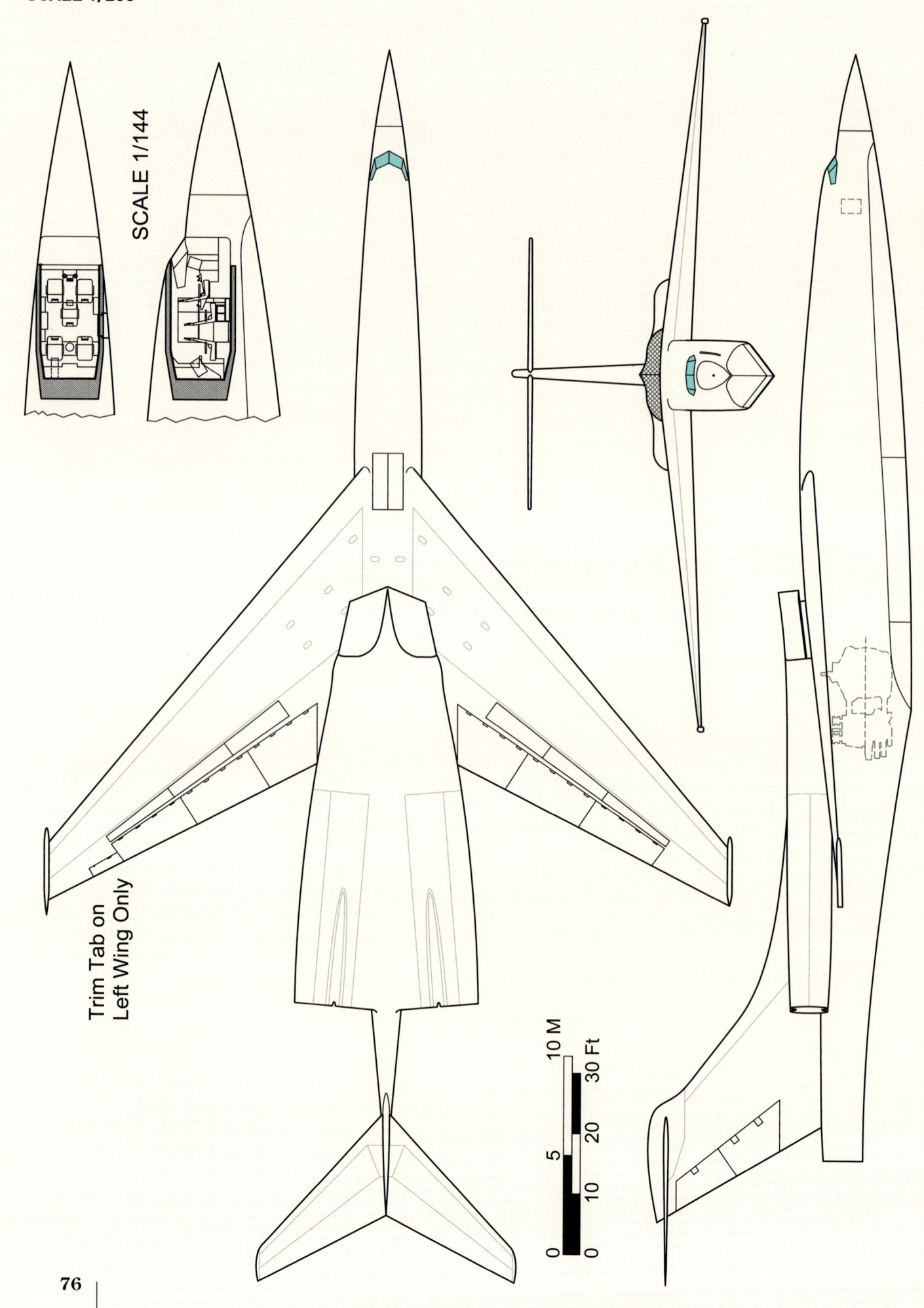

Convair Model 23B
SCALE 1/250

SCALE 1/144

Trim Tab on Left Wing Only

Nuclear Powered Seaplane Supersonic Bombers

Convair Model 23B-1
SCALE 1/325

0   5   10 M
0   10   20   30 Ft

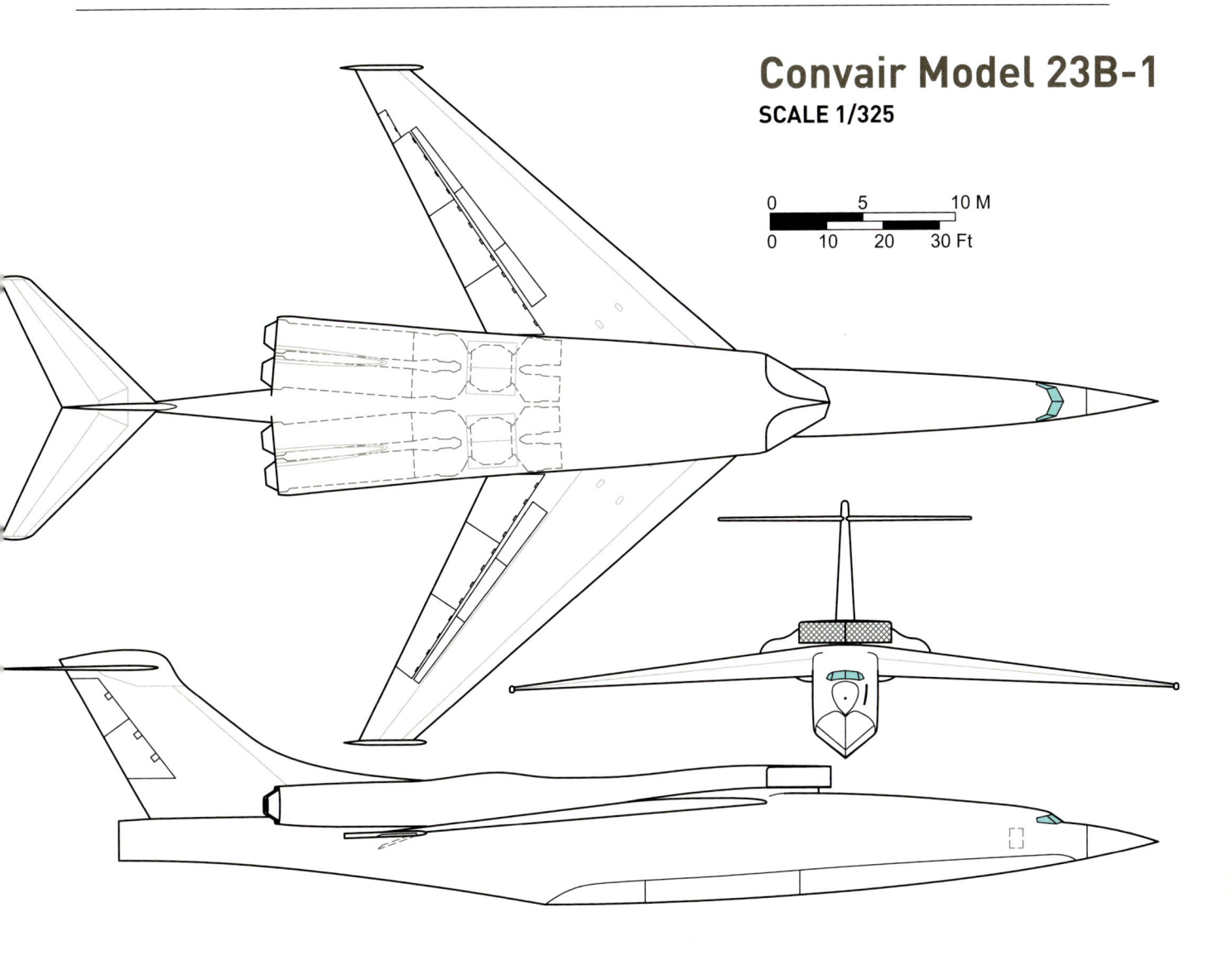

Convair Model 23B-1

The design initially designated Model 23B-1, from June 1956, was a geometrically identical variant of the Model 23B with conventional chemical jet engines (Pratt & Whitney JT-9s) rather than the nuclear engines. With the reactor and shielding removed, a substantial mass of jet fuel could be stored within the fuselage. While performance – in particular range and endurance – would not be as impressive as for the Model 23B, the Model 23B-1 could be built sooner and cheaper, allowing the airframe and aerodynamics to be verified while the nuclear propulsion systems was being developed.

Another aircraft designated Model 23B-1 came along in August 1956 and replaced the chemically fuelled concept. The new Model 23B-1 was geometrically similar to the Model 23B, but replaced the four NJ-2B engines with two GE AC-110 engines. This swapped out a single reactor located within the fuselage for two separate reactors located within the engine nacelles, shifting the aircraft's centre of gravity upwards and slightly aftwards and necessitating a number of minor changes to the configuration. The most obvious (basically the only obvious) change was to the inlets; these stayed atop the fuselage but were moved well forward of the wing leading edge.

Convair WS-125

Weapon System 125A was the most important programme to develop an operational nuclear powered aircraft. The primary design studied by Convair for WS-125A was a large landplane, described in the Nuclear Powered Bombers chapter. But never a company willing to ignore a possible alternative, Convair put forward a supersonic flying boat design in 1956.

While it is repeatedly described in various publications as a "seaplane version" of the WS-125A landplane, there are no obvious points of design commonality apart from the engines. It appears to be a wholly separate creation. In fact, two different seaplanes were designed. Both designs share clear family heritage with the Model 23 designs; while the exact chronology of each is unclear, the diagrams for the Model 23 designs were generally dated a few month prior to those of the WS-125A designs.

77

Convair WS-125
SCALE 1/288

AGM-28

15 M / 50 Ft

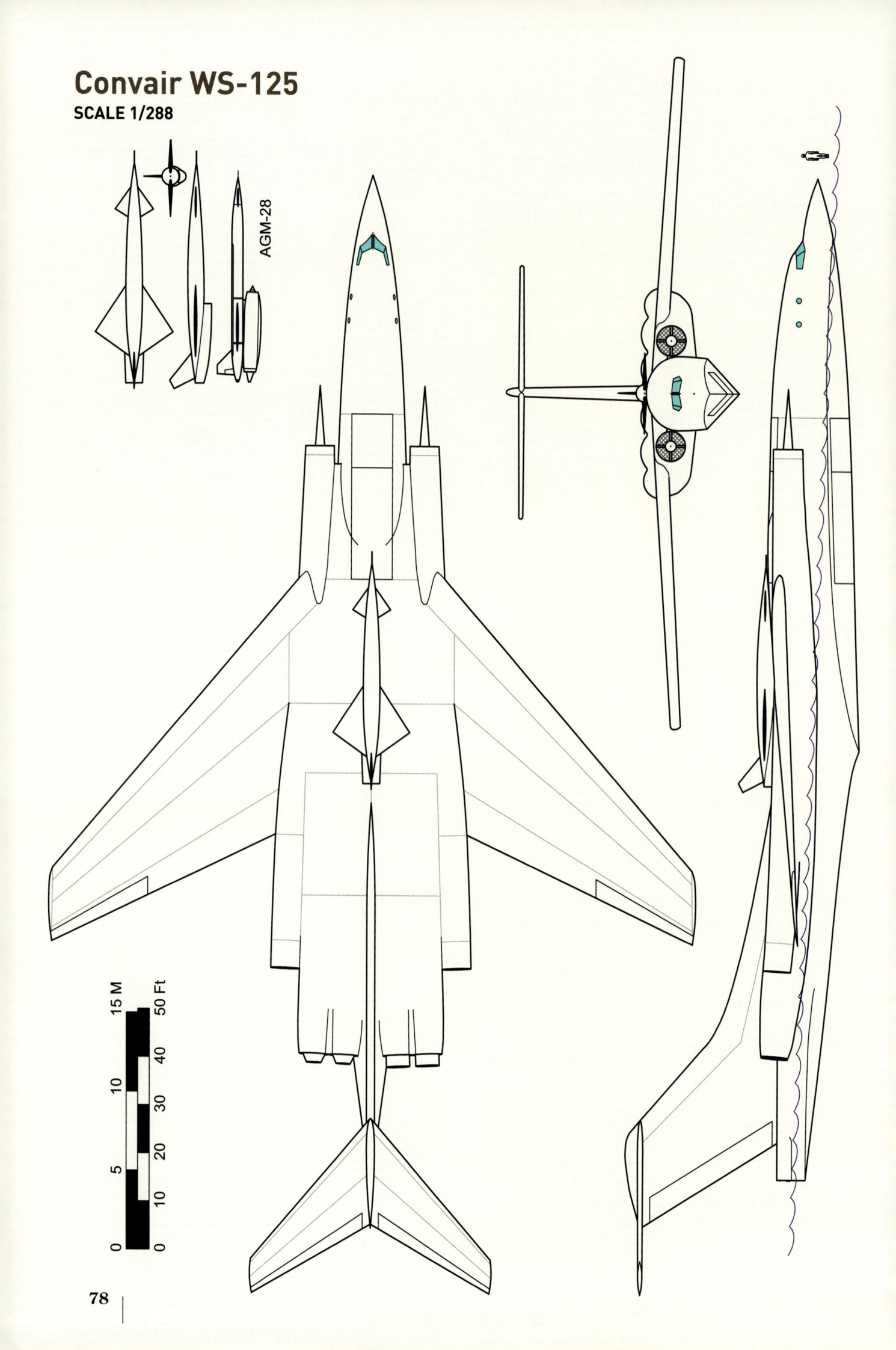

78

The first of the Convair water-based WS-125A designs had delta wings and a single Pratt & Whitney JT-9A turbojet in a nacelle ahead of and below each wing; as with other Convair designs (in particular the water-based B-58, which was a design stablemate), the nacelles would angle upwards to clear the water. A pair of GE AC-110 nuclear engines took up the rear fuselage, fed by a pair of wing-root inlets with long ducts. The fuselage had a straight underside and a single large hydroski.

The second design seemed to get a bit more attention. Designed with a planing hull (no hydroski) and markedly swept wings, this design also used two General Electric AC-110 nuclear turbojets and two Pratt & Whitney JT-9A chemical turbojets. The nuclear turbojets were located inboard and well aft. The conventional turbojets, used for boost during takeoff and for high speed over dangerous territory, were outboard of the nuclear engines and slightly forward. All engines were angled outboard to clear the vertical stabilizer.

The horizontal stabilizer was placed far up atop the vertical stabilizer to keep it out of water spray and the wake from the wing at high angles of attack. The circular wing root inlets were equipped with sharp spikes that could translate aft entirely within the inlet or well forward of the inlet to shape the inlet flow field for the Mach number.

Performance for the seaplane version of the WS-125A was to be the same as the landplane version: mission radius was 11,000 miles, the bulk of which would be carried out under pure nuclear power. A Mach 0.9 cruise at 30,000ft would be under pure nuclear power, and a dash speed of Mach 2.2 at 60,000ft over a total distance of 2,000 nautical miles used the chemical engines for boost.

Additional thrust was available for takeoff in the form of a 60,000lb thrust hydrogen peroxide monopropellant rocket engine (doubtless the same rocket proposed for Model 23) located in the extreme tail end of the fuselage. 10,000lb of hydrogen peroxide would be carried.

The aircraft had two internal weapons bays. Located behind the heavily radiation-shielded cockpit was a bay for defensive missiles (type unknown, though the size of the bay gives a maximum length of 125in). Behind the defensive missile bay was a bomb bay of 275in length. While the weapons would drop through doors on the bottom in the conventional manner, they would be loaded through doors on the top side of the fuselage while the aircraft floated.

The primary weapon of the WS-125A bomber was a missile designed specifically for it by Convair-Fort Worth. An evolution of the single-engined missile that graced the earlier six-Engined Nuclear Powered Attach Seaplane, this missile was somewhat similar in layout to the AGM-28A Hound Dog. The WS-125A missile had trapezoidal wings and canards and a pair of underslung afterburning GE SJ-113 turbojets fed from a common inlet. Performance data is lacking; range was in the area of 500 nautical miles and it was intended to be launched at (and would presumably maintain) Mach 2.5 and 55,000ft. The payload was 6,482lb of warhead and fusing. The WS-125A missile had a fuselage length of 45.4ft and a wingspan of 17.4ft.

The WS-125A seaplane was intended to be serviced as much as possible while on the open water, using shielded boats and barges. Additionally, the seaplanes could be based not just at widely dispersed locations around the Pacific, but also at landlocked continental US bases. To accomplished this, long, wide and adequately deep water-filled canals would need to be constructed for the aircraft to take off from and land on. While a substantial construction project, Convair estimated that this would cost no more than the construction of the wide and thick concrete runways needed by the landplane equivalents. A cracked runway requires expensive repairs; disturbed water does not.

Convair Submersible Nuclear Ramjet

History is filled with ideas for vehicles that could operate in several wildly different media. Flying boats, roadable airplanes, amphibious cars. There have even been designs for flying submarines (or submersible aircraft, depending on capabilities). In order to do two very different things, the vehicle necessarily has to be a compromise... a flying boat has to be more ruggedly built that a land plane, with some notable and unfortunate aerodynamic problems tacked on; a car that can fly has to be built much lighter than a regular car, less capable of withstanding even the slightest of fender benders. This is why multi-media vehicles are generally rare, and often seem quite unusual.

Almost certainly one of the most outlandish concepts for a vehicle meant to operate in two different environments was dreamed up at Convair in 1960-61: a nuclear powered supersonic flying submarine. The available data on this is as yet fairly lean, coming from two presentations devoted to then-ongoing design work for atomic powered aircraft being done for the US Navy. The Submersible Nuclear Ramjet aircraft was apparently something of an afterthought; compared to the unmanned nuclear VTOLs meant to operate from carrier decks and the giant nuclear seaplanes and the Mach 3+ carrier based nuclear powered strike aircraft, the Submersible Nuclear Ramjet must have seemed a bit outlandish and consequently received a relatively cursory explanation.

Convair Submersible Nuclear Ramjet
SCALE 1/225

Drag brakes deployed

Polaris SLBM to scale

Project Pluto Nuclear Ramjet

Drag brakes deployed

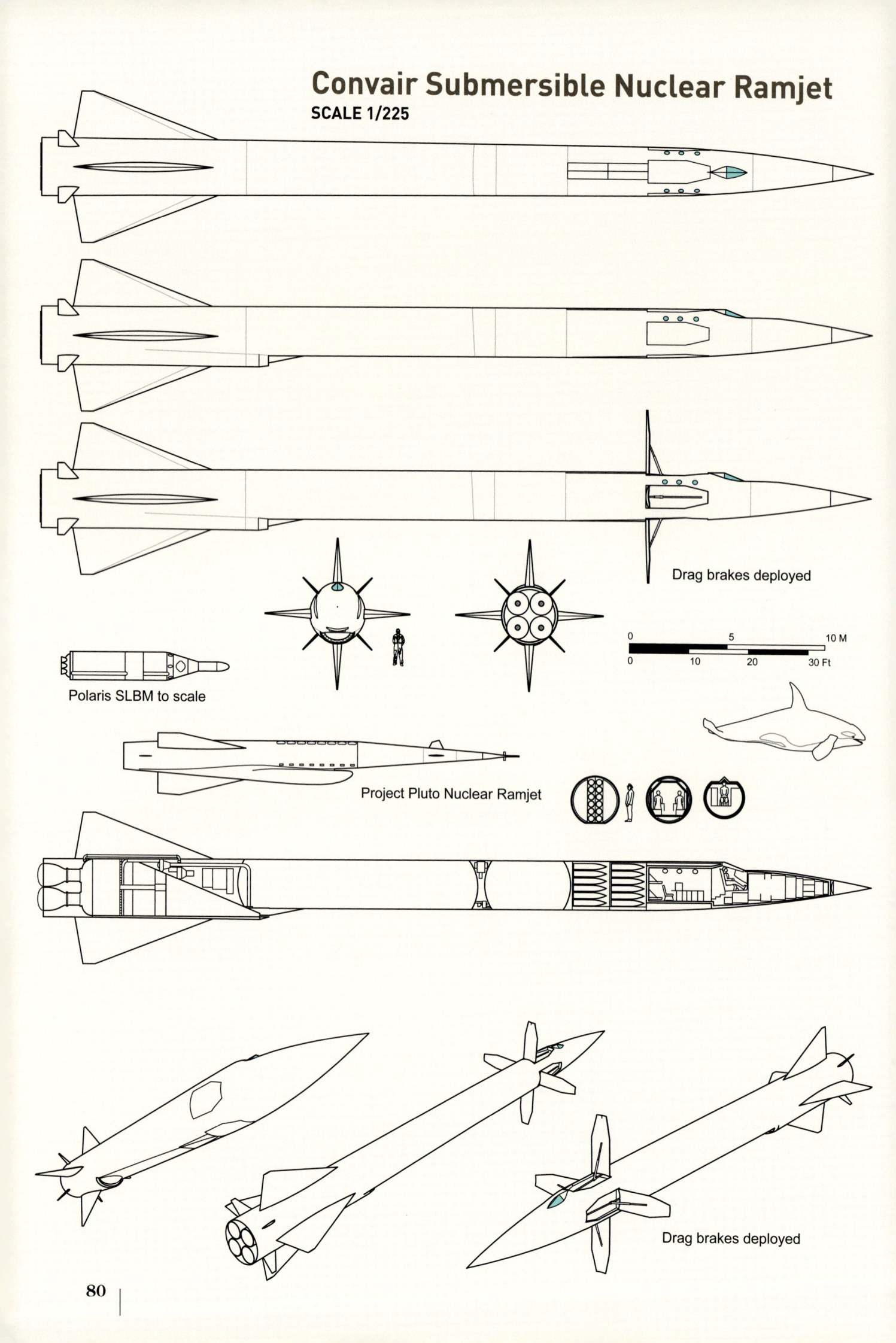

80

The two presentations mentioning this vehicle provide somewhat contradictory and very incomplete information. The reason for this seems to be that the earlier one describes an idea that was at that point not yet well detailed, while the later one provides some detailed diagrams but no accompanying hard data. The reconstruction shown here is assembled from a top view, an inboard profile and a few cross sections; the precise cockpit and inlet geometries are based on incomplete views.

As described in the earlier report (which has only a very simple sketch of it), the vehicle was to be pencil-shaped, eight feet in diameter and 180ft in length. While submerged with much of its internal volume filled with seawater, the vehicle would weigh 350,000lb; in flight with the tanks largely emptied it would weigh 240,000lb. While underwater or on the surface, propulsion would come from using the nuclear reactor at low power as a water ramjet, heating seawater to steam and ejecting it for thrust. Maximum submerged speed was estimated at 100 knots. While this may have been possible, it presented more than a few technical and military challenges. A propulsion system like that would, obviously, hardly be stealthy; it would be by far the loudest submarine at sea. At 100 knots it would be easily tracked from an ocean away; it would deafen whales at doubtless disturbing distances. Additionally, using salt water as a reaction mass is a prospect fraught with difficulties; boiling the water would tend to deposit salt onto the solid surfaces. And the troubles that would result from the engine ingesting plankton, algae or fish can be readily imagined.

It should be noted that this design was apparently not the only one to consider this propulsion system. Circa 1959, the Defense Advanced Research Projects Agency studied a nuclear-powered hydrojet torpedo... a nuclear-tipped underwater missile using a nuclear ramjet propulsion system to attain 100 to 250 knots for intercontinental ranges. Little is known of this other than the basic idea for a nuclear reconnaissance/attack torpedo and the project code name: NAUCRATES DUCTOR. As dramatic as that name sounds, it's merely the scientific name of the pilot fish.

The Submersible Nuclear Ramjet would lurk for extended periods of time underwater, either cruising about at sea or simply sitting quietly. Due to the long duration of the missions, there would be a crew of nine packed into a relatively small, heavily shielded compartment. If the command came to initiate a mission, the voluminous internal water tanks would be pressurized and the water expelled through the nuclear reactor; run at full power (3,600 megawatts), the water would be vaporized, the super-hot steam creating enough rocket thrust to launch the craft vertically out of the water like a submarine launched ballistic missile.

The engine would continue to operate as a rocket as the vehicle climbed, pitched over and accelerated to ramjet velocity, whereupon the reactor would transition from internal water to air as the reaction mass. The vehicle would fly at high speed and low altitude while over enemy territory, using radar to automatically hug the terrain to stay under radar detection.

The Submersible Nuclear Ramjet was in design and operation very much like the Project Pluto Supersonic Low Altitude Missile, except with a live crew and none of that boring "sitting around on dry ground before launch" stuff. Payload would be 20,000lb of laydown nuclear weapons – bombs designed to be parachute retarded so that they would survive impact with the ground. The bomb would come to rest and stop for some pre-determined length of time, presumably just a few seconds, enough time for the aircraft to clear the danger zone. Presumably the bombs would be jettisoned out of the top of the fuselage rather than the bottom; this way the bomb would have a little bit more time to hit the ground and it would not disturb the Mach 3 airflow into the underslung inlet. In the case of the Submersible Nuclear Ramjet that time would be quite short compared to most aircraft as its cruising speed would be Mach 3 plus.

At the end of the mission, the craft would find a safe patch of open water and the ramjet would throttle down. As the craft slowed it would pull up into a vertical climb; as it stalled, drag brakes located near the nose would extend, allowing the vehicle to be dynamically stable as it dropped tail first towards the water. The nuclear engine would transition back to rocket power for a final deceleration, safely lowering the vehicle into the water. After splashdown the internal tanks would again fill with water, letting the aircraft submerge beneath the waves while simultaneously providing shielding for the crew.

It should be noted that this landing process is used by the SpaceX Falcon 9 booster, including the deployment of aerodynamic controls near the 'nose'. The Falcon 9 has even made soft landings in the ocean itself; these landings would be quite like those of the Submersible Nuclear Ramjet. In the case of ocean landings (early test flights of the Falcon 9), the boosters were allowed to simply flop over onto their sides; it's not clear if that was intended with the SNR, but it could hardly have been otherwise in practice, an event the crew doubtless would have found 'exciting'.

The later description of the vehicle includes no data. The previously described 8ft diameter lines up well with what's shown in the inboard profile, but if that's accurate the vehicle length is a full 40ft shorter than in the earlier description. The inboard profile shows two separate propellant tanks. Presumably the larger aft tank is used for the rocket launch and acceleration, while the smaller forward tank remains filled with water throughout the mission to serve as shielding and only comes into use as propellant during the final rocket phase as the craft lowers itself back into the sea. The top speed for this later design was bumped up to potentially Mach 4. The vehicle and payload weights are not given, but the inboard views depict 24 distinct weapons.

While Project Pluto stood a chance of being built, the Submersible Nuclear Ramjet seems to not have risen above the level of preliminary design. Still, the similar requirements in performance – Mach 3+ flight at near treetop levels – led to similar designs. Both craft featured long, slim fuselages, no true wings and a series of sizable control surfaces at the tail. At the speeds and altitudes these craft were to fly, the lift generated just by the fuselages would be more than sufficient to keep them in the air. The Pluto was by necessity to be heavily built from advanced high temperature materials and, as mentioned, the forward fuselage was to be coated in gold to help dissipate heat. It is interesting to consider that Convair's slightly more insane idea would have received similar treatment.

At cruise conditions the leading edges would likely have glowed from air compressed to incandescence; the sonic boom would have been monumental. It seems likely that in actual practice the vehicle would have been covered in some sort of paint or coating appropriate for submarine duty, probably something dark blue or gray to help hide the craft under the waves. But it would have to be a coating that would peel or burn off cleanly as the vehicle accelerated. In order to preclude bits of the coating from being ingested into the nuclear reactor, the underside would probably be left uncoated. The end result would be a vehicle with an interesting colour scheme.

After a mission, any paint it had originally started off with would almost certainly be gone. A giant golden submarine rocketing through the sea would be difficult to hide, but after a nuclear strike mission it would hardly matter anymore... there would be few people left to go after the vehicle, and few places for the vehicle to find to call home. After a mission where the reactor has been activated to full power, the radiation spilling from the vehicle would be immense and long lasting. It's not clear just what the crew would be expected to do with their radioactive deathtrap. Plans for Project Pluto called for test flights over the Pacific Ocean that ended with a plummet into the Marianas Trench, sinking the airframe and reactor to the deepest part of the sea... but a living crew is hardly likely to be all that thrilled with a mission which ends up with an intentional death-plunge. And tootling up to dock with a reactor that is close to meltdown and being attacked by salt water and diatoms is not a good way to make oneself popular with the folks in port.

Left wholly unshown and undescribed in the available literature is some sort of low-speed underwater propulsion system. Doubtless it must have had such... a propeller or water-jet powered by electric motors, able to move the craft around at modest speeds. Running off modest reactor power, this would have allowed the vehicle to cruise the seas with some semblance of stealth; running on battery power, it would have allowed the craft to manoeuvre near other vessels or in port without roasting the neighbours. It's difficult to see how the nuclear water-ramjet could be used at anything but high speeds.

CHAPTER 4: VTOL Bombers

Perhaps surprisingly, the history of American supersonic bomber development has not been full to overflowing with vertical takeoff configurations. Fighters, yes… quite a number of books could be filled with designs for VTOL supersonic fighters. Such aircraft have been designed back to the early 1950s, often and with great enthusiasm and one (the F-35) has even entered service. But it is easier to make a fighter capable of vertical lift than a bomber. Fighters are generally smaller than bombers, have shorter mission durations and less range.

Trying to lift something like the B-70 off the ground vertically would be a heroic effort and would greatly mangle the performance of the aircraft. And with greater range, it's more likely that the bases the bombers will take off from will be further from the front lines, and thus their extensive runways are more likely to remain reasonably intact.

All that said, supersonic bombers capable of vertical lift have been designed from time to time.

Boeing Model 809-1012

The Boeing Model 809 series from 1957 is sadly poorly documented, but quite interesting. It appears to have been a catch-all designation for a series of bomber and transport designs using unconventional propulsion systems (see *Boeing B-47 Stratojet and B-52 Stratofortress: Origin and Evolution* for Model 809-1004-1, a heavily modified B-52 with a jet-flap wing with up to 38 engines).

Model 809-1012 was a VTOL supersonic bomber using a propulsion system that would have been familiar to many VTOL aircraft designers of the time, a mix of tilting engines and dedicated lift jets. The aircraft configuration was fairly conventional for a supersonic aircraft… stubby trapezoidal wings married to a flattened and pointed fuselage, small canards and a large, swept vertical tail. A single turbojet nacelle was mounted to the tip of each wing, and one more to two aft-fuselage pylons; these engines could rotate 90° for vertical or horizontal thrust. Further forward, a bank of 24 smaller jet engines were fixed in position to provide vertical thrust.

The lift jets were the conventional General Electric J85, perhaps best known for powering the Northrop F-5 and T-38 aircraft. The main engines, though, were to be General Electric X275Es… this was the then-contemporary designation for what would become the J93, which would power the North American XB-70. It's therefore not too surprising that the top speed of the Model 809-1012 was to be Mach 3.

Unfortunately, no other performance data is available. And even though nearly half the gross weight of the aircraft was to be fuel, and the payload would have been a fairly paltry 3,000lb (in the form of a single weapon), it can be assumed that range would not have been spectacular without in-flight refuelling. The landing gear shown in the fairly basic diagram did not seem to have wheels, just pads; this would have simplified the design and lowered the weight, but also made it so that every takeoff and landing would have had to have been vertical.

Boeing Model 809-1013

Designed alongside Model 809-1012, the -1013 dispensed with the hidebound conventionality of the preceding configuration. The structural design would have been far simpler; no rotating engines, no banks of lift jets tucked behind doors. Instead, the Model 809-1013 would have been a tailsitter like the Convair XFY-1, the Lockheed XFV-1 or the Ryan X-13.

A cluster of eight GE X279E turbojets, two rows of four, would provide both vertical and horizontal thrust for the delta winged aircraft. The aircraft would have sat on its tail and towered around 110ft over the surroundings; the bomb bay would have been several storeys high, the crew compartment higher still. Never mind the difficulties that tailsitters have always had with landings... simply re-arming the aircraft and getting the crew on board would have been logistical nightmares. The available diagram showing Model 809-1013 is quite simple and low in detail… quite probably because the designers knew that the idea was never going to fly.

Still, the sight of an aircraft with two more of the engines than the XB-70 had, lifting off vertically under full afterburner, would doubtless have been spectacular.

NACA VTOL Bomber

Described in several NACA and early NASA Research Memoranda are a number of wind tunnel investigations

Boeing Model 809-1012
SCALE 1/200

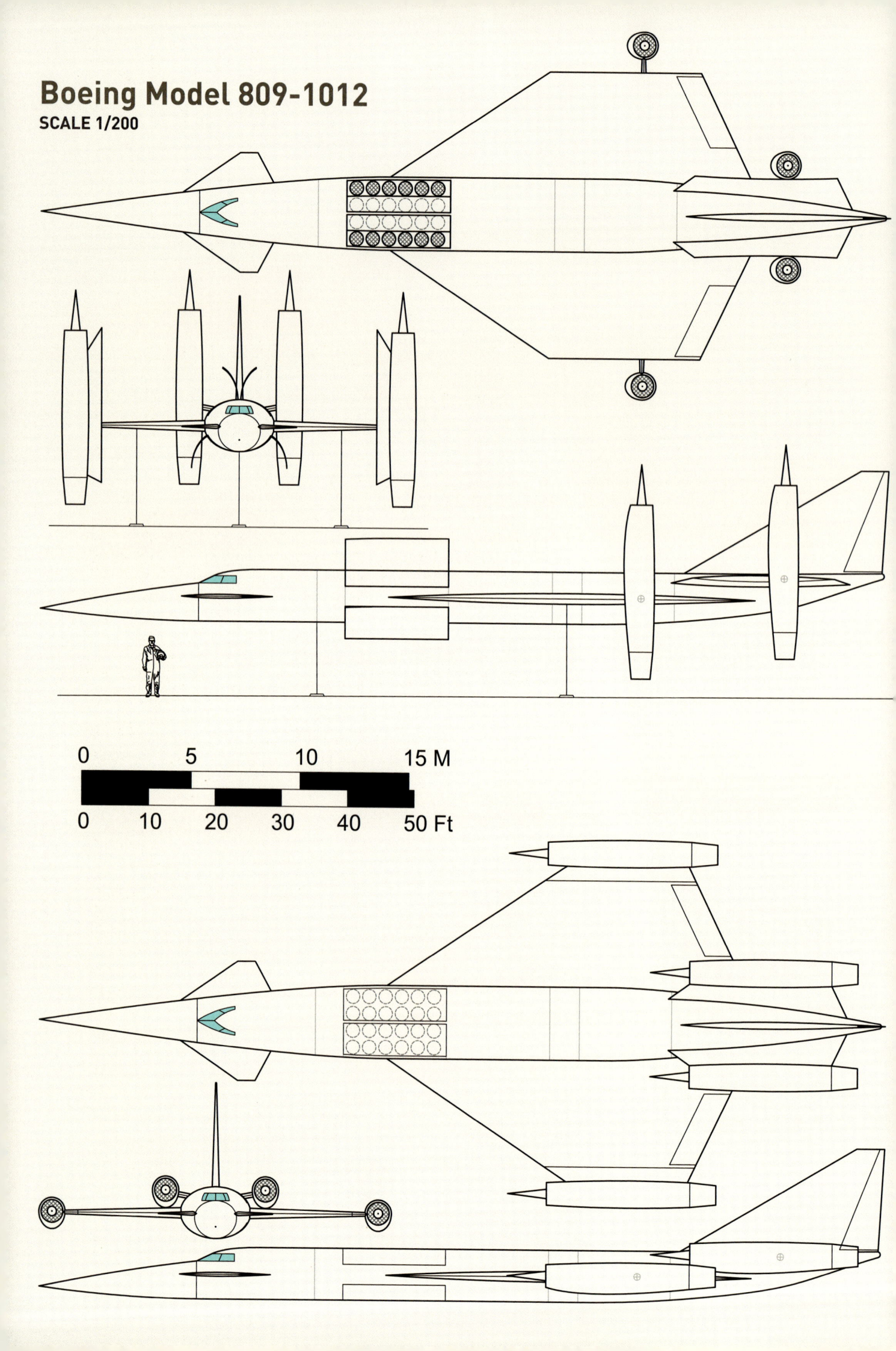

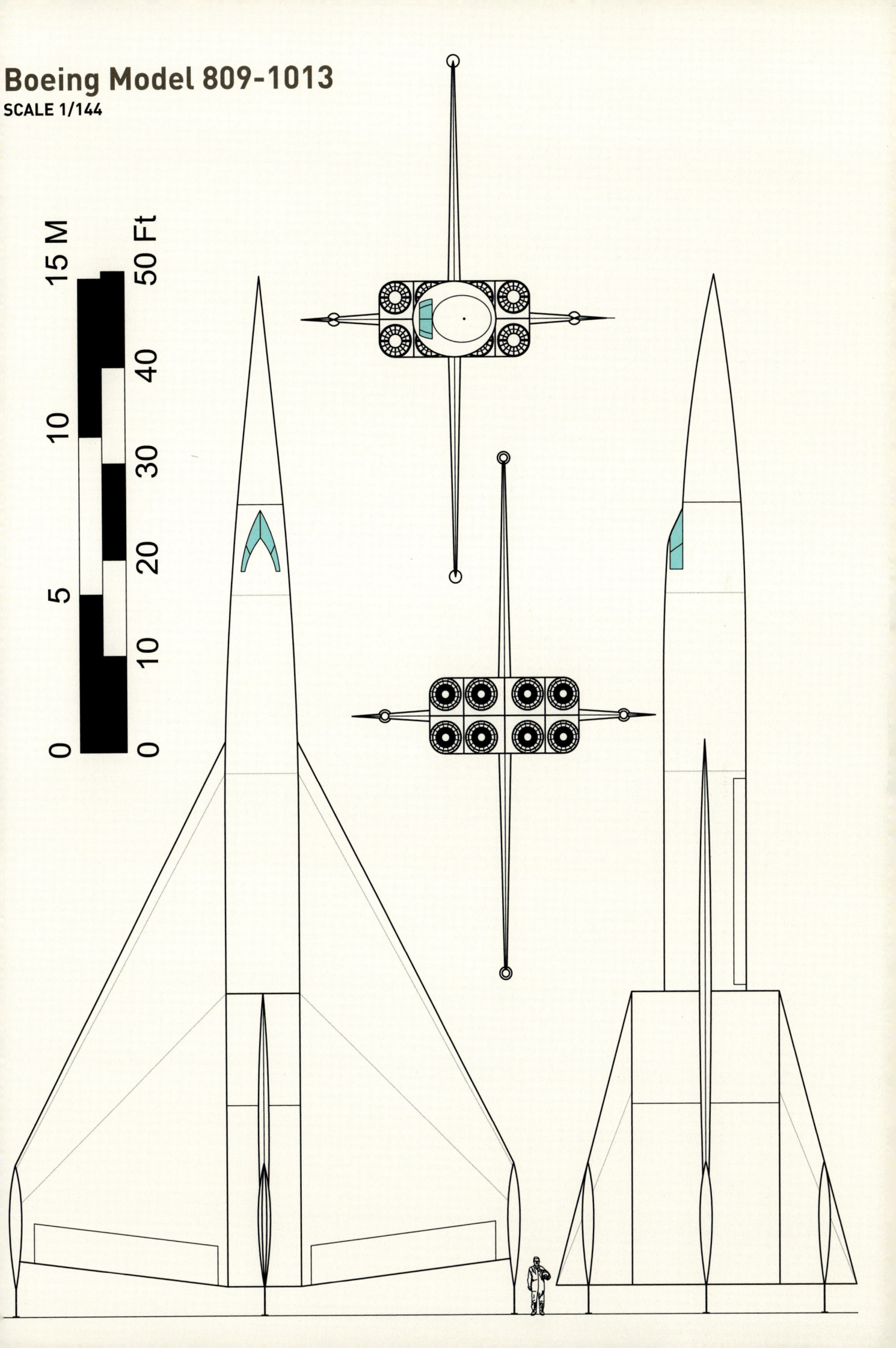

Boeing Model 809-1013
SCALE 1/144

15 M — 50 Ft
10 — 40
— 30
5 — 20
— 10
0 — 0

of an unbuilt VTOL project, described in very general terms only. It is unknown to the author whether this design came from a contractor or originated within the NACA. Also unknown was whether there was a USAF request for such a vehicle or whether it was unsolicited.

This aircraft was a supersonic jet bomber, not an unusual vehicle for the NACA to study at the end of the 1950s. However, it was unusual in that it was designed for vertical takeoff and landing. To achieve this, it had six turbojet engines buried within the stubby rectangular wings which could rotate upward to provide vertical thrust. The fuselage was spindle-shaped with a high fineness ratio, resembling the Lockheed CL-400 'Suntan' recon plane. A great many tail and canard configurations were experimented with.

Along with uncertainty regarding the aircraft's origin, uncertainty also exists regarding the size of the full-scale vehicle. The Research Memoranda describe the wind tunnel models in great detail but leave out direct references to their scale. However, through analysis of what information is available the size of the aircraft can be approximated.

The best reference describes a model with a 3ft span, and says that this is "considered approximately 1/10 scale." Unfortunately, the model described is a greatly simplified version. Another report describes wind tunnel tests of a remotely piloted model, and gives a wing span for the model of 32in. While this is certainly arguable, a reasonable guess for this model would be 1/12 scale, giving a wingspan of 32ft. The vehicle length would therefore be 112ft.

The length of the full size vehicle is close to the 107.4ft length of the SR-71. The size assumption is partially confirmed by noting that the gross weight of the SR-71 is 152,000lb, with a landing weight of 67,500lb, are also very similar to what is given for the full scale VTOL bomber.

Boeing Model 818-104, -105

As the Model 809 designation covered a wide range of unconventionally powered bombers and a few transports, the Boeing Model 818 designation covered the field of tactical fighter bombers, as well as battlefield surveillance platforms. Model 818-255 would end up being the designation used for the design Boeing submitted in June 1962 for the TFX programme (see *US Supersonic Bomber Projects Volume 1*). This was a swing-wing fighter-bomber similar in concept to the General Dynamics F-111 that eventually resulted from the TFX programme. But some earlier designs, from before the TFX programme was really nailed down, were quite a bit different.

The complete history of the Model 818 series is unknown... and will likely remain unknown. As well as the usual dreary list of things that cause aerospace knowledge to be lost in the mists of time, there is the additional issue that in December 1960 the building housing the records of the then-ongoing Tactical Fighter Project burned to the ground, taking many of the records with it. Nevertheless, a number of records of these earlier designs exist.

Model 818-1 from June 1958 was a VTOL fighter-bomber with a dozen engines. It is currently known to this author solely from a single diagram devoid of any details, including dimensions, but it set the configuration that would appear on later, more detailed designs. The design was much like that of Model 809-1012 from the year prior, but with the forward lift jets replaced with lift-cruise engines. Model 818-105, from September 1958 (essentially the same design as Model 818-104 from June), had a long, slim and aerodynamically unadventurous fuselage married to stubby, broad-chord aft mounted wings.

In lieu of the canards needed to offset the pitch problem created by the aft wings, on either side of the forward fuselage the aircraft had two side-by-side turbojets. At each wingtip was a long, thin pod that projected well ahead of the wingtip leading edge; outrigger landing gear would retract into the pods. A more important role of the pods, though, was to serve as the pivoting mounting point for a quartet of turbojets, all laid side-by-side. In forward flight, this cluster of engines would face fore and aft, and would serve as a rectangular endplate on the wingtip, as the pair of engines on each side of the forward fuselage would serve as canards. But for takeoff and landing the engine clusters would all rotate 90° upwards to provide vertical thrust. All 12 engines were Pratt & Whitney JT12s (J85s for the Model 818-104) without afterburners.

The landing gear specified was unsurprising for the company that had produced the B-47 and B-52. Along with the relatively small landing gear that was produced from the wingtip pods, 'bicycle' landing gear, fore and aft, were stored within the fuselage. All tyres were low pressure for use on unimproved strips; the central landing gear took 70% of the aircraft weight. The vertical stabilizer did not have a rudder; instead, spoilers would be used for directional control and could serve as speed brakes.

Unusually, Model 818-105 was to be equipped with its own special weapon, a glide bomb with an infrared seeker. This would have been a small weapon... weighing only 300lb, the yield would have been a trifling – for a nuke – two kilotons. Of course, it's not a sure thing that a target would necessarily have a unique infrared signature, but the Model 818-105 would take care of that: prior to jettisoning the glide bomb, the 818-105 would first make a run at the target and from an altitude of 350 to 1,000ft and launch a marker rocket

NACA VTOL
SCALE 1/185

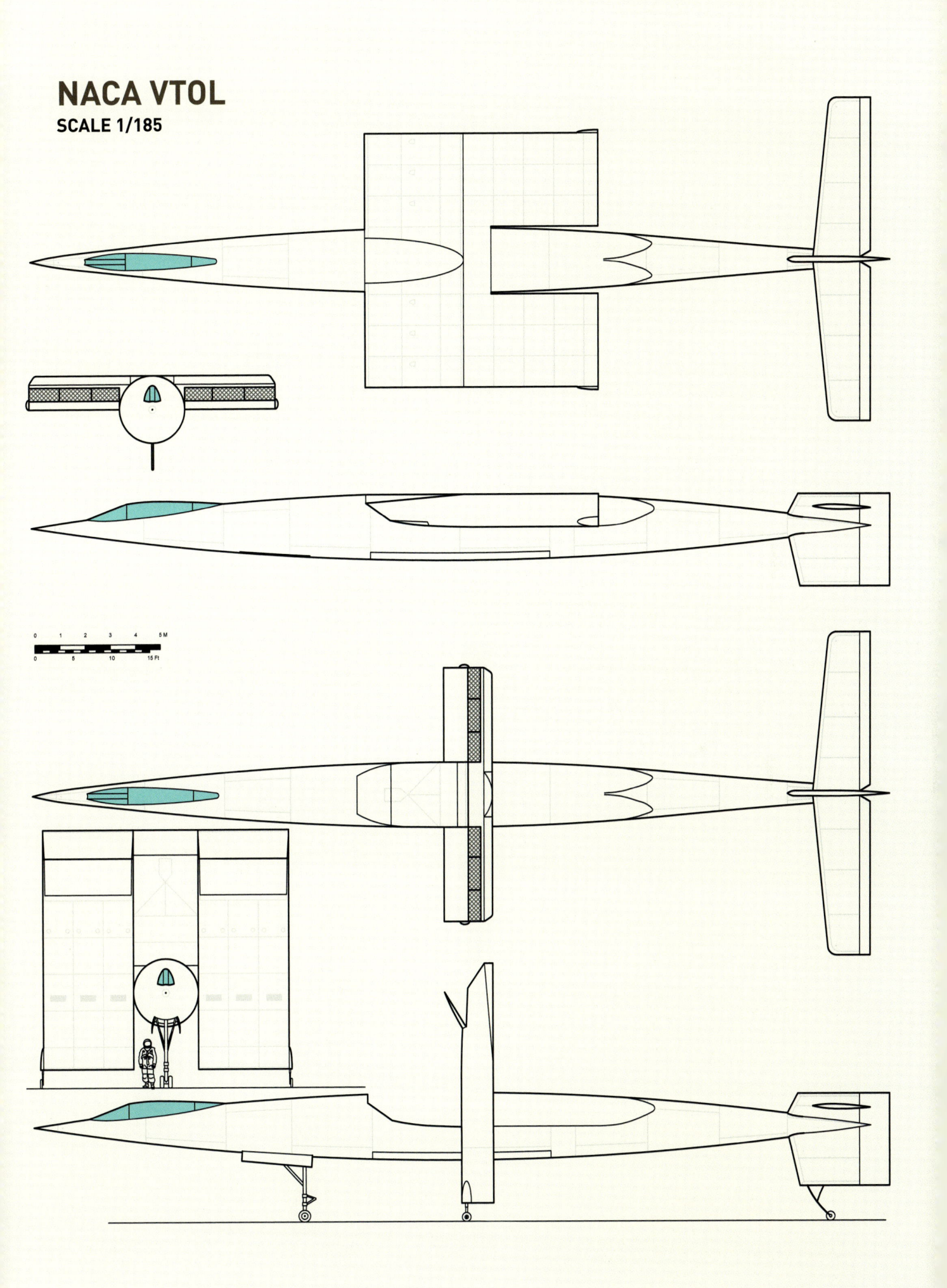

Boeing Model 818-104, -105
SCALE 1/125

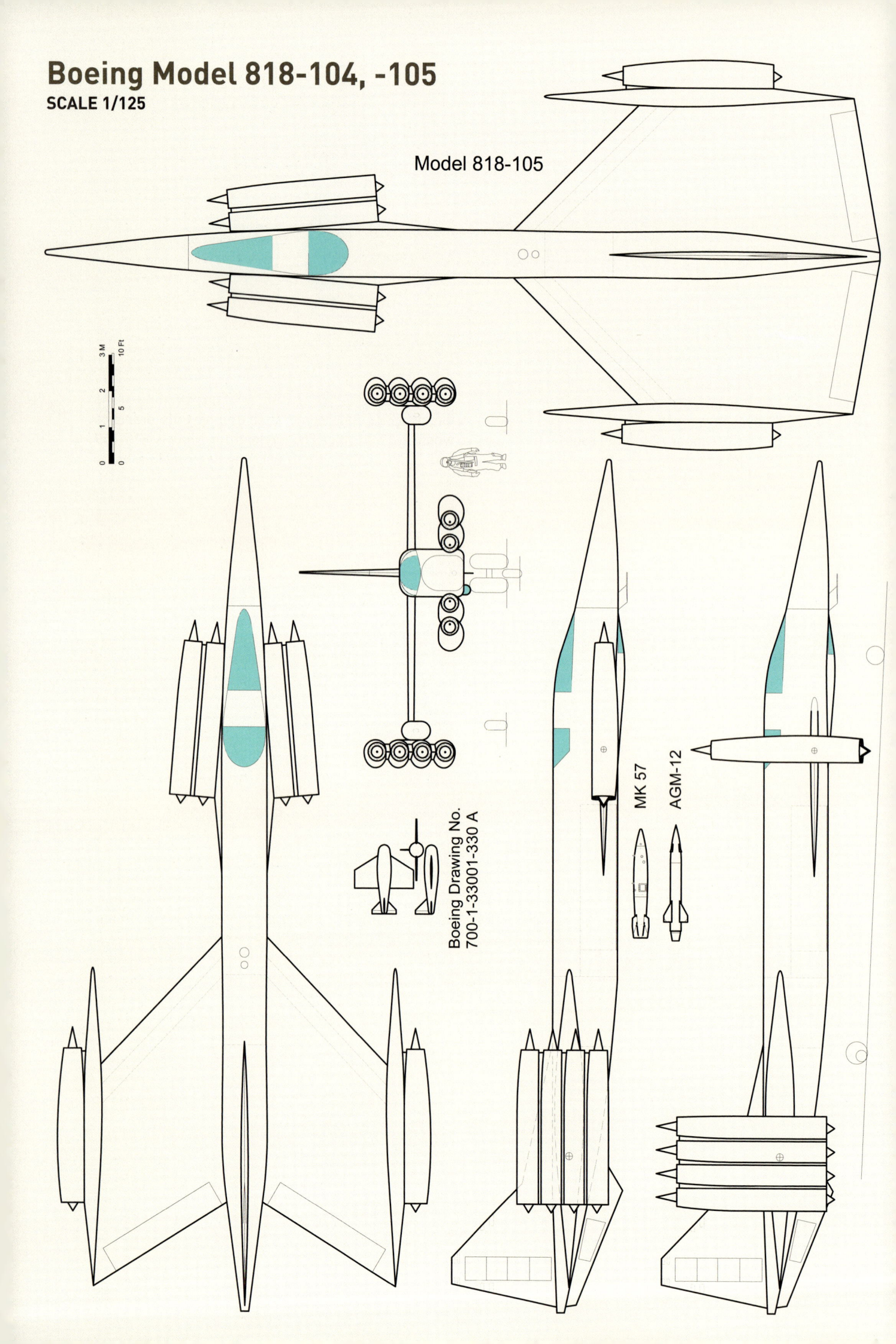

Model 818-105

Boeing Drawing No. 700-1-33001-330 A

MK 57
AGM-12

at it. A special flare would provide the targeting heat source the bomb would need.

The glide bomb would be released as the aircraft passed over it; with the seeker off, it would begin a pre-programmed turn back toward the target. The seeker would activate and steer the bomb towards the target, homing in on the flare with a claimed circular error probability of 100ft. The benefit here would presumably be that if the marker rocket missed, the nuclear weapon need not be deployed. How many marker rockets were to be carried is not described in the available documentation, but the aircraft could carry two glide bombs. Alternate weapons loads included:
  1 TX-43 nuclear weapon
  4 delayed fall weapons (2 kiloton each)
  1 Mk 28 nuclear weapon
  4 500lb conventional bombs

In addition to these, the weapons bay doors would serve as rocket launchers, holding a total of forty-eight 2.75in unguided rockets. For the fighter mission, four Sidewinder missiles could be carried. No gun or provision for one was provided. A TV camera was provided offset under the nose; it is unclear if this was meant for bomb aiming, VTOL operations or both.

Boeing Model 818-159

Dating from mid to late 1959, Boeing's Model 818-159 had an unusual configuration. Evidence indicates that it was a minor study... a study that resulted in the design of a strike-reconnaissance aircraft with almost no wings whatsoever. Essentially a lifting body, the 818-159 was a slim triangular dart with two crew in a cockpit at the extreme nose and two GE J79-X220 turbofan engines at the extreme rear, topped with a large vertical stabilizer equipped with spoilers rather than a conventional rudder.

Six GE J85 lift fan-jets were embedded within the fuselage just aft of the cockpit; together with thrust vectoring of the main engines (by closing off the nozzles and opening louvered nozzles on the underside), these provided the thrust needed for VTOL performance. The aircraft was designed specifically for sea level performance, thus the extreme miserliness in terms of any feature likely to create drag at high subsonic speeds in the thickest atmosphere. But at higher altitudes it could reach Mach 2.5.

Boeing Model 818-168

Designed alongside Model 818-159, Model 818-168 was a somewhat more conventional sort of configuration, somewhat like the Convair B-58 Hustler with a slim pointed fuselage, shoulder mounted clipped delta wings and a single podded turbofan (P&W J52) engine under each wing. Where it differed from the B-58 was, apart from having half as many turbojets, the use of two vertical stabilizers... and three lift fans for VTOL operations.

The lift fans would be driven – likely via tip-turbines – using exhaust tapped from the turbofan engines. One of the lift fans would require a passage through the middle of the fuselage; the other two through the wing. No indication is given to the fans being covered by doors or louvers during forward flight, though that seems likely as top speed was to be Mach 2.5.

Model 818-168 was a one-man aircraft with all-weather recon-strike capability, designed to cruise supersonically at high altitude then dive down to the deck for the last 50 miles of penetration to the target. The cruise home after dropping its ordnance would be subsonic. The payload for Models 818-159 and -168 was left vague, but was described as being nuclear, high explosive, chemical or even biological. For nuclear payloads, inertial/data link guided air-to-surface missiles with small nuclear warheads could be used, or guided gravity bombs or lay-down weapons.

Lockheed CL-407-80

In 1956 Lockheed studied a range of VTOL fighter-bombers for the USAF Tactical Air Command. The presumption was that by the 1964-65 timeframe both the US and USSR would have sufficient ICBMs to destroy the other nation, but not the accuracy to take out the enemy's weapons. This, presumably, would lead to less likelihood of all out war and increased likelihood of limited wars... a belief that proved more or less true, as seen by Vietnam. Consequently, Lockheed began a study of strike-reconnaissance aircraft suitable for limited wars, capable of being based virtually anywhere and with fast reaction. Supersonic VTOL aircraft were the choice, intended to deliver useful weapons with high accuracy and provide rapid intelligence.

The CL-407 series was designed to fill this role. Intended to be based in dispersed, minimal facilities, they would be difficult for the Soviets to target. Being capable of vertical takeoff, they would not need long, vulnerable runways. Being equally capable of both bombardment and surveillance and reconnaissance, using side-looking radar, optical and infrared cameras with quick-developing film, the CL-407 would be able to quickly find enemy targets such as armour columns, mobile missile units, ammunition dumps and the like. Such targets would be numerous, widely separated and important to hit, but not a good use of strategic bombers or ICBMs.

So the nimble and smallish CL-407 would, it was claimed, be highly useful in spreading out and sowing destruction among the enemy, launching from hidden, small bases. The weapons proposed for use by the CL-407 would be small inexpensive nuclear air-to-surface missiles. ('Inexpensive' and 'nuclear' don't generally

Boeing Model 818-159
SCALE 1/100

Boeing Model 818-168
SCALE 1/80

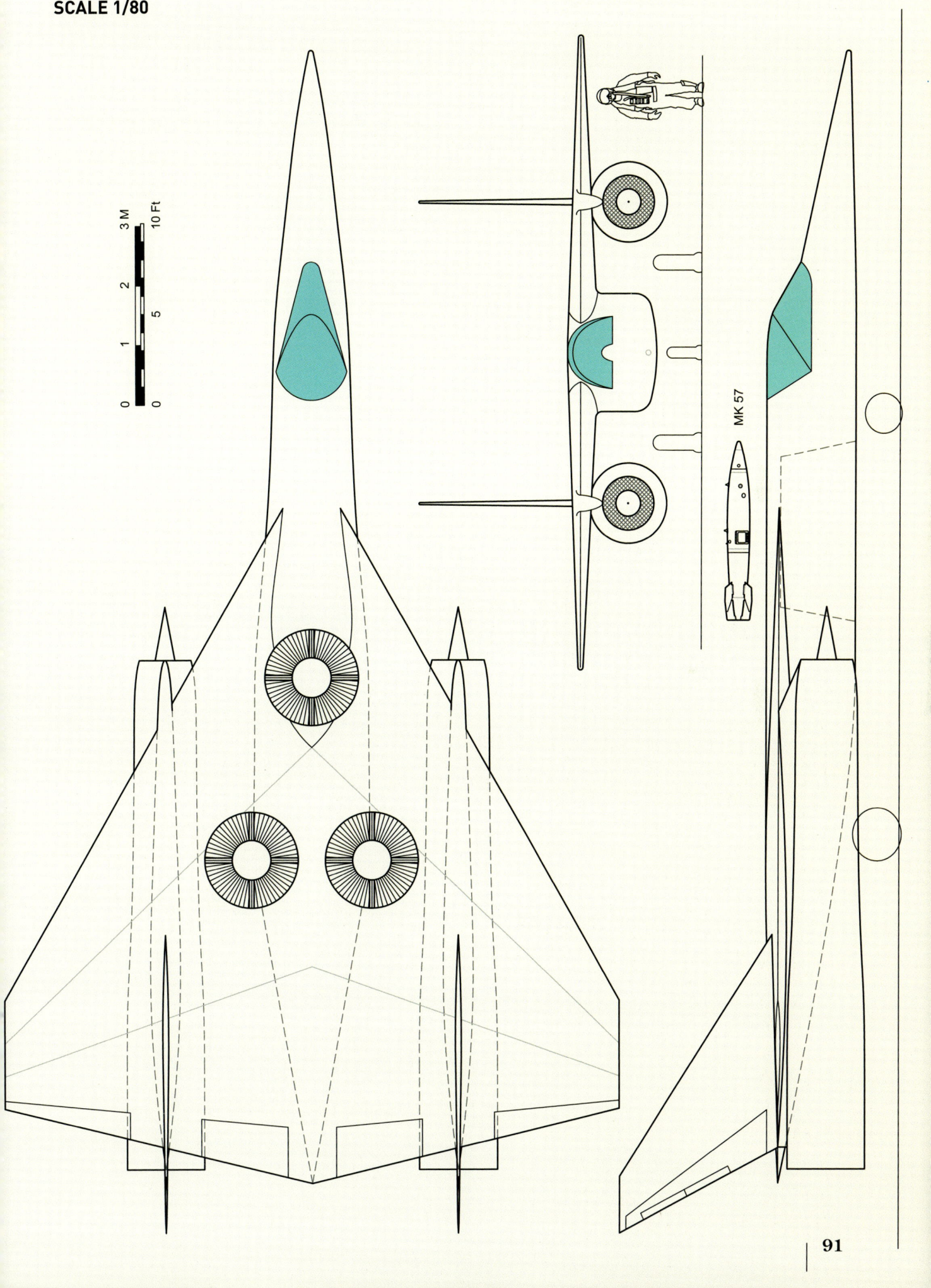

MK 57

91

Lockheed CL-407-80
SCALE 1/125

MK 57

92

go together, but this was the 1950s…) The CL-407 would also be able to take out larger fixed installations such as airfields and oil fields and submarine pens with megaton-class thermonuclear weapons. Additionally, the reconnaissance potential of the aircraft was increased by use of a real-time data link, allowing for targets that the Air Force *really* didn't like to be quickly struck with surface-to-surface missiles.

Ten variants of the CL-407 are known with their sub-designation indicating the approximate gross VTO weight of the aircraft. The CL-407-80, for instance, had a gross VTO weight of 80,280lb. All used a mix of lift jets and lift/cruise engines to achieve VTOL performance and high speed flight. And all did away with lift fans and diverter valves and vectoring nozzles with the lift/cruise engines by the simple expediency of tilting the entire engine… even when it was embedded deeply within the fuselage.

The engine (or engines, as several designs featured two main turbojets) was well embedded within the aft fuselage for horizontal thrust, but for STOL or VTOL performance the engine – and the fuselage structure above and below it – would rotate upwards 75°. A bank of lift jets located in the forward fuselage would provide further vertical thrust. The lift jet would achieve full thrust first, pitching the aircraft up on its landing gear 15° nose-up; the main engines, now pointed directly vertically, would increase thrust and the aircraft would rise.

For short takeoffs, the lift jets would again pitch the aircraft 15° upwards, but the main engines would rotate only a fraction as far, about 30°. Somewhat concerning, as the main engines rotate upwards, they transition from easily drawing air through the fixed inlet ducts, to drawing air through the open faces of the compressors… but there is a short phase when the upper edge of the inlet structure obscures the engines. This would doubtless have been 'interesting'.

CL-407	Crew	Engines	Ordnance	VTO GTOW (lbs)
-27	1	1- J79-X207 + 2 J85	1000	27,210
-32	1	1 J79-X207 + 3 J85	1000	31,860
-37	2	1 J79-X207 + 4 J85	2000	36,510
-40	2	2 J52 + 3 J85	2000	40,536
-48	2	1 J58 + 4 J85	2000	48,129
-54	2	2 J79-X207 + 4 J85	2000	54,420
-63	2	2 J79-X207 + 6 J85	2000	63,720
-68	2	1 J58 (fan) + 6 J85	2000	68,100
-80	2	2 J93 + 6 J58	2000	80,280
-87	2	2 J58 + 6 J58	2000	86,940

CL-407-80 was configured like most of the designs: a pointed fuselage, highly swept triangular canards, aft mounted swept wings and two vertical stabilizers, each mounted at about half-span on the trailing edges of the main wings. The inlet was above the mid-fuselage, an inverted variable ramp, feeding two turbojets side-by-side in the rear fuselage. In the case of the -80, those turbojets were General Electric J93s, the engines that powered the XB-70. And appropriately too: the CL-407-80 was designed for a top speed of Mach 3.

The canards were to be retractable at subsonic speeds and deployed at supersonic, maintaining the aerodynamic centre position as it would otherwise shift aft through transonic into supersonic. A single weapons bay was located on the underside just aft of the lift jets. It could contain two 1,000lb air-to-surface missiles (with a range of 20 miles, using inertial and TV guidance or a radiation seeker, and with a warhead ranging from 2-10 kilotons) or two nuclear gravity bombs.

To either side of the weapons bay was a 16ft-long side-looking reconnaissance radar antenna. In the event of a catastrophe, the fuselage forward of the lift jets would jettison using a sizable solid rocket motor to serve as an escape capsule. For increased range, external fuel tanks could be used; the capacity for inflight refuelling does not seem to have been included.

There are a few other known CL-407 configurations whose sub-designations do not correlate to takeoff weight; these presumably are early configurations or minor side-studies. Some of the non-weight-correlated designs differed in configurations from all the rest. The CL-407-42 (VTO gross weight 39,800lb) did not have canards, but instead barely-swept wings more akin to those of the F-104 and a conventional tailplane; a nacelle at mid-span held two J85-5 engines that would tip up for vertical thrust.

Three J85-5 Phase II aft-fan engines were provided in the forward fuselage for VTOL use and one more in the rear fuselage. The CL-407-47-2 (gross VTO weight 55,300lb) had delta wings and a canard, but the inlets were on the side of the fuselage, not the top. One CL-407-48 – there seem to have been two – was a highly modified F-104 Starfighter turned into a VTOL technology testbed with four J85 lift jets in the fuselage behind the cockpit and a J79 main engine modified with a thrust diverter for VTOL operations.

Bell D188A

The USAF initiated SR-141 for a V/STOL tactical fighter-bomber in 1956. Bell responded with the D-191, a design similar in layout and concept to the D-109 of five years earlier: a seemingly conventional fighter with straight wings, but with wingtip engines that could tilt for vertical thrust. Bell won the evaluation, but development was precluded by lack of USAF funds.

At the same time, the US Navy had high hopes that technology had progressed to the point where a

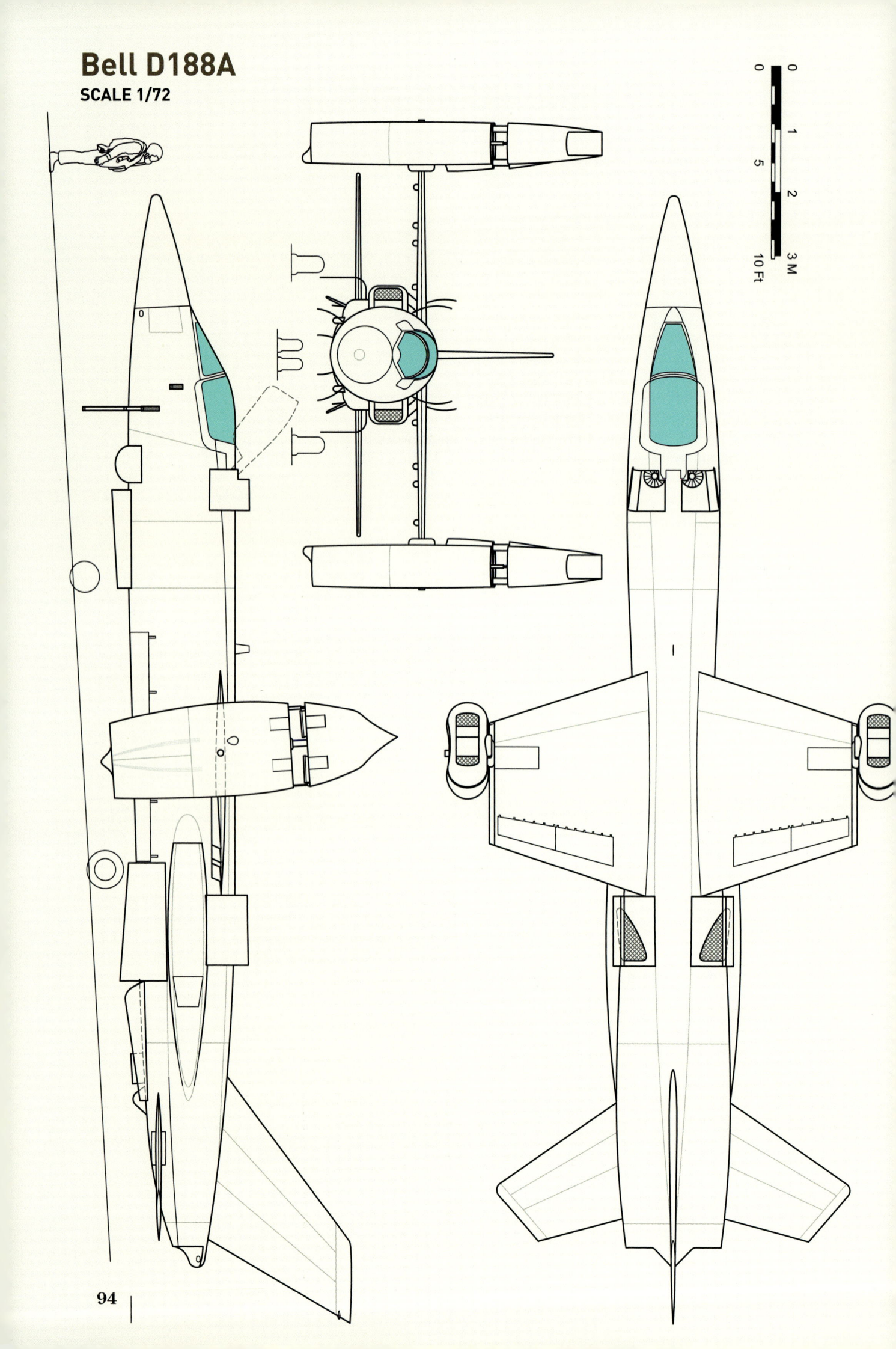

Bell D188A
SCALE 1/72

94

practical vertical takeoff and landing fighter could be designed and built. Such aircraft could be deployed to smaller carriers or even to ships not previously intended to carry fighter craft, such as destroyers.

Without the need for long runways and catapults, small decks little larger than the aircraft itself could be used. Bell Aircraft Corporation, with its long history of VTOL aircraft design and development, was selected by the Navy to design a practical VTOL fighter. Bell continued with its ongoing D-188 studies... but an odd twist occurred. The D-188 was a fighter of fairly conventional layout, but equipped with a multitude of vertical lift jets. D188A was the configuration that Bell decided to proceed with, but D188A was a derivative of the D-191, not the D-188. In June 1957, Bell began the preliminary design of the D188A for the US Navy under BuAer Contract NOas 57-836c.

Early concepts for the D188A featured at least two fuselage mounted jet engines and at least two wingtip mounted jet engines; the fuselage engines were equipped with thrust diverters and the wingtip mounted engines were permitted to swivel. Many configurations with as few as four and as many as eight engines were studied. The design – which was also granted the project designation Model 2000 – started to come together with two engines in the wingtip pods, but variability in the number of fuselage engines.

One design featured two fuselage mounted jet engines, with extremely long (and horribly inefficient) exhaust extensions leading to the aircraft's tail. A thrust diverter was located just aft of each engine, which provided vertical thrust near the aircraft centre of gravity. Two further engines were located in pods on each wingtip; each engine was fitted with its own individual circular inlet with a shock cone spike in the inlet for supersonic flight. This would have produced good high speed performance, but poor inlet performance at low speed. The fuselage engines had chin inlets and short S-ducts. All engines were fitted with afterburners.

The design continued to evolve and the number of engines grew. A mockup was built and an informal inspection held in early January 1958. The D188A design had taken nearly its final form... a single seat, eight engine fighter-bomber with four wingtip mounted lift/cruise engines in two pods, two fuselage mounted lift jets (located just aft of the cockpit) and two fuselage mounted jets that could be used for both lift and forward thrust. These latter engines had been moved much closer to the tail; the inlets for these engines were located beneath the trailing edge of the shoulder mounted wings. The fuselage was given a very distinct 'Coke-bottle' shape for area rule drag reduction. The configuration has often been compared to that of the Lockheed F-104 Starfighter... but was in fact derived from that of the Bell D-109 of 1951, and owed nothing to the F-104.

The D188A was equipped with six afterburning J85-GE-5 engines (two in the aft fuselage, and two each in rotating wingtip pods) and two non-afterburning J85-GE-5 engines (mounted aft of the cockpit). The engines just aft of the cockpit would be used solely for vertical lift. The wingtip engines would rotate to provide both horizontal and vertical thrust. The aft fuselage engines had diverter valves installed ahead of the afterburners to permit both vertical and horizontal thrust.

Control in hover would be provided by reaction control thrusters located at the aircraft extremities. The thrusters would be compressed air 'puffers', with the air provided by engine compressor bleed.

Vertical liftoff and transition to pure horizontal flight was a process expected to take 60.5 seconds and 9,050ft of range. The transition from pure forward flight to hover was expected to take 41 seconds and 4,430ft. The D188A was perfectly capable of conventional rolling takeoffs when conditions permitted, meaning lower fuel consumption and heavier payloads. At 19,110lb weight, Mach 2 and 35,000ft, the maximum sustained load factor was 3.65g. This equated to a turn radius of 33,000ft.

The D188A is sometimes claimed to have been designated the F3L for the US Navy. While Bell called it that in promotional material, there is no evidence that the US Navy accepted that designation. Similarly, Bell used 'XF-109' in promotional material aimed at the USAF; in the decades since the aircraft has become well known as the F-109. But the Air Force never officially granted the D188A the F-109 designation; this was solely Bell corporate optimism and good, effective PR.

In December 1957, the United States Air Force officially entered into the development programme and provided funds on an equal basis with the Navy. However, funding problems caused the US Navy to back out of the programme, while the USAF continued. By February 1959, the design had been revised and a mockup was ready for review. Bell had not built a production fighter since the P-63 of Second World War vintage. To offset some of the expected production problems, Bell went into partnership with Convair; Convair's fighter assembly facilities, as well as its experienced employees, would be used to build production aircraft. However, the USAF ceased financially supporting the effort in March 1959... but Convair and Bell continued development on internal funds.

As well as the complexity and cost of the aircraft, the USAF's interest was shifting away from the idea of a Mach 2.3 VTOL fighter to a slower STOL fighter, more of which could be built for the same cost. This concept eventually led to the TFX programme and the F-111 (see *US Supersonic Bomber Projects Volume 1*). The revised Air Force design differed from the December 1957 design. There were major changes to the tailplanes, and the aft fuselage contours were quite different (the fuselage was widened considerably), but in major respects, it was recognizably the same aircraft.

The wingtip engine inlets were optimized for high speed flight, and were not well suited for low speed or vertical flight. To get around this, they were designed to translate 10in forward, creating a sizable secondary inlet. The translation was automatic based on the angle of the nacelles. Doors covered the inlets and nozzles of the forward fuselage lift jets when not in use as well as covering the secondary vertical thrust nozzle on the fuselage lift-cruise engines. The rear fuselage engines were provided with two inlets each... a conventional vertical tamp 'scoop' on the fuselage sides under the trailing edges of the wings, optimized for high forward speeds, and a secondary inlet just ahead of and above the engines, used during vertical thrust.

The side inlets would be closed off; as they were close to the ground, foreign object ingestion would be a concern, and the secondary inlets on the upper side of the rear fuselage would be not only aerodynamically more efficient, they'd be much less likely to swallow rocks and bolts. In the event of an engine failure during vertical flight, the diagonal engine would also be shut down. This meant that the aircraft would no longer be capable of climbing vertically or even hovering, but control would be maintained during descent.

Control at low speed was achieved by a combination of engine thrust differential (pitch) and reaction control jets (roll and yaw). The reaction control jets were located on the engine nacelles; four variable exit nozzles were provided on each, fed from a manifold system hooked up to the entire eight-engine system. The thrust available to the reaction control system amounted to 5% of the total engine thrust. Controls at high speed included all-moving slab stabilizers: the horizontal tailplanes as well as the vertical stabilizer. Two small ventral strakes were located under the aft fuselage to provide added stability. Spoilers were the only aerodynamic control surface fitted to the main wings.

Construction was to be primarily aluminium with some use of stainless steel and titanium.

While the US Navy wanted their D188A to take off from ships smaller than aircraft carriers, the USAF was interested in an aircraft that could operate from dispersed, rapidly prepared facilities. In essence, the D188A would be spread throughout seemingly random locations in central European forests, requiring only a few truck or helicopter loads of supplies to be transported to small clearings. Some preparations would be needed for the launch pad itself... eight turbojet exhausts mere inches from the ground would damage conventional pavement, never mind soil.

Sadly, the Air Force was not entirely impressed by the design. The cost and complexity were high, and led to an aircraft with a fairly low weapons load. The basic armament was all contained within a bay (12ft long, 2.5ft deep, 4ft wide) in the underside of the fuselage below the wings at the centre of gravity. No gun was to be carried; after all, this was in the era when missiles were going to do all the work of bringing down other aircraft, a belief that would be sorely tested a few years later in Vietnam.

For fighter missions, the armament bay would contain a trio of Sidewinder air-to-air missiles. For strike missions, two Bullpup missiles could be carried; these would be modified versions with folding fins for more compact stowage. Other weapons loads included 16 cluster bombs, or 16 Zuni rockets, or four 250lb unguided bombs or two 500lb napalm bombs or two 1,000lb unguided bombs or two 1,000lb nuclear bombs. These weapons could be mixed: for example, a 1,000lb bomb and a Sidewinder. In addition, the armaments bay could be equipped with reconnaissance systems; a side-looking antenna could take the place of one weapon while providing space for one air-to-ground missile of the Bullpup variety.

Depending on range requirements, wing pylons could also be fitted with one missile each or 400-gallon fuel tanks. The mission range could be expanded through the use of inflight refuelling using a probe that would deploy from the forward fuselage. The D188A could be turned into a buddy-system tanker with the addition of a module that would plug into the armaments bay, connecting to the aircraft's fuel system and diverting it to a deployable hose-and-drogue system contained on a reel in the belly module.

For the use of nuclear weapons, the D188A could employ laydown weapons (which use parachutes to slow descent and reduce the impact of hitting the ground, then 'lay down' on the ground for a moment to give the aircraft some time to escape the blast radius) or a 'toss' technique that would release the bomb while in a fast vertical climb, again granting the aircraft a chance of running away from the impending Earth-shattering kaboom. Bomb aiming would be aided by the onboard radar systems, including ground mapping and terrain clearance, systems to track enemy radar and other electronic emissions, and a Doppler-inertial navigation system.

In 1959, an additional version was designed that was to use more advanced versions of the J85-5 engines. These more advanced engines would increase the cruise speed from Mach 2 to Mach 2.3, and give a maximum dive speed of Mach 2.5. Maximum internal fuel went from 9,750lb to 13,500lb with a fuselage length increase of about a foot. Vertical takeoff was possible with all eight engines at full thrust and the

Bell D188A
SCALE 1/72

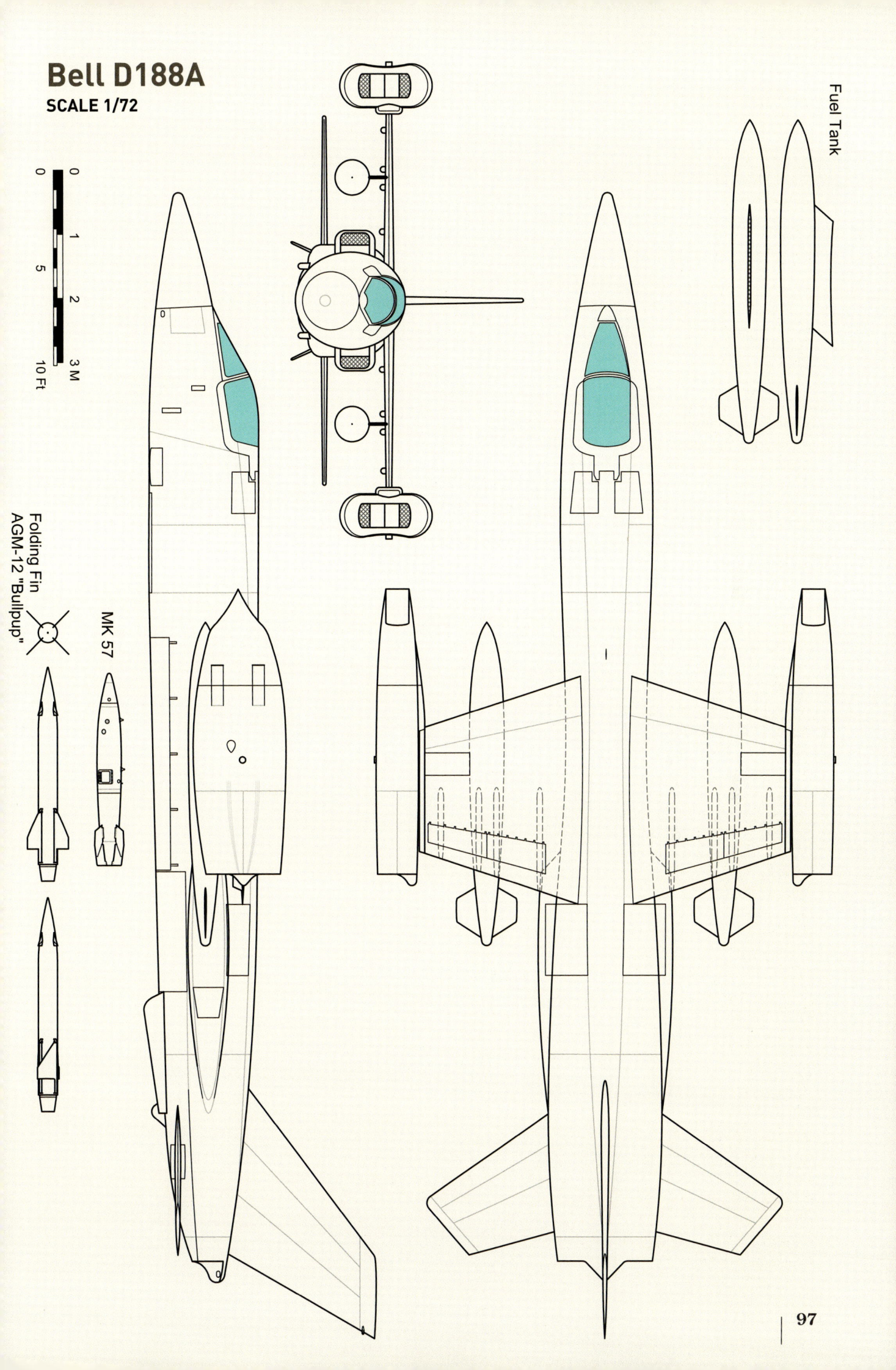

Fuel Tank

Folding Fin
AGM-12 "Bullpup"

MK 57

97

Bell D188A
SCALE 1/72

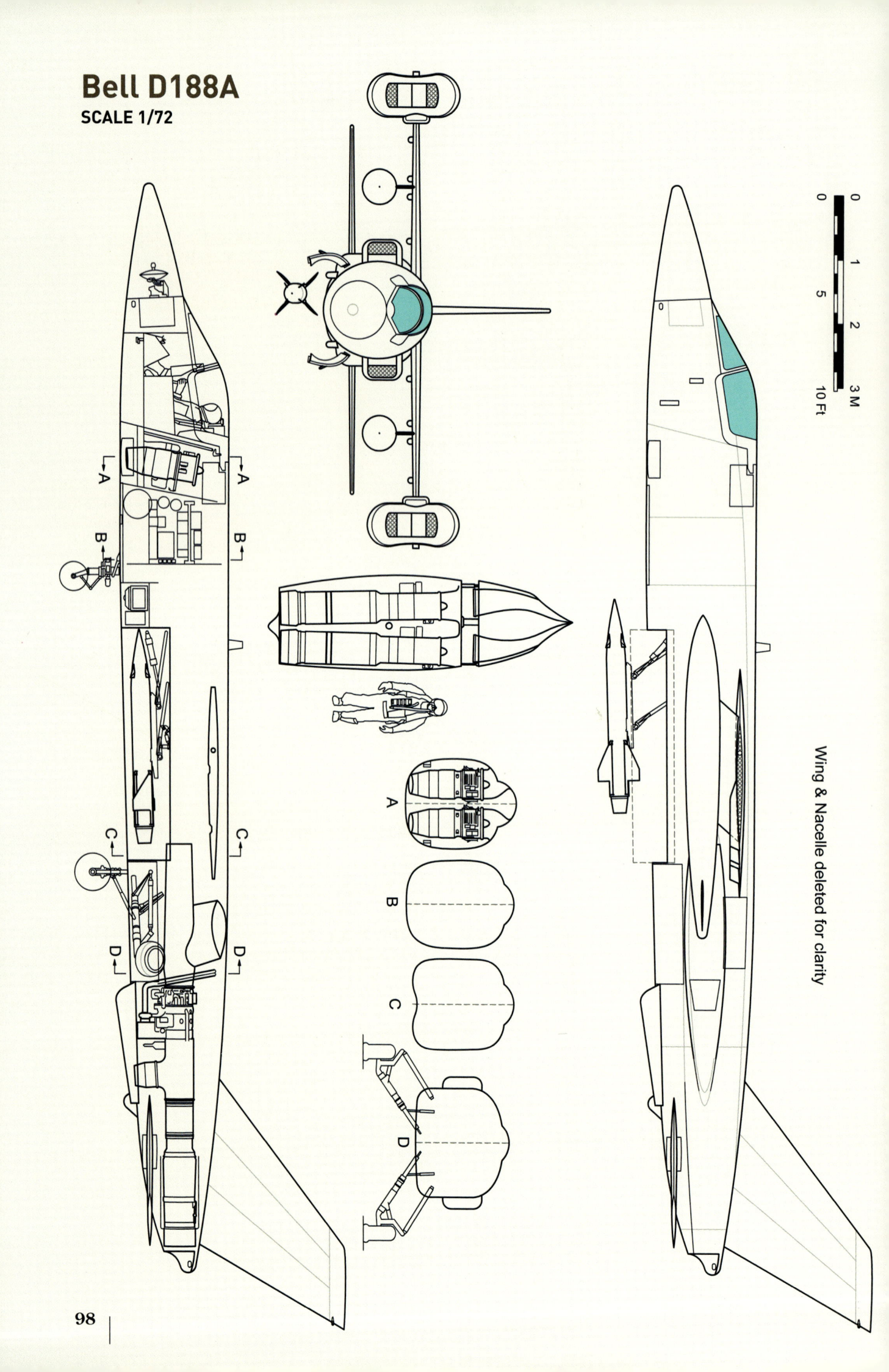

Wing & Nacelle deleted for clarity

nacelles tilted a full 90°, but a short takeoff would reduced fuel consumption if a runway was available.

For short takeoffs the run would begin with the nacelles fully forward; the six horizontal-thrust engines would accelerate the aircraft down the runway and then suddenly divert the rear engines into partial vertical lift and tilt the nacelles partially upwards. This would 'jump' the aircraft into the air with substantial forward airspeed; the engines would then return to full forward thrust.

At the time the D188A was being refined, the battlefield most expected was Europe being invaded by the Soviets. The D188A would, unlike conventional fighter-bombers, be able to be dispersed virtually anywhere. Runways would not be needed, only relatively small, quickly prepared takeoff and landing pads. These could be anything from existing concrete lots to pads hastily assembled from metal gratings made for the purpose. Along with trucks and trailers supplying fuel, ordnance and maintenance components, such widely dispersed aircraft could be quickly hidden in and near the forests of Europe, camouflage netting being useful for the cause.

In peacetime these sites would be set up around conventional landing fields used by conventional airlifters. The range of the D188A even with vertical takeoff was sufficient to not only attack the satellite nations surrounding the USSR, but well into the USSR itself. From NATO territory, and using either a two-D188A 'buddy' refuelling system with vertical takeoff or a single aircraft with conventional runway takeoff, one of the aircraft could *almost* reach Moscow with a 1,000lb nuclear weapon. This of course assumes a planned return to base, but in the event that nuclear weapons are being tossed around by single-seat fighter-bombers, it's not unreasonable to assume that the pilot might well be okay with a one-way mission, thus assuring sufficient range to reach Moscow.

However, if the point came that one-man tactical aircraft are being used to drop H-bombs, Moscow would very likely have already been converted into a glass-coated memory by way of ICBM or strategic bomber. With short takeoff and buddy refuelling, a single D188A could penetrate well beyond Moscow and return to West Germany.

If the D188A was based close to the combat zone, thus negating the need for great range, the payload or loiter time could be greatly increased. This would allow the aircraft to be used for ground support, using conventional weapons such as the Bullpup, rockets or bombs to take on enemy troops, logistics and armour. Had history gone the D188A's way, it might have ended up in Vietnam serving in that capacity, based in relatively small forward sites to support ground operations. However, Vietnam played hell with complicated American weapons systems; how well the D188A would have actually fared would have depended greatly on how well it was designed.

With eight jet engines, it doesn't sound like something that would have been fault tolerant. Swallowing bugs and leaves and dirt and rain, not to mention catching all manner of ground fire, doesn't sound like something such a craft would have shrugged off. But as with many weapons systems, early problems may well have been learned from and corrected, leading to successful aircraft. The D188A was to be designed and built with the assumption of being based not at major airfields but at dispersed sites; thus maintainability would have been a driving factor.

The D188A had the range to self-ferry from the United States to Vietnam in several stages without in-flight refuelling, or it could have made it in one go with refuelling. One LST would have had the cargo capacity to transport enough material – 1,500 tons – to support one squadron of D188As through 170 strike missions.

Bell was convinced that the D188A was an aircraft worth having and spent a further $2,500,000 of company funds to continue the effort. Assuming an engineering go-ahead in January of 1959, Bell claimed that the first prototype could fly by December 1960 and, assuming all went well, the first squadron would be available in the middle of 1963. Bell stated that the decision by the DoD to fund the D188A would determine whether or not the United States would field a supersonic VTOL fighter before the early 1970s. The D188A continued on into 1961, but no more Air Force or Navy funding was to be had. The concept died as the Air Force lost interest in VTO in favor of less exciting concepts such as the TFX.

The D188A, while a failed attempt, pointed the way to a future that almost was. In the early 1960s, NATO held a competition to procure a supersonic VTOL strike-fighter. One of the companies to bid was EWR of West Germany; that bid what was, in essence, a stripped down D188A. With assistance from Bell, the EWR VJ-101 C fighter, which was eventually built and successfully flown, looked like nothing so much as a D188A with the tail engines removed and faired over. But even though the design proved itself, it was replaced by yet another VTOL fighter project, the VJ-101 D, which used fixed lift jets for clean high speed aerodynamics. However, this aircraft never left the drawing board.

Republic AP-100

Reported on in mid-1959, the Republic Aviation Corporation AP-100 was the result of about five years of effort to design a VTOL combat aircraft. Prior designs had used pure jet-lift, with resulting high fuel consumption and damage to the ground from the high velocity jet exhaust. But the development of the General Electric X-353-7C propulsion system seemed like a way to solve these problems.

Republic AP-100A
SCALE 1/120

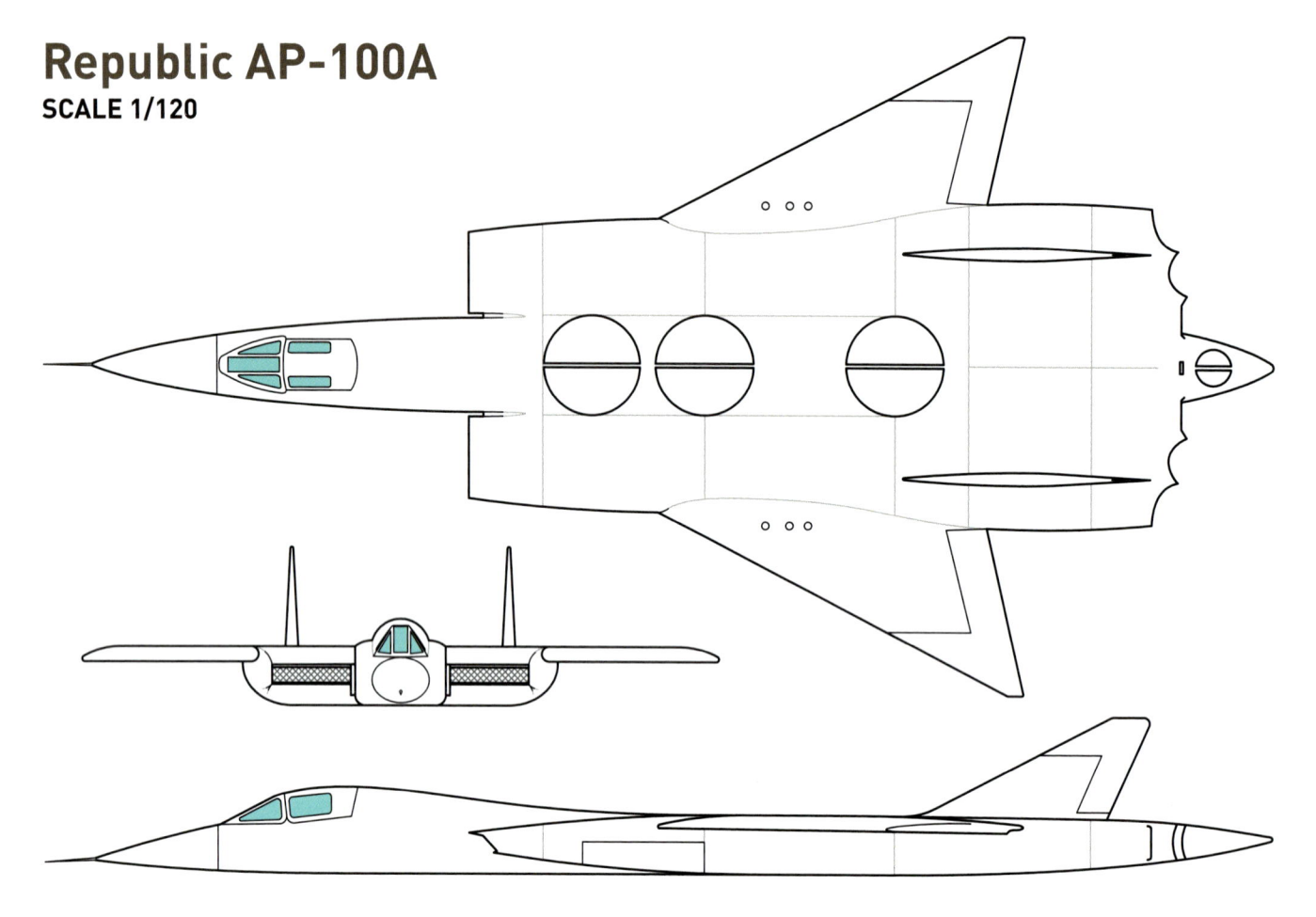

Instead of simply aiming the exhaust downwards, the exhaust from a turbojet would be diverted into ducts that would pass it tangentially through 'scrolls' around the rim of a large diameter lift fan. Around the rim of the fan would be a multitude of small turbine blades; the high velocity exhaust gases would spin the lift fan. The high velocity exhaust would be converted into a low-velocity exhaust through the lift fan… but the actual mass flow rate would be substantially increased. This would make for a cooler, less damaging exhaust.

Ground erosion and foreign object damage would be greatly reduced. In addition, thrust would also be increased: the maximum thrust of two GE J85-5 Phase II turbojets was 9,620lb, while the thrust of the lift fan driven by those two engines was 14,160lb. The AP-100 was designed around this new VTOL propulsion system, using six turbojets for forward thrust and to drive three lift fans.

The engine planned was a J85 modified specifically for VTOL use. An additional compressor stage was added to the front, while the turbine and nozzle diameters were increased in order to deal with the increased air flow and to improve high altitude, high speed performance.

The six J85s were laid side-by-side at the rear of the fuselage, creating a wide, thin lifting body. Behind each engine was a long duct terminating in an afterburner, but between the engine and the afterburner was a diverter valve. For vertical thrust the valve would close and the exhaust would be sent to the lift fans, each buried in the fuselage in a line behind the cockpit. The lift fans covered the centre of gravity of the aircraft, accounting for shifts caused by fuel and weapons loading; by separating the vertical from the horizontal thrust components, the base drag of the aircraft could be reduced, allowing reasonably efficient (for the time) supercruising with afterburner. The exhaust from two engines was diverted to each fan.

As the three fans were arranged in a straight line, they provided no roll or yaw control in hover (yaw control would be available through the louvers covering the outlets of the fore and aft fans on the underside). For hovering roll control, a trio of jets were located above each wing root using gases tapped off the engine exhaust. At the tail was a small pitch control fan and a pitch control jet nozzle. It was expected that in normal operations the AP-100 would climb vertically to 200ft then begin to transition to horizontal flight; it would descend to around 180ft in the process before beginning to climb again in conventional forward motion.

The fans would gradually shut down as the diverter valves opened the horizontal thrust nozzles. The aircraft would be fully conventionally powered about 57 seconds after liftoff, at an airspeed of about 160 knots,

Republic AP-100B
SCALE 1/120

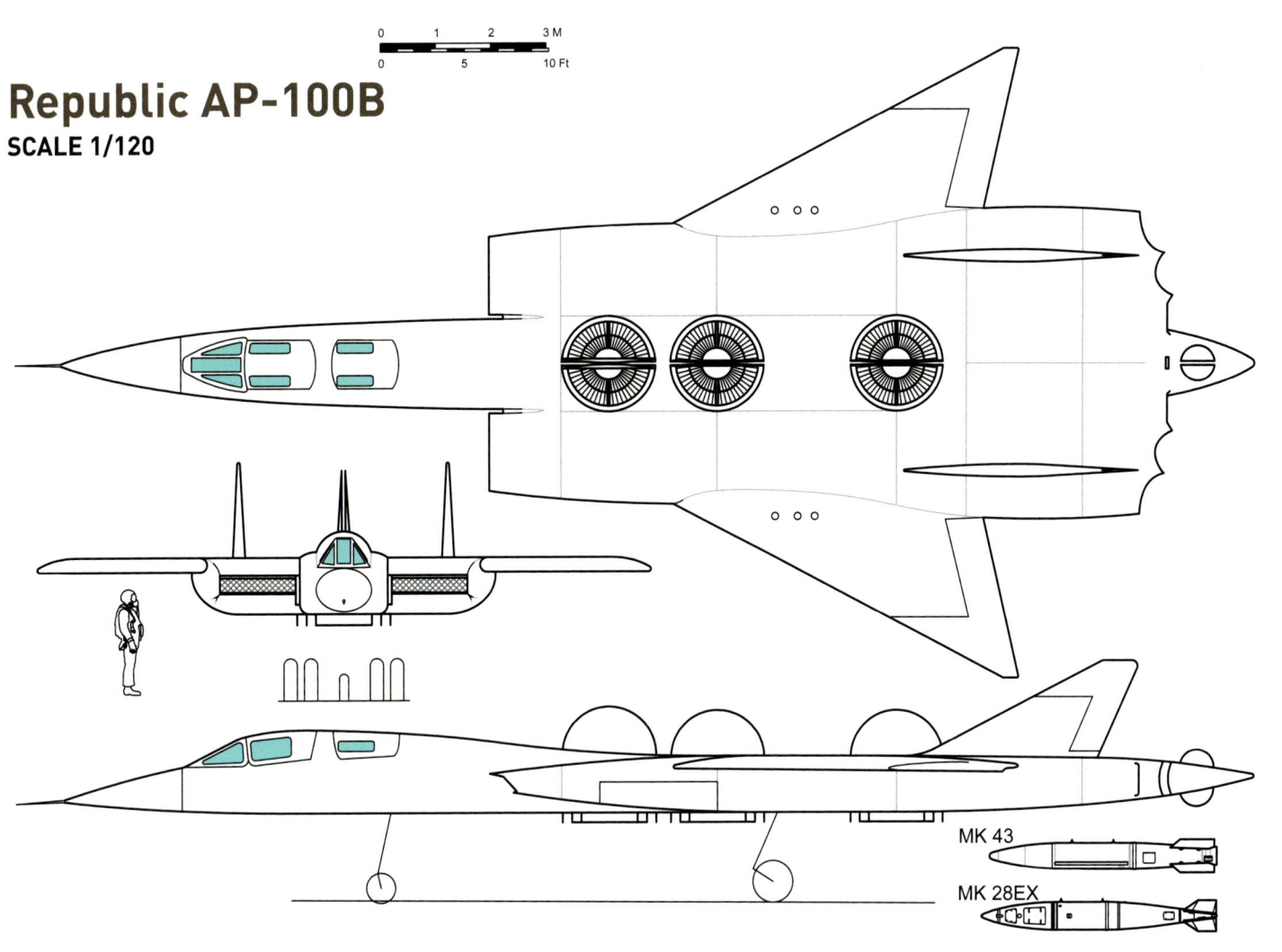

nearly 8,000ft downrange. Landing would be similar though reversed, and without a dip in altitude: it would maintain about 180ft in altitude as it decelerated and transitioned to fans, then would drop straight down.

The AP-100 was presented to the USAF in mid-1959 as a tactical fighter-bomber that could operate from either hardened sites or austere bases in all weather conditions. Prior to the outbreak of war (presumably in Europe) the aircraft would be kept in individual hardened shelters able to withstand 50psi overpressures from nearby nuclear detonations; thereafter they would operate from the now presumably flattened forested areas. Seemingly random locations would be pre-stocked with fuel, repair parts and ordnance for quick use. The weapons bay, able to house a single 1,000lb nuclear weapon, was in the rear fuselage.

The AP-100 would be capable of bombing from low altitude to high altitude – sea level to 75,000ft – with different levels of accuracy. Using radar guidance of the aircraft and unguided gravity bombs, a 1,000lb nuclear weapon would have a circular error probability of 1,690ft when dropped at Mach 2.3 from 70,000ft, or 440ft when dropped at Mach 1.4 and 15,000ft. A 1,000lb conventional bomb would have a CEP of 130ft when dropped at Mach 0.9 and 1,000ft; a TX-43 nuclear bomber would have a CEP of 250ft when dropped at the same condition.

In this case the TX-43 would serve in the lay-down role to give the aircraft a chance of escape. Other ordnance packages could include two LAU-3 rocket pods, each pylon-mounted to the underside of the fuselage; or four GAM-83 'White Lance' air-to-surface missiles (the Bullpup), with two suspended beneath the fuselage and one under each wing.

Ferry range was 3,300 nautical miles, long enough to be largely independent of tankers. Inflight refuelling would be possible for long-range missions.

Mach 2.3 was determined to be the optimum maximum cruising speed of the AP-100. Above this velocity aerothermal heating begins to make the use of aluminium problematic; the high temperatures soften the metal and require that structure be made from steel or titanium. The former metal was heavy while the latter metal was, in 1959, very hard to forge, machine or even acquire in industrial quantities. Republic found that an otherwise identical aircraft would need to be 75% larger to cruise at Mach 3 rather than Mach 2.3, and would cost at least twice as much. The AP-100 would have a brief dash capability of Mach 2.5 at 70,000ft, and could attain Mach 1.3 at sea level.

As seen from mid-1959, if the go-ahead was given in October 1959, the mockup inspection could be held in the second quarter of 1960 and the first prototype would fly in December 1961. The first operational aircraft would begin to arrive in May 1964, the first Tactical Air Command squadron in September and the first wing of 80 aircraft by November 1965. Production could range from five to twenty aircraft per month.

Two versions of the aircraft were proposed. The AP-100A had a single-seat cockpit while the AP-100B put in a second seat for a navigator. The AP-100B, while doubtless being a more accurate bomber, would also have had less fuel capacity and thus range.

Despite considerable study, including wind tunnel testing at both Republic and NASA (including 'flying' scale models in VTOL using lift fans powered by compressed air piped in through hoses), the AP-100 was not built.

Republic D-24

In late 1961, NATO produced NBMR 3 (NATO Basic Military Requirement), which called for a standard NATO-wide strike-recon plane capable of supersonic speed at low altitude. To that extent, the concept was similar to the TFX requirement… but the aircraft was to have the capability of not just short-field performance but vertical takeoff. A number of proposals were put in by a number of countries and companies. Republic joined with Fokker of Holland to produce a design they called the D-24 Alliance. The internal Republic designation for the basic design was RAC 758-1A30.

The Republic-Fokker design competed against a fairly wide field of qualified contestants. The British aircraft industry pinned their hopes to the Hawker P.1154, a supersonic evolvement of the Hawker P.1127 Kestrel (aka the Harrier jump-jet). The British engine industry, however, was split, pinning part of their hopes on the French Dassault Mirage 3V, a derivative of the Mirage with eight Rolls-Royce RB.108 lift engines embedded in the fuselage. The Italians proposed the Fiat G.95-6, and Lockheed proposed an F-104 with lift-jet pods on the wingtips. The Germans proposed the VJ.101D and the Focke-Wulf FW.1262. General Electric proposed aircraft using lift fans.

A single seater, the D-24 used a layout similar to that of the Republic TFX entry (see *US Supersonic Bomber Projects Volume 1*), a slim pointed fuselage married to a highly swept shoulder mounted delta wing. Small wing panels would be stowed above the delta wing at high speed, but would rotate outwards at low speed to increase wing area and move the centre of lift forward.

For propulsion the Alliance incorporated a single Bristol Siddeley BS.100 engine. The BS.100 was similar to, but more powerful than, the BS.53 Pegasus engine used on the Harrier, and included four vectorable nozzles for both lift and forward thrust. The BS.100 used plenum burning (essentially afterburning) in the two forward rotatable nozzles to greatly increase thrust. The engine was fed air through two 'chin' inlets below the cockpit. The landing gear gave the aircraft a distinctly nose-up attitude.

A weapons bay capable of holding one 1,000lb nuclear weapon was situated in the fuselage aft of the main engine. Another compartment was located forward of the engine; this was normally occupied by a fuel tank, but reconnaissance equipment could be installed. It does not appear that any guns would be mounted internally, and given the time the design was made it is probable that no gun armament was planned, much like the Bell D188A. Available documentation shows no armament beyond the single bomb; it is possible that, as with the TFX design, external pylons for additional weapons could be fitted. Given the configuration, it would be simpler to do that to the D-24 than the F-111, as the pylons would not have to rotate as wing sweep changes.

For STOL, rather than VTOL, missions, a single 212 gallon external fuel tank on a pylon could be fitted. For long range ferry flights, two 150 gallon fuel tanks could be fitted external to the forward fuselage, and two 300 gallon tanks below the wings.

Information is available regarding the expected maintenance issues the D-24 would have with the BS.100. Each aircraft would fly 30 hours each month, with missions of 1.5 hours duration, with a major overhaul of the engine every 1,000 hours. A wing of 30 D-24 aircraft would require 2.5 spare engines per month and would need 450 hours of inspections. This compares favourably to a comparison (made at the time) with the Mirage 3V, which was estimated to needs 66.7 spare engines per month per 30 aircraft, and need 1,800 hours of inspection.

NASA wind tunnel tested several versions of the D-24, including a revised configuration of its own. After wind tunnel testing showed some unsatisfactory minimum drag, revisions were made to the design. These included lengthening the nose and simplifying the planform. Unlike many aircraft concepts that never left the drawing board, the D-24 Alliance received a fair amount of press at the time, with appearances of concept art and display model photos appearing in a number of aviation magazines.

Ryan Model 186-C

The Ryan Aeronautical Company proposed its Model 186-C and 187-C in early 1965. The two were designed at the same time, both using the same lift fan VTOL propulsion system previously examined by

Republic D-24
SCALE 1/72

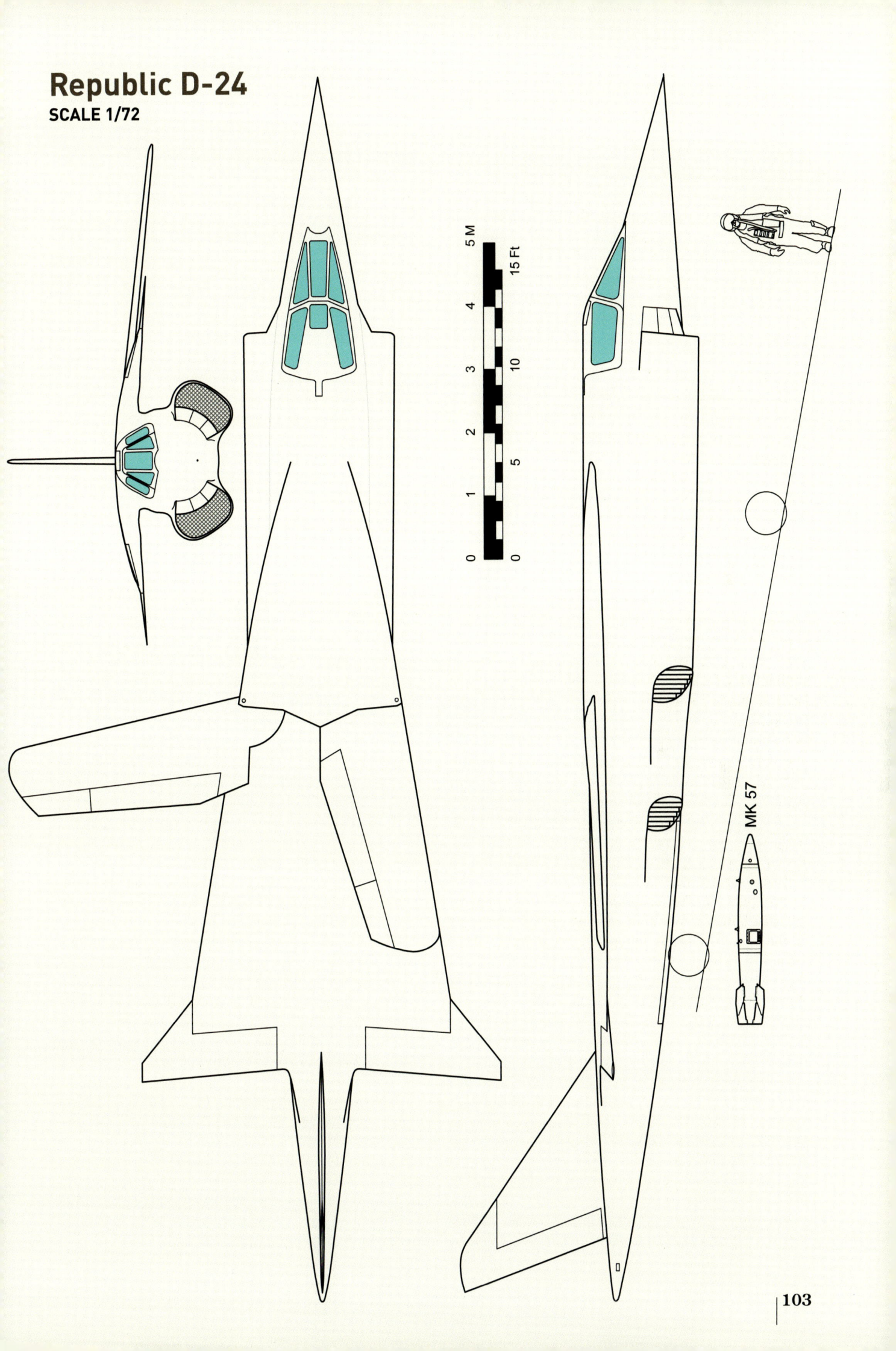

MK 57

Republic for its AP-100. Ryan had the added benefit of experience with the Ryan XV-5A Vertifan VTOL experimental aircraft. The XV-5A was equipped with three lift fans and first flew in May 1964. Where the AP-100 had three fans driven by six J85-5 engines, the smaller XV-5A had its three General Electric X353-5 lift fans driven by only two J85-5s.

Ryan was contracted by the US Army to develop the XV-5A (alongside the Lockheed XV-4 Hummingbird) in 1961, when the Army could still have fixed-wing combat aircraft. The XV-5A was a distinctly subsonic aircraft, but Ryan believed that it would make a creditable operational ground-attack platform in the form of the Model 177. This would remain a subsonic VTOL vehicle, with two crew seated side-by-side and capable of carrying a 2,000lb payload.

Ryan designed several other aircraft using the Vertifan VTOL propulsion system. The Model 182 was a VTOL transonic strike-fighter, not quite able to go supersonic; looking vaguely like a Douglas A-4 with a glandular problem, the Model 182 had a total of five lift fans. Two were mounted in the wings; one in the fear fuselage and two in the forward fuselage. All were fixed in place and were driven by a pair of turbojet gas generators.

The Ryan Model 186-C strike fighter was designed for supersonic flight and carried all of its lift fans within the wings. And it required substantial wing real estate to do this: the aircraft was fitted with eight 40.5in diameter lift fans. The wings were highly swept with a broad chord ('gothic' planform) where they met the fuselage, running from the tail up alongside the cockpit, with small extended panels at the tips. This provided not only a great deal of area in which to accommodate the lift fans, it also resulted in a design suited for high supersonic flight, reaching a maximum of Mach 2 at about 40,000ft, and about Mach 1.25 at sea level. The leading edge of the wing root was hinged and actuated to serve as a flap during low speed flight.

The aircraft had only two turbojet engines; each had a single variable ramp inlet under the wings for good efficiency at high forward airspeed. During hover, and especially when near the ground, auxiliary inlets located on the upper surface of the wings would open. The engines were not well defined, being simply "1968" technology-level "GE-1" engines with 5,240lb of thrust dry, 7,300lb of thrust with afterburner. With these it would have a ferry range of 2,000 nautical miles; perhaps oddly, no inflight refuelling capability is in evidence.

The Model 186-C could serve in either fighter or bomber role. For both missions it had a decently-sized internal ordnance bay, capable of fitting either a single Mk 84 2,000lb general purpose conventional bomb or two Mk 82 1,000lb general purpose bombs. Given how much of the wing was taken up by the lift fans, it looks unlikely that much if anything in the way of ordnance or additional fuel could be carried under the wings. The two crew were given ejector seats in a conventional tandem cockpit.

Ryan Model 187-C

Designed alongside the Model 186-C, the Model 187-C was simultaneously more and less conventional. Equipped with the same propulsion system, it was not as capable of achieving the same speed… but it could seemingly do more.

The overall configuration was fairly straightforward and would have looked at home alongside many other supersonic strike fighters of the time. It had a normal, though rather square cross-sectioned, fuselage, married to somewhat small mid-mounted swept wings. Two afterburning turbojets exhausted below the rear fuselage, each fed from an inlet under the wing roots that looked much like the inlets of the General Dynamics F-111. But as with the Model 186-C, this aircraft achieved VTOL flight through the use of eight lift fans.

Unlike the Model 186-C, the lift fans in the Model 187-C were stowed vertically in the fuselage during horizontal flight; only at low speed did they deploy, folding out horizontally. This allowed the wing to be small and unobstructed. And while the lift fans took up space in the fuselage, the aircraft was not stretched in length compared to the Model 186-C. It was slightly wider, which allowed for the cockpit to have side-by-side seating akin to the F-111. Unlike the F-111, the crew of the Ryan Model 187-C were given individual ejector seats rather than an escape capsule.

Like the Model 186-C, the 187-C had an internal weapons bay capable of carrying one Mk 84 2,000lb general purpose conventional bomb or two Mk 82 1,000lb general purpose bombs. Unlike the Model 186-C, the Model 187-C had additional weapons. An M61 Vulcan cannon was fitted into the lower port side of the forward fuselage; while useful for air-to-air combat, strafing ground targets would be a more likely role. Additionally, at least one hardpoint was available under each wing; Ryan diagrams depict it carrying a single Bullpup missile under each wing.

The Model 187-C had the same two hypothetical engines as the Model 186-C and the same lack of inflight refuelling capability. The ferry range was extended to 3,300 nautical miles, no doubt made possible by the aerodynamically cleaner configuration. However, the top speed was a little slower, Mach 1.8 at 40,000ft.

Ryan artwork of the Model 187-C generally depicts it in either USAF markings or in West German markings, sometimes both in the same illustration. A vehicle like this would, in the mid-1960s, have made much more sense to be based in West Germany than in the United States, as it would have been a better strike platform than bomber-interceptor due to the relatively low maximum speed of Mach 1.6.

Ryan Model 186-C
SCALE 1/72

105

Ryan Model 187-C
SCALE 1/100

0 1 2 3 M
0   5   10 Ft

CHAPTER 5
Hypersonics

Once past the 'sound barrier', there are few firmly definable thresholds in terms of speed. At Mach 1, very interesting things happen that set 'above' definitively apart from 'below'. But there is no such physical distinction at Mach 2, 3 or anywhere else. The benefits of flying ever faster come from the increased speed. The benefits of breaching another Mach number are largely psychological; the practical differences between Mach 2.99 and Mach 3 are vanishingly few.

As aircraft attained ever-increasing Mach numbers, some new phenomena were discovered. Starting above Mach 2, aircraft structures started encountering aerothermal heating… not, as is commonly thought, the result of friction with the air, but of the air ahead of the aircraft being highly compressed by the aircraft shoving its way through faster than the air could get out of the way. Air can only move at the speed of sound; something plowing through it faster than that cause the air to bunch up, with localized pressure spikes. And as pressure increases, temperature increases.

By the time an aircraft reaches Mach 3, designers need to start looking into exotic materials that can survive not just the pressure of high speed flight, but extended periods of being heat-soaked. And beyond Mach 5 or so, the heating and pressure become so severe that the air can dissociate (for example, the O_2 molecule can be curbstomped into two separate, independent oxygen atoms… highly reactive, ready to cause a ruckus), and atoms can be ionized (electrons ripped off). This means not only heat and pressure, but also chemical effects that can play hell not only with aircraft structures but with propulsion systems.

So aerodynamicists dubbed speeds above Mach 5 as not just 'supersonic' but 'hypersonic'. As troublesome as hypersonic issues can be, Mach 5 has the advantage of being *really* fast. It makes a hypersonic aircraft is hard to hit. It makes a hypersonic aircraft quick to reach a target. And it means that extremely long range missions can be achieved in a handful of hours, not the better part of a day or more. Crews need not necessarily be overly fatigued by spending long hours trapped in an uncomfortable chair. So it is hardly surprising that over the years military aircraft have been designed for hypersonic flight. This has included a number of bombers, generally meant to strike targets far away in very short order.

As glitteringly sci-fi as a hypersonic bomber is, the fact has long been that the concept is terribly impractical. Airbreathing propulsion systems that work at subsonic and low supersonic speeds begin to fail as Mach numbers increase; aircraft begin to rely on the very simple but fuel-thirsty ramjet for flights faster than Mach 4 or so. And much beyond Mach 5 to 7, the need turns to scramjets… supersonic combustion ramjets. These are, like ramjets, theoretically simple; but like nuclear fusion powerplant, scramjets have been just on the horizon for generations.

Making an engine that feeds air through at supersonic speeds, manages to get stable combustion with high mixing efficiency, generates substantially more thrust than drag and doesn't tear apart has proven to be a very difficult thing indeed, with demonstrated run times in actual practice tending to top out as a matter of a few seconds. Their day will doubtless come, but that day is not yet. And while aircraft designers have struggled to produce an aircraft, any aircraft, that can cruise along faster than Mach 5 and perform a useful mission, rocketeers many decades ago developed ICBMs that can hurl bombs halfway across the planet at near-orbital velocities.

Many designers skipped right over the hypersonic flight regime and went straight to designing orbital bombers. Such craft are hardly discussed these days, given that basing weapons of mass destruction in space violates international treaty. But the mere fact that an orbital bomber, or at least a sub-orbital bomber that pops out above the atmosphere to save itself the wear and tear of hypersonic flight, is basically a whole lot easier than a hypersonic cruiser has likely caused many designers and planners to abandon the concept before the design process could really get underway.

Boeing Model 813

Throughout much of 1958, Boeing-Seattle studied the feasibility of manned hypersonic bombers for strategic missions. These aircraft, intended for the 1970-1975 time frame, were produced under the Model 813 designation and varied substantially across a number of layouts, including both single and two-stage configurations. This work was done under SR-170 as the Extended Range High Speed Strategic Bomber Study and was presented to the ARDC in January of 1959.

The goal was an intercontinental range bomber capable of striking any target with a substantial military payload, and to be essentially invulnerable both on the ground and in flight. While the coming age of strategic missiles was foreseen in this study, Boeing argued that military targets, which were both heavily hardened against attack and often difficult to locate with precision, needed a man in the loop to carry out precise real-time aiming.

At least 30 configurations were studied by Boeing for this role, ranging from 100,000 to 500,000lb gross weight and from Mach 3 to Mach 10. While engine and wing configurations changed, sometimes wildly, a few things seemed more or less constant. The fuselage for most configurations was long, narrow and extremely pointed; the three crewmen sat one behind the other. They did not have windows with which to see the outer world, but would have a number of sizable screens giving them visual data from radar, infrared and visible light sensors.

The various sensor systems would provide different resolutions at a distance of 50 miles: radar would have a resolution of 50ft; infrared, 125ft; television, 75ft, and direct optical, 2.5ft. It was expected that with experience to be gained from the Dyna Soar programme, radar with a resolution of 5ft from a range of 500 miles might be achievable. The crew were not meant to serve as pilots per se, but in a decision-making and bomb aiming role. The aircraft would be as automated as possible otherwise, including being able to land itself. If need be, though, the crew could directly control the aircraft. The crew were to be composed of one "Battle Commander" and two "Reconnaissance Officers".

The crew compartment, including the nose and a portion of the wing, would be jettisoned as an escape capsule if the need arose. Despite the horrific conditions in which the aircraft would find itself, the crew compartment was to be a shirt-sleeve, comfortable environment. There would be no need for special pressure suits or even oxygen masks.

The Model 813 would operate not from a conventional airfield, but from something akin to early ICBM launch complexes. There would be a central facility surrounded by 13 remote sites, separated by a distance of some five miles, distant enough to prevent a single enemy bomb from taking out more than one or two sites. Each Model 813 aircraft and booster would be housed in a semi-hardened underground bunker. The bunkers would have upwards-sloping floors upon which the boosters and aircraft would rest, pointing skywards; overhead would be a large translating door that would protect the craft and crew from attack, weather and reconnaissance. Each remote site would be connected to the rest of the world via a modern road network, sized and rated to tow the booster and aircraft from nearby landing fields.

The boosters would themselves have boosters. Solid rocket motors would lob the aircraft into the sky directly from their underground revetments with a zero-length launch; the airbreathing or rocket main boosters would then continue to push the aircraft higher and faster.

Model 813-1001 was a boost-glide system… a dart-like manned stage without an airbreathing propulsion system, it would be lofted skywards and downrange via a rocket booster stage. It had a relatively small rocket engine of its own; while performance details are lacking, it clearly would not provide for a long-term, high-thrust system.

Model 813-1001A was configured much the same, but dispensed with the rocket engine and instead had two ramjet engines suspended under the wings. An unpublished NASA memorandum discusses hypersonic bomber aerodynamics, showing both a hydrogen-fuelled and a hydrocarbon-fuelled configuration; the hydrocarbon design is very clearly the Boeing Model 813-1036. While the memorandum, like most NACA/NASA wind tunnel reports, is vague on the details of the design such as where it actually came from, it's reasonable to assume that both designs came from Boeing as the requirements described are the same. Consequently, it appears that there was another Model 813 but designed for liquid hydrogen fuel. The configuration is similar to other Model 813's but with a far more voluminous fuselage.

Boeing Model 813-1002

The next design was rather different than most others. While the planform was consistent with the rest of the Model 813 line, it was unique in having a raised cockpit canopy, giving the pilot at least some forward vision. This argues for the Model 813-1002 perhaps not being the speed demon the other designs were. Additionally, there was no dorsal vertical stabilizer; the role was performed by two relatively small ventral fins flanking a rectangular box that contained four square-section ramjet engines. Landing gear consisted of a pair of nosewheels; the tips of the ventral fins would serve as skis. No indication is given of any shock absorbing capability at the tips of the fins, suggesting that landing would be uncomfortable.

Boeing Model 813-1032

Model 813-1032 set the stage for the most developed configuration. It was a clipped delta in planform with a narrow fuselage that extended to the vertex of the wings; at the rear sat a sizable dorsal vertical stabilizer. Seen from the front the wings were gull-shaped, rising up from the fuselage shoulder to a little past half-span, then angled back down. Below the bend, and at the trailing edge of the wing, was one podded hypersonic ramjet

Boeing Model 813-1002
SCALE 1/240

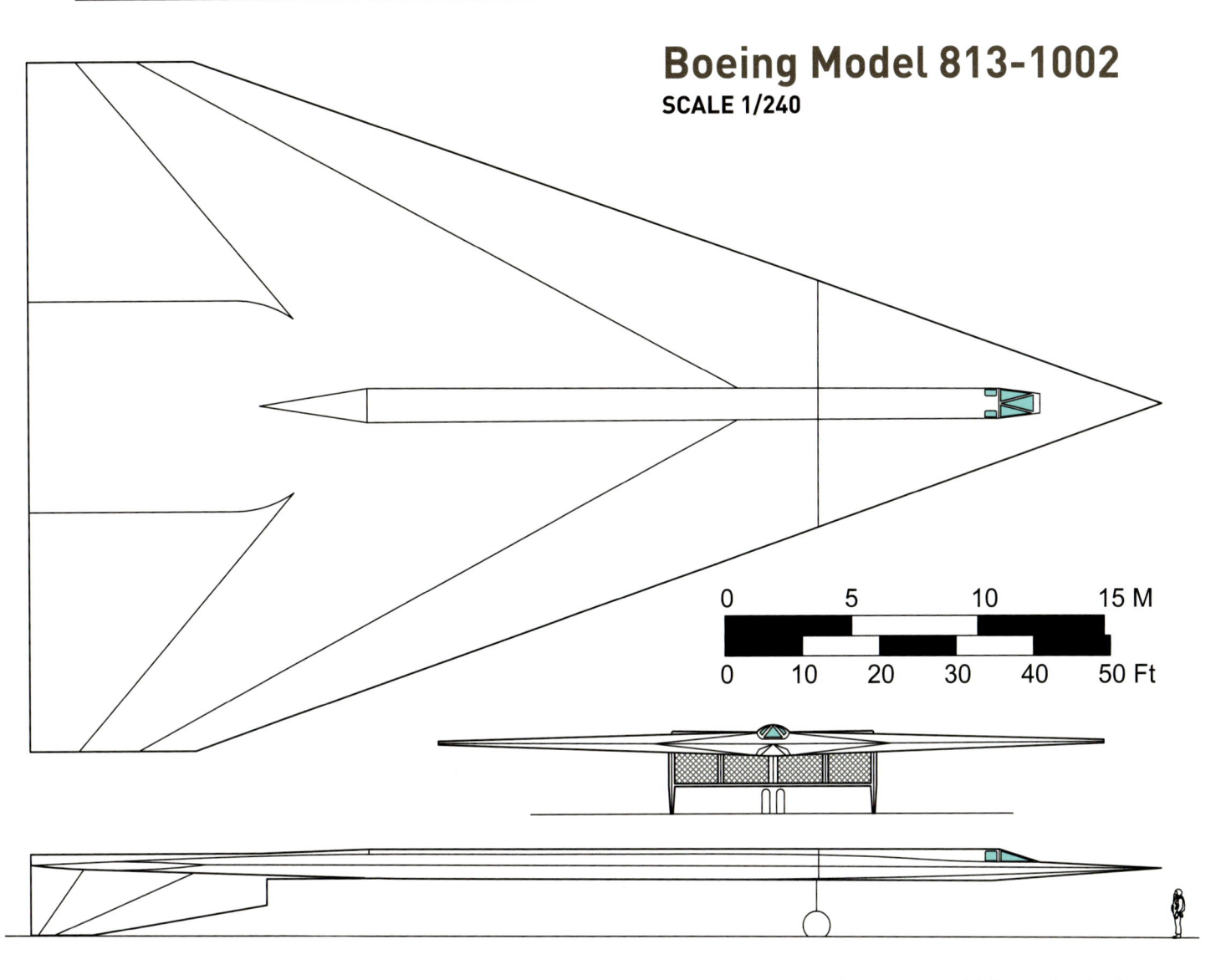

engine. Again it had a pair of nosewheels; a pair of skis would be deployed from the mid-fuselage to serve as the main landing gear. For launch the Model 813-1032 would be fitted with two Model 813-3032 solid rocket boosters. Simple and reliable, boosters such as these would, like a Minuteman ICBM, be ready to go at a moment's notice. They would not, however, be reusable. While this would be unlikely to be a problem in the event of global thermonuclear war, it would certainly make training flights expensive.

Boeing Model 813-1036

This appears to have been the design given the most study, and was the design presented to the Air Force. The manned stage was much like that of Model 813-1032; it was, however, slightly longer, with the fuselage nose projecting ahead of the wings. More importantly, instead of expendable solid rockets it used a reusable flyback booster.

The aircraft had a pair of hypersonic ramjets for sustain propulsion. These were seemingly simple machines with no moving parts… a large inlet spike ahead of a short conical frustum of an engine which consisted of a short convergent section and a short divergent nozzle. A perforated shroud surrounded the engine, permitting air to cool the thin walls of the combustion section; this would, it was felt, have allowed the engine to not need regenerative cooling.

The engines, burning JP-6 fuel, would permit Mach 6 cruising at 60,000ft. The total range of the aircraft would be a bit over 8,500 nautical miles burning JP-6; if it used boron-based high energy fuel if should be able to reach around 11,300 miles. Both fuels would permit the cruise phase to begin at about 80,500ft altitude and slowly climb, as fuel burned off, to about 100,500ft while maintaining Mach 6.

Two distinct boosters seem to have been designed. Both were unmanned recoverable and reusable aircraft that were little more than engines, fuel tanks and some control surfaces. Both boosters used six high Mach capable turbojets. These engines were highly hypothetical; it was thought that pure turbojets might have been used all the way to Mach 6, but a dual cycle (turbojet and ramjet, akin to the engine cycle used by the

Boeing Model 813-1036
SCALE 1/220

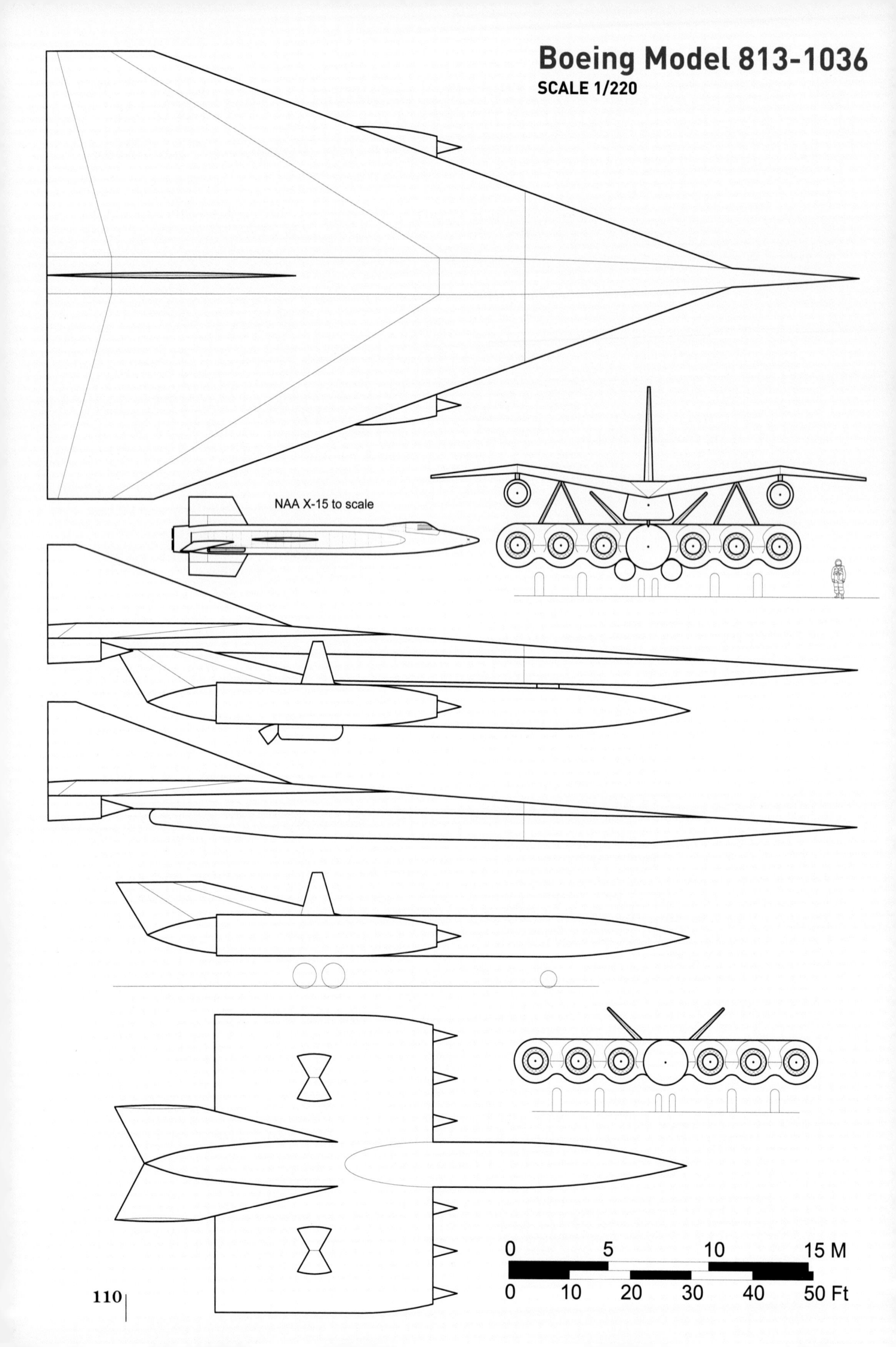

NAA X-15 to scale

0 5 10 15 M
0 10 20 30 40 50 Ft

110

SR-71) would probably be needed. The engines would produce around 40,000lb of thrust each on the runway; this would increase to well over 50,000lb after Mach 1, continuing past Mach 3. From there thrust would drop off. At Mach 6, the engines were expected to only produce about 10,000lb of thrust.

Both booster designs laid the six engines side-by-side, the package forming a simple low aspect ratio wing. One design – shown more commonly in the available documentation – had only the engine pack, a cylindrical fuselage with an ogival nose and a butterfly tail; the other design had a long tapering conical fuselage, highly swept stub wings outboard of the engine pack and a pair of vertical fins. Both would be equipped with conventional landing gear strong enough to support the fully fuelled composite aircraft. Both would also be fitted with solid rocket boosters powerful enough to lob the vehicle into the air from within the submerged revetments; unfortunately, details of these boosters are not available.

The lower wing surface of the cruise aircraft was expected to reach up to 1,300°F, necessitating the use of nickel-based J-1610 alloy. The leading edge would reach up to 1750°F, which the J-1610 alloy would handle. The upper wing surface would be cooler at 900°F, allowing the use of titanium-vanadium alloy B-120 VCA. Processed silica aerogel insulation would be used around the fuel tanks to keep the fuel from boiling. Unfortunately, the documents available to this author on the Model 813-1036 are incomplete; missing are discussion of the fuselage structure and materials. However, it is certain that the nose would have seen extreme temperatures.

Due to the extreme speed at which the aircraft would cruise, it would not fly a circuitous path like the B-52 might have. Instead, it would be relegated to flying a 'strip', a narrow rectangular piece of territory. Curiously, illustrations suggest that once the aircraft had deployed its weapons it would simply turn around and fly home, covering the same territory. This would indicate a very tight turning radius... an incredible achievement for an aircraft flying at Mach 6.

The bomb bay doors opened inwards, keeping them out of the Mach 6 airstream and driving the fuselage to be an isosceles trapezoid in cross section, wider at the bottom. This allowed the bomb bay doors to hinge up and in and clear of the bomb load. The offensive payload could be a single 50 megaton bomb, eight two-megaton bombs or four two-megaton air-to-surface missiles. The bomb bay was located right behind the landing gear bay.

The main gravity bomb would be a bluff shape with a variable-length nose 'probe'. This curious feature would be used to adjust the drag of the bomb while in flight; this would be used to dial in range, though not side to side travel. It was expected that the 750lb, two megaton device would have a circular error probability of 2,500ft,

giving an 80% probability of killing a target hardened against a 100psi blast.

Along with offensive weaponry, the aircraft would carry defensive systems. Part of this would be a pair of Model 813 decoy missiles, kept in a bay just ahead of the main landing gear. These were much smaller than the aircraft but, equipped with similar ramjet propulsion systems, they would present much the same radar return as the aircraft and would hopefully distract Soviet air defense systems. The infrared radiation from the decoys would be ten times lower than from the aircraft; the decoys would nevertheless remain important targets because the Soviets, it was surmised, would not be able to distinguish the decoys from air-to-surface missiles.

Another role envisioned for the Model 813 was ICBM-killer. While taking out ICBM sites on the ground is an obvious role for a strategic bomber, the thinking was that by carrying Mach 8-capable air-to-air missiles, the Model 813 could be used to take out Soviet ICBMs while in boost phase. The difficulty, of course, would be getting the Model 813 interceptors deep into the USSR in time to intercept the missiles. This would seem to be a capability that could only be used as the opportunity arose, but it's unclear how much of the offensive payload would need to be sacrificed to make room for the anti-missile missiles.

The testing programme would require 15 airframes and boosters. Five of the aircraft would be equipped with dual cycle engines, allowing them to fly without the need of boosters. These test planes would of course not reach the speed and range of the boosted versions, but they would permit early testing of the aircraft in slower regimes and landing.

Unlike many proposals of the time that promised operational aircraft in a timespan comfortably measured in months from go-ahead, this time the Boeing designers suggested that nine years and three months would elapse between go-ahead and the first delivery of operational craft.

Republic Mach 7

Alexander Kartvelli's presentation on future supersonic aircraft, including the Mach 4 nuclear ramjet design and the AP-100 VTOL previously described (see Chapters 1 and 4 respectively), also included a hypersonic bomber. This design used a modified tailless delta configuration with two triangular vertical stabilizers; overall it was a fairly standard hypersonic shape of the time, composed largely of straight lines, sharp edges and planes.

Propulsion was provided by two turbojets capable of accelerating the craft to Mach 3; at that point ramjets would take over and move the plane up to Mach 7. Both engine systems would burn JP-7. The entire lower fuselage is devoted to the needs of the ramjet inlet and exhaust systems, with the underside of the

Boeing Model 813-1036
SCALE 1/175

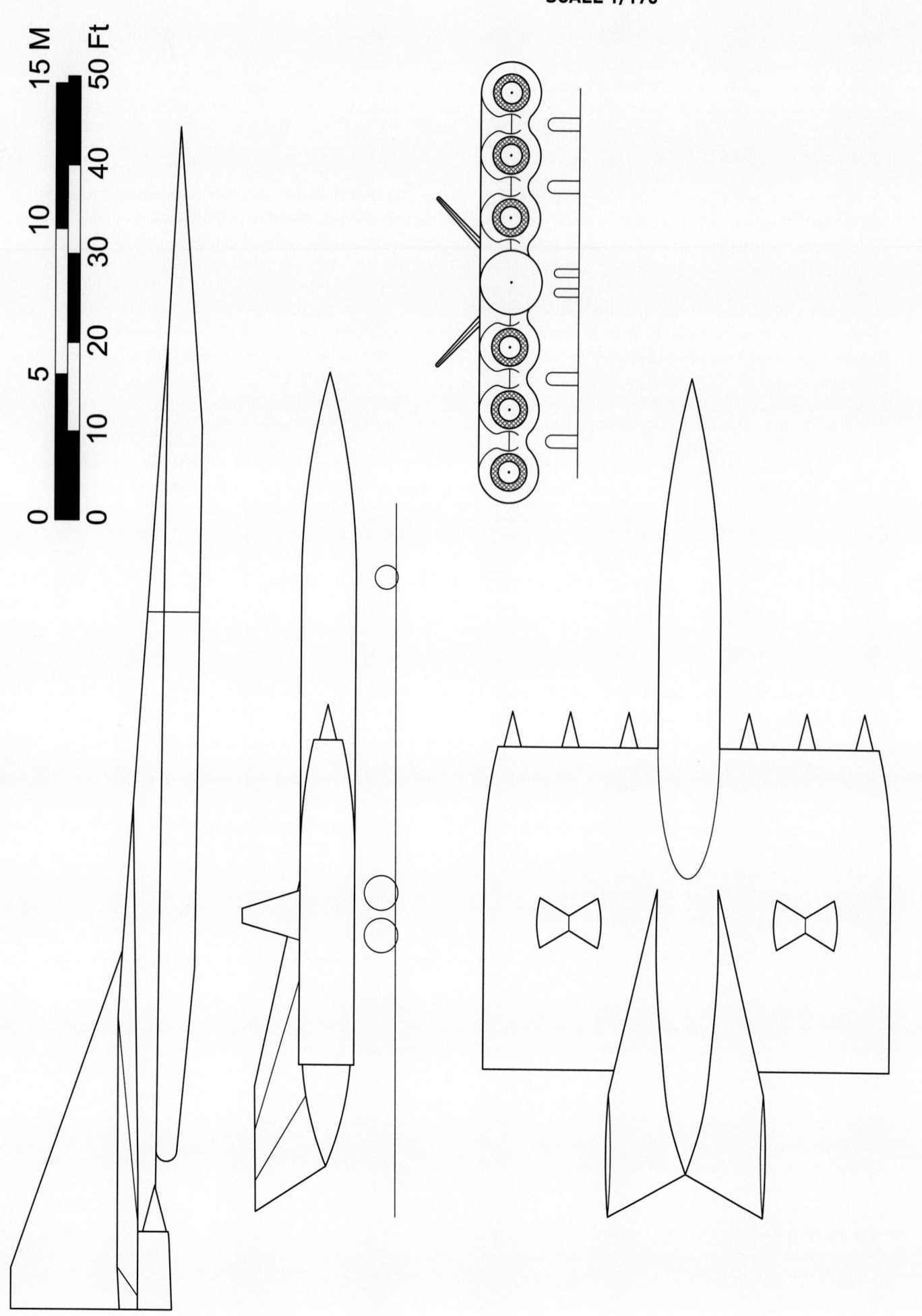

Boeing Model 813-1036
Booster Model 813-2032
SCALE 1/175

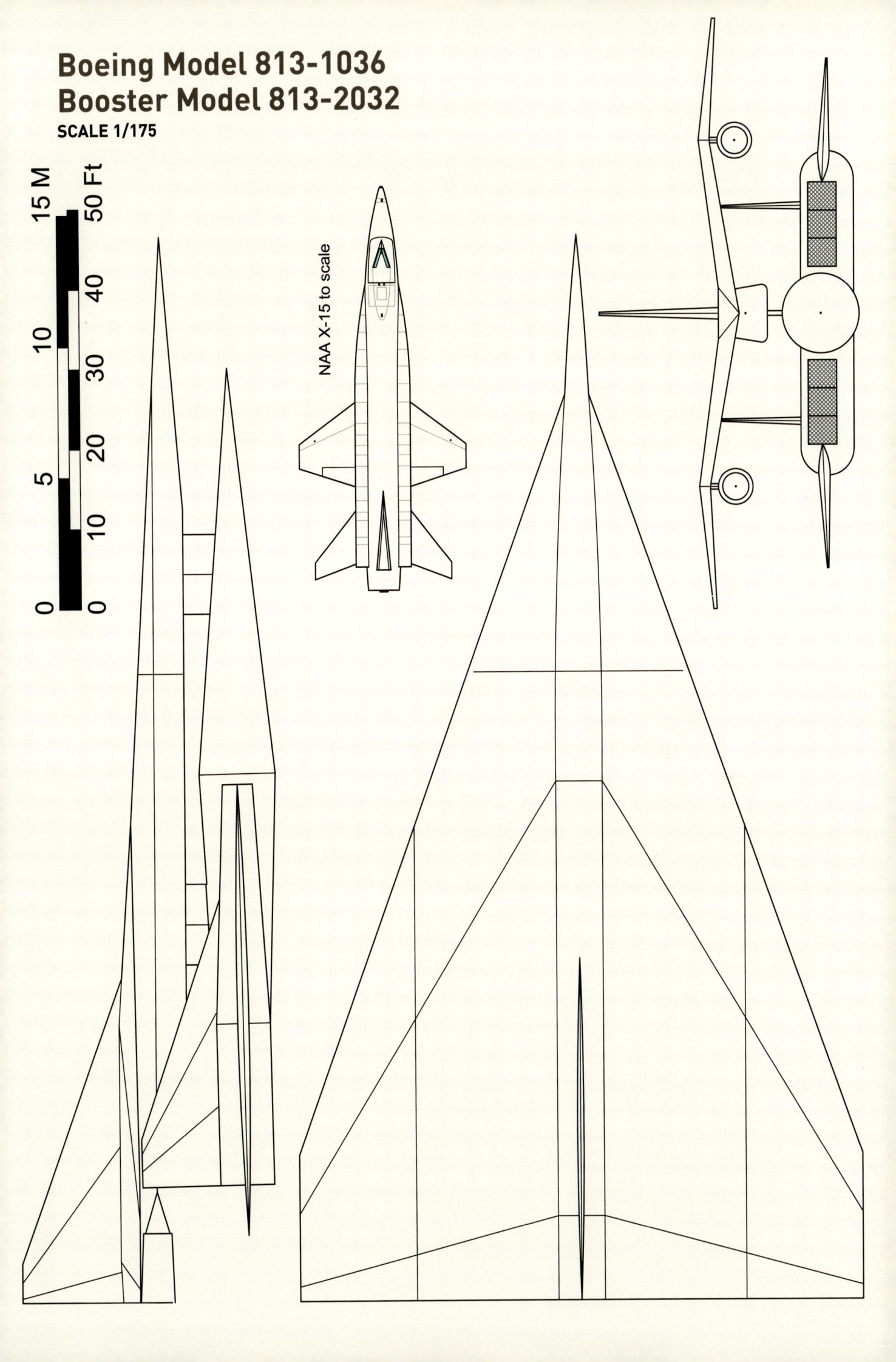

NAA X-15 to scale

Boeing Model 813-1036
Booster Model 813-2032
SCALE 1/175

Boeing Model 813 Decoy

Boeing Model 813-5000

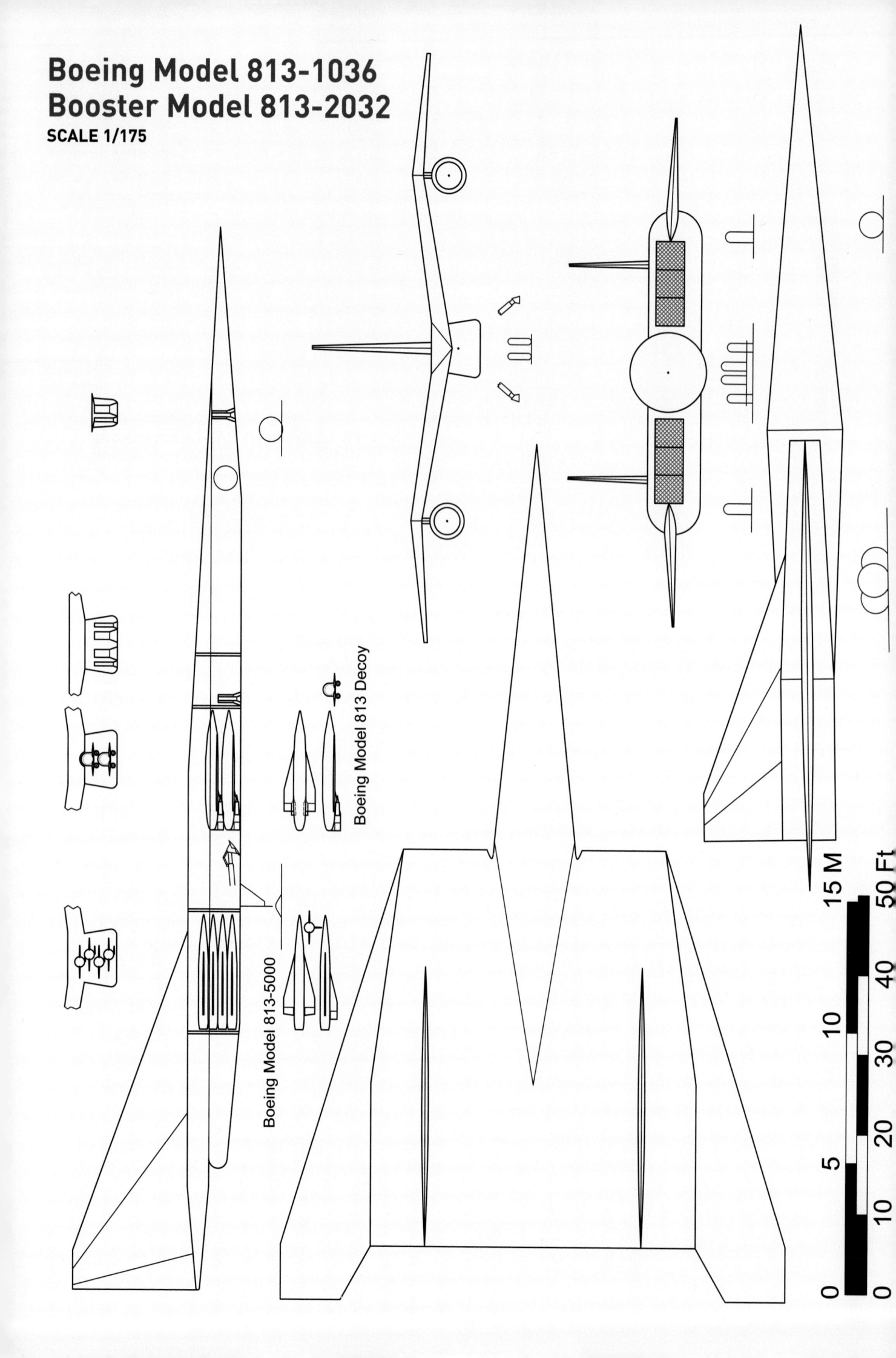

forward fuselage serving as inlet ramps and the entire aft underside of the fuselage serving as exhaust nozzles.

The turbojets and their inlets and exhausts are mere subsets, with the turbojet inlet being behind a door in the ramjet inlet. The doors to the turbojets would close as the ramjets came up to power; the ramjets were fed through smaller circular inlets that the concave forward fuselage faces fed into. The ramjet engines would serve as afterburners for the turbojets.

The payload was contained in a single narrow bay that was squeezed between the engine systems; the main landing gear in the spaces just outboard of the engines. The single weapon looks like a stretched gravity bomb, but would doubtless have been a rocket powered missile of some kind.

Little other data is available. The plane was relatively small and seemed to have a cockpit sized for only a single pilot.

Lockheed CL-2103

It may seem odd that there are so few hypersonic bomber designs when there are so many hypersonic passenger transport designs. Merely supersonic bomber concepts seem to outnumber supersonic passenger aircraft concepts, but once projected airspeeds get to Mach 4 or so, the bombers start to thin out. This may be due to technical or political issues leading to relatively few hypersonic bombers having been designed, or it may be due to the fact that a hypersonic bomber is one of those things that the United States Air Force would want to keep a lid on. It may not build one for itself, but that doesn't mean it wants other countries to use American design data to build their own hypersonic bombers.

Whatever the reason, at least once there was overlap between hypersonic passenger transports and hypersonic bombers. The Lockheed CL-2103 from 1980 was one such design. In 1979 Lockheed worked under contract to NASA on the Hypersonic Cruise Aircraft Propulsion Integration Study which resulted in the design of a series of passenger transports capable of Mach 6 flight. These designs were meant to carry 200 passengers over a distance of 5,000 nautical miles with an initial operational capability to occur in the year 2000.

Produced under the internal CL-1725 designation, the five 'HYCAT' designs differed considerably in configuration and engine arrangements, but all had long, slim, flattened fuselages and used liquid hydrogen for fuel. The tradeoffs led to the adoption of the HYCAT-1A as the baseline design. The HYCAT-1 had been a tailless delta design, but the HYCAT-1A stretched the rear fuselage and added small horizontal stabilizers. These were found necessary to provide trim for relative changes in centre of pressure throughout the speed range; they also allowed the use of drooped ailerons for low speed lift.

The HYCAT-1A used two propulsion systems: from runway to Mach 4.5, four turbojets provided thrust; beyond that, scramjets took over. A series of ramps and doors adjusted the inlet for the turbojet until at Mach 4.5 when the inlet was closed off entirely. The turbojets and scramjets used a common nozzle system for exhaust. The majority of the fuselage was stuffed with multi-lobe liquid hydrogen tanks; the passengers were in a relatively small three-deck module (two passenger decks, one lower cargo deck) located in the mid-fuselage. This cut off the cockpit entirely from the rest of the aircraft.

The CL-2103 from the following year is known from somewhat minimal information. However, what is known is that it was a long range hypersonic bomber configured very much like the HYCAT-1A, but scaled up somewhat. The HYCAT-1A was already a large aircraft, with a fuselage length of 337ft; but transformed into the CL-2103, it became truly immense with a fuselage length of 399ft, the swept tail extending it further still. Crew was to be only two; with a cruise speed of up to Mach 7 and a range of 5,000 miles, mission times would be on the order of one hour.

Curiously, the simple inboard profile of the CL-2103 shows the same layout of propellant tanks, include an empty space where the passenger section would have been on the HYCAT-1A. The main difference was that the aft fuel tanks were truncated, leaving the rear fuselage available for the payload. On one hand this makes sense, as there are few other logical options given that the underside of the craft is a finicky and precisely tailored inlet and exhaust for the engines. On the other hand, this position would seem to be well aft of the centre of gravity, meaning a substantial pitch-down when the bombs or missiles were dropped.

The main strike mission would be strategic nuclear attack, with a payload of 50,000lb carried well aft. The details of what would constitute that payload are unavailable, but it would have to be something that could survive being ejected or dropped while flying as fast as the X-15 ever managed to attain. Propulsion was via scramjets and, presumably, turbo-ramjets that are undefined in the available literature.

The CL-2103 was one of several long range combat aircraft that Lockheed designed at the same time. The CL-2102 was a spanloaded flying wing, a subsonic design intended for stealthy low-level operations; Lockheed suggested that the CL-2102 and CL-2103 could operate in tandem.

With Soviet air defences focusing on the blisteringly obvious hypersonic bombers some 26 miles up, the stealthy flying wings would theoretically be able to stalk the vast regions of the USSR unleashing unpleasantness almost unopposed. CL-2104 was a lifting body spaceplane (based on the FDL-7 configuration) capable of being put into orbit with a bombardment payload of

Republic Mach 7
SCALE 1/160

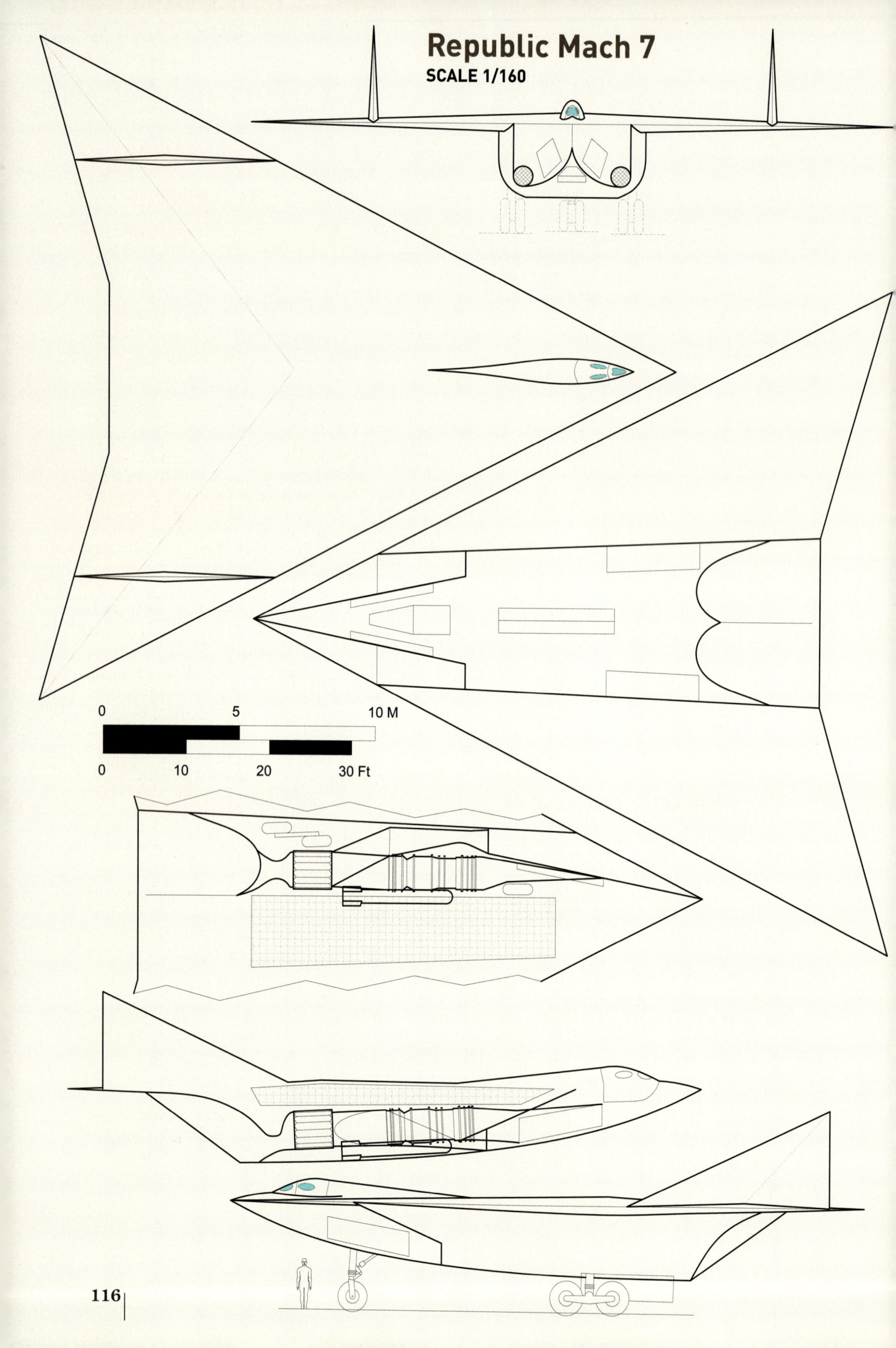

0 5 10 M
0 10 20 30 Ft

116

Lockheed CL-2103
SCALE 1/475

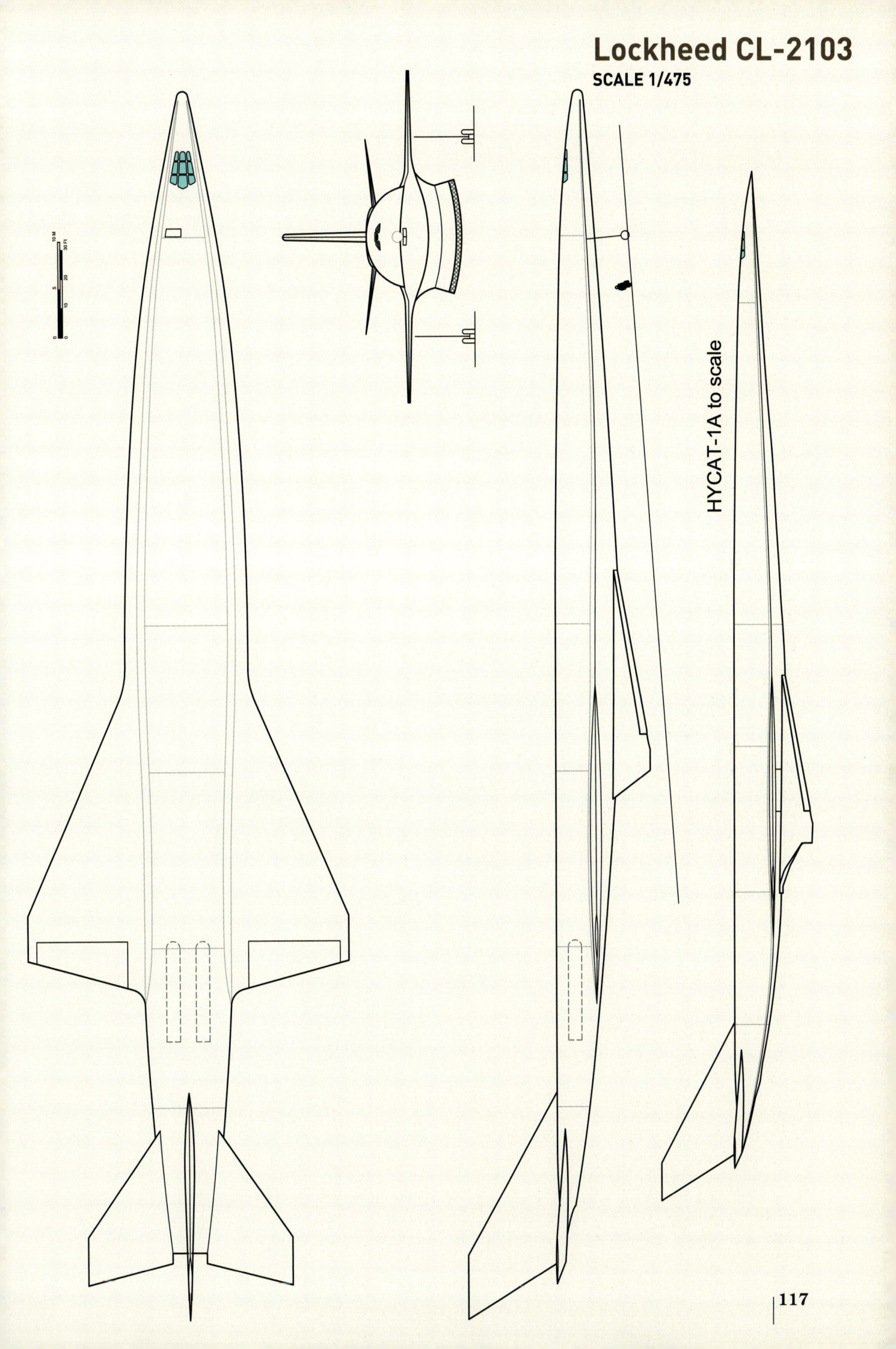

HYCAT-1A to scale

117

20,000lb; CL-2105 comprised at least two designs for surprisingly pedestrian subsonic bombers with heavy payloads.

As well as strategic nuclear strike missions, the CL-2103 could also be used for reconnaissance. Flying twice as fast and seven miles higher than the SR-71, while carrying a truly vast sensor payload, the CL-2103 could clearly provide an important intelligence capability. But there is of course no possibility that the aircraft could slip by overhead without being seen; the infrared signature alone would light up Soviet air defence systems for hundreds of miles. Another proposed role was interception of Soviet AWACS systems. That does seem perhaps a bit much for a vehicle such as this.

General Dynamics Configuration 902

The X-30 National AeroSpace Plane (NASP) was one of the biggest and most advanced launch system development programmes, and as has happened all too often it was cancelled after billions were spent, progress was made and financial difficulties were encountered. The idea was to develop a single stage to orbit 'airplane' that could fly from runway to orbit using only internal fuel. This would require the development of truly astounding scramjet engines; these would need to function not just at dull, pedestrian speeds like Mach 5 or even Mach 10, but virtually all the way to orbital speed... about Mach 25. This was a technical problem of monumental proportion, and in the end one that it could not be solved within the budget or political timeframe allowed.

Begun in 1986 and cancelled in 1993, NASP built on numerous prior programmes, perhaps most obviously the Air Force's Aero Space Plane (ASP) of the early 1960s. ASP was even more ambitious: a similar goal of an orbital aircraft, but with the technology of 25 years earlier. ASP was not restricted to scramjets and was not restricted to a single stage; ramjets, rockets, multistage, inflight and even supersonic refuelling schemes were all examined for ASP. Both ASP and NASP were perhaps too demanding of the technology available; had NASP been open to ASP-type technologies, it's interesting to contemplate whether the programme might have succeeded. But in any event, both programmes were cancelled... and both suffered from some vagaries about just what they were for.

NASP was sold as a means of providing low-cost regular space transportation, though the immense development cost and likely equally immense maintenance requirements of the air breathing vehicle would have made a mockery of the idea of affordable economics. An air breathing launch system might sound great on paper... oxidizer is often the single heaviest line item on a launch vehicle's weight statement, and breathing air would seem to get rid of that. But the tradeoff is that the relatively simple cylindrical body of a conventional rocket is replaced by a painstakingly crafted structure designed to precisely funnel air into the engine at all flight conditions, from runway to orbit.

And where a rocket climbs, at least initially, virtually straight up, getting out of the atmosphere as soon as possible and then doing the great bulk of the acceleration to orbital speed while above the air, an airbreather necessarily must do all of that acceleration while in the atmosphere. Instead of avoiding the troubles of aerothermal heating, an airbreather like NASP wallows in aerothermal heating. By definition it blasts through the air at velocities that any other aircraft would consider terminally insane.

In order to help the NASP programme make some kind of financial sense, the technology was sold as being multi-purpose. If an aircraft could fly to orbit with a small payload, it could fly across the world at lower speed with a larger payload. In this case, 'lower speed' would have been respectable velocities such as Mach 10. This 'Orient Express' would have opened a new era in air travel, where flight times across oceans would have been measured in minutes. For the lucky traveller who could afford to hop an Orient Express from Los Angeles to Tokyo, doubtless far more time would have been spent waiting for his luggage than the actual flight. This aspect of the programme received a great deal of publicity.

Not as well publicized was the fact that a hypersonic passenger transport made possible a hypersonic reconnaissance aircraft or, relevantly for this book, a hypersonic bomber. Given that much of the NASP programme remains shrouded in secrecy (for example, decent enough diagrams of the X-30 NASP were published, but nowhere did anyone in the know actually say precisely how big it would be), it's hardly surprising that military applications of the NASP and NASP derivatives are even murkier. This author is only aware of a few such designs, though it's a dead certainty that others, perhaps many others, were produced, studied and in the end memory holed.

One such design is the General Dynamics Configuration 902. This was described in 1991, and was visually nearly a carbon copy of the official X-30 NASP design. Like the NASP, it had a long flattened lifting body fuselage with an underslung propulsion package. The long forward fuselage served as a flat inlet ramp, directing air into the rectangular inlet. At low speed, thrust is provided by four Pratt & Whitney F119 turbofan engines (the same that power the F-22), while at higher speeds the inlet geometry gradually changes and by Mach 2.5 shifts the propulsion work over to a bank of four ram/scramjet engines. Unlike the X-30, the Configuration 902 'only' had to run at Mach 10. The JP-8 fuel tank for the turbofans was quite small, especially in

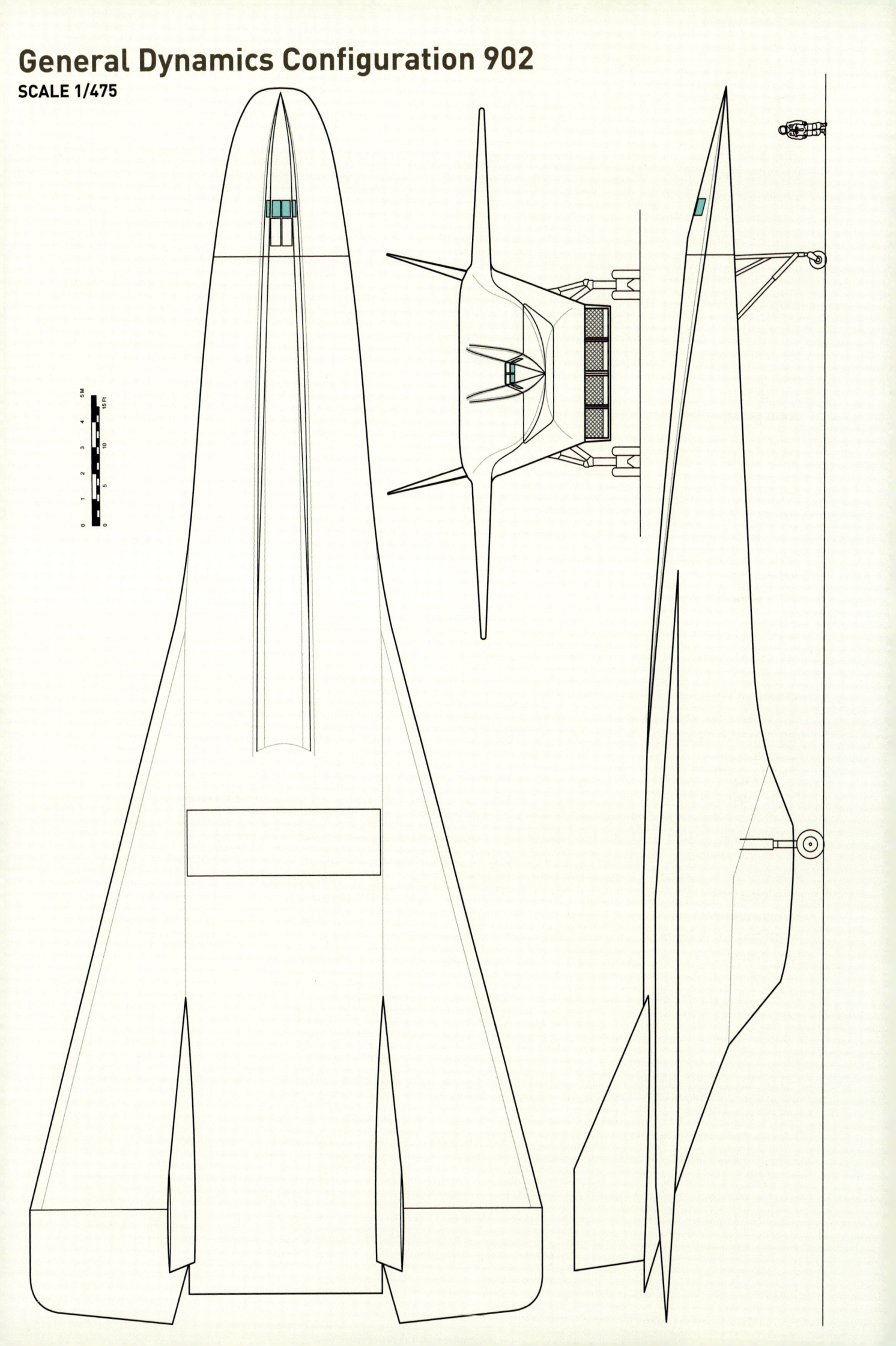

General Dynamics Configuration 902
SCALE 1/475

comparison to the liquid hydrogen: virtually the entire interior volume of the aircraft's fuselage was reserved for liquid hydrogen stowage. Still, the density difference meant that the comparatively tiny hydrocarbon fuel tank held a surprising amount of fuel compared to the vast, fluffy liquid hydrogen: 39,000lb to 90,000lb.

The payload bay was almost an afterthought, deploying weapons up and out the back of the aircraft. Unfortunately, details of the weapons to be deployed and the actual means of deployment are not available. The crew of two sat in a shirtsleeve environment cockpit with a slightly raised canopy. Crew escape was not described, though it can be assumed that the forward fuselage would jettison as an escape module.

The cryogenic tanks were to be made from graphite epoxy composite, while the lower temperature structures were to be titanium. The higher temperature structures were to be titanium matrix composite, with reinforced carbon-carbon in selected areas; the leading edges would be actively cooled using heat pipes taken directly from the NASP programme. These would flow liquid hydrogen through pipes to draw heat from the leading edges and use it to warm the fuel just prior to injection into the scramjet.

Several mission trajectories were proposed. Flying out of Montana, the aircraft could reach Eastern Europe in 55 minutes, and then return to base; launching from Florida it could reach the Middle East in 75 minutes, continuing on to a landing on Diego Garcia. And a California launch could reach the Far East of Asia in 50 minutes, followed by a landing in Australia. Along with strike missions, the aircraft could perform rapid reconnaissance flights over ground targets; it could pop up into space (though far from orbital velocity) to do close flyby inspections of foreign satellites; and it could launch upper stages to send small payloads into orbit... or launch anti-satellite weapons. A further advantage of the Mach 10 cruise speed is extended crossrange of glide weapons; from the launch point at an altitude of 100,000ft, with a modest lift to drag ratio 3.5, weapons could glide forward another 1,050+ nautical miles, and reach out to the sides nearly 600 nautical miles.

Perhaps optimistically, perhaps *fabulously* optimistically, General Dynamics estimated that the time from an aircraft landing from one mission through inspection, refurbishment, refueling, rearmament and launching the aircraft again would be about five hours. Equally optimistically, General Dynamics believed that if given the go-ahead in 1991, flight tests could begin as early as 1997. Given the ongoing difficulties in getting scramjets to work reliably at hypersonic speeds, this seems astonishingly aggressive. With this schedule, low rate production of operational vehicles would begin in 2003.

Lockheed Configuration 710A 'Hypercruiser'

When the General Dynamics facility in Fort Worth was sold to Lockheed in 1993, some of the projects that had previously been worked on continued. This appears to have been the case with the Configuration 902, for as of the middle of 1993 Lockheed-Fort Worth was pushing Configuration 710A. This design, dubbed 'Hypercruiser', was similar in mission and performance to Configuration 902, and appears to have been a descendant of the design, though substantially changed. The programme was still ongoing as of spring 1995.

Configuration 710A was slimmer than Configuration 902 and no hard information is currently available as to why the later design has a lower Configuration number than the earlier... perhaps an effect of the sale to Lockheed. Another possibility is that these designs both may have emerged from the INCAAPS programme ('Inlet and Nozzle Concepts for Advanced Air-breathing Propulsion Systems') which produced an apparently vast series of Mach 5+ configurations.

A display model – possibly only one – was built of this concept. No clear photos of it seem to have come to light as yet.

The diagram shown here is based on a top and side view of Configuration 710A. Unfortunately the available documentation did not include a front view, so that view is somewhat speculative.

The Configuration 710A strike variant could deliver 30 independently targeted weapons anywhere in the world within two hours. The exact nature of the weapons is unclear; illustrations depict a dart-like hypersonic glide vehicle designed by General Dynamics around 1987. Presumably they would be armed with nuclear warheads, though in years subsequent to this design there were numerous proposals for hypersonic glide weapons armed not only with nuclear warheads but also conventional high explosives and bunker penetrators. Lockheed estimated that the Hypercruiser could begin development circa 2004, and enter initial operational capability in 2015.

McDonnell-Douglas/Boeing DF-9

While the X-30 NASP programme ended in 1993, the companies that devoted a great deal of effort to it were not in a hurry to throw that work away. More to the point, they were often in a hurry to convince the government to fund spinoff programmes. Beginning in early 1995, McDonnell Douglas (St Louis) began studying a dual-fuel hypersonic aircraft for NASA-Langley's Systems Analysis Office, a vehicle clearly derived from NASP design studies.

This craft was meant to be able to fulfill two very different roles... space launch and long-range, high-speed strike missions. The cruise speed was to be Mach 10, thus hydrogen was a necessity for a scramjet

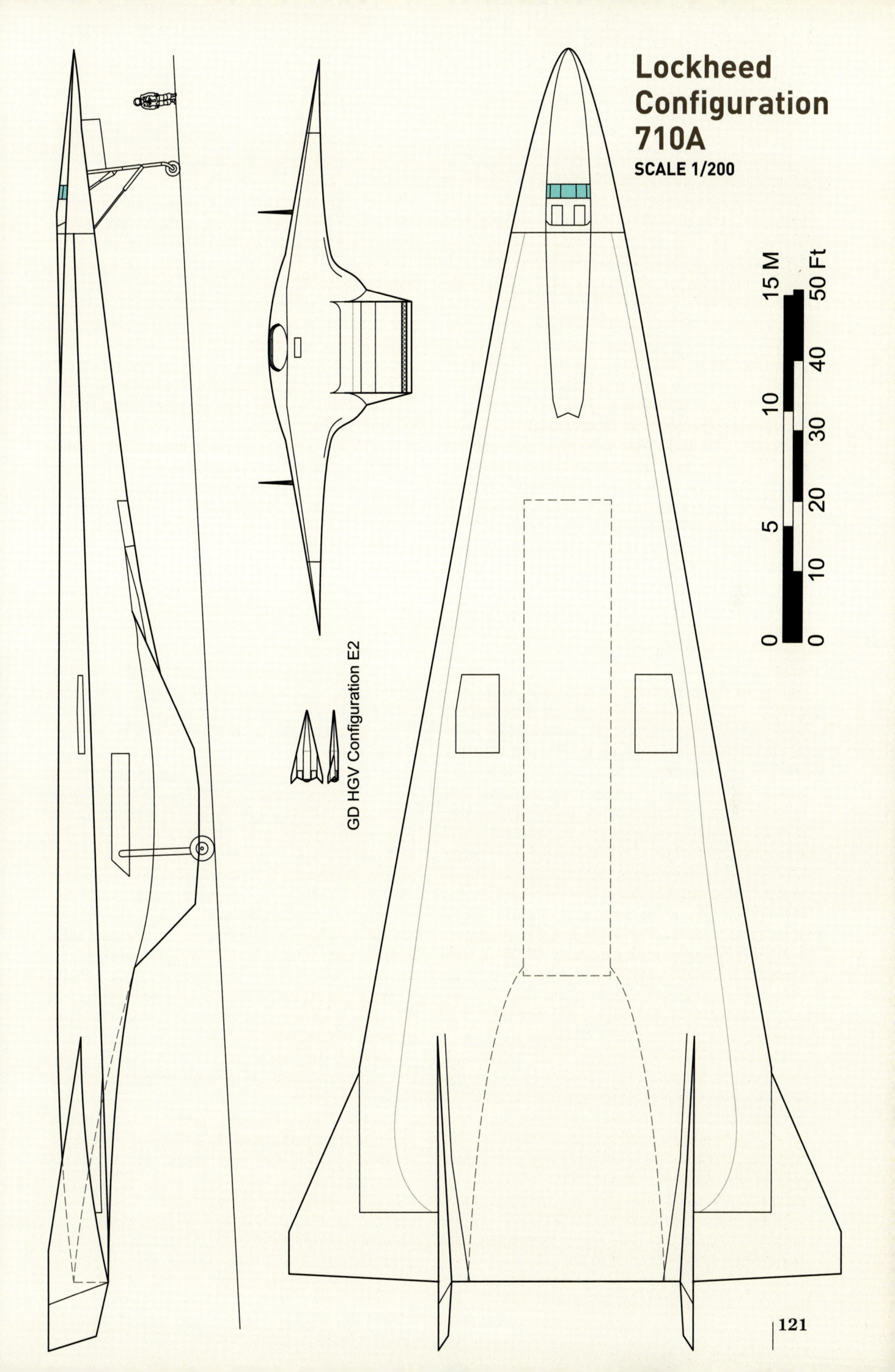

Lockheed Configuration 710A
SCALE 1/200

GD HGV Configuration E2

propulsion system. But the extremely low density of liquid hydrogen would drive the volume – and thus drag – of the aircraft much too high. So by using both hydrogen and a dense hydrocarbon, the best of both worlds could be achieved.

The McDonnell Douglas team studied a flattened lifting body configuration (the 'DF-9', from 'Dual Fuel'), similar in many respects to the General Dynamics Configuration 902, though slimmer with much smaller wings. Given a 'spatula' nose, this configuration provided sufficient lift and control at low speed and adequately low drag at high speed. The broad nose and flat underside served as a long, wide inlet for the airbreathing engines.

Several completely different engine systems were to be used. For low speed flight up to Mach 4.5, four Pratt & Whitney Air (core enhanced) Turbo Ramjets were employed, burning the relatively dense JP-7 hydrocarbon fuel. From Mach 4 and above, three Pratt & Whitney hydrogen-burning ramjet/scramjet modules provided thrust. While the systems shared a common inlet, ramps within the engine module would shift geometry during flight to provide best airflow between the propulsion systems. At high speed, the AceTR system would be completely closed off. The system was designed for a Mach 10 cruise on scramjet power.

In most descriptions of the vehicle, the role of reconnaissance is generally given greater prominence than the strike role. However, the cargo bay is in the same location regardless... in the upper surface of the fuselage, directly above the engines. This would at first blush seem to indicate that the recon role would have been a tricky one: optical cameras either would have had to look through the underside of the forward fuselage, which at the time was serving as a compression inlet for the scramjet engines; or they would have had to look upwards through the upper fuselage, meaning the aircraft would have had to roll over onto its back, very unlikely given that it was in powered airbreathing flight at the time. Doubtless the problem of looking through the ventral flow field would have been solvable... but it seems likely that chucking a bomb out of the back of the aircraft would have been an easier thing to do.

A modified version of the design was considered for space launch. It was largely similar to the Mach 10 cruiser, but used a linear aerospike rocket engine along the trailing edge of the central fuselage expansion ramp. This aerospike, which would become associated with the Lockheed X-33 and VentureStar, was derived from prior X-30 NASP work (the NASP was almost never depicted with this engine in public artwork, but a substantial rocket propulsion system would be needed to boost the airbreathing vehicle into orbit).

In the case of the DF-9, the rocket engine, with a thrust of 150,000lb, would be used to loft the vehicle at Mach 10 to an altitude of 280,000ft, essentially above the atmosphere. At that point, a cargo bay door on the back would open and release a pop-up upper stage. Ten feet in diameter, 30ft long and weighing 30,000lb, this rocket powered upper stage would boost into Earth orbit with 5,000lb of payload. It would be akin to the Centaur upper stage, with a single modified RL-10 rocket engine. After staging, the DF-9 would drop back down into the lower atmosphere following a ballistic arc. The propulsion system would not start up until the craft was subsonic. It would then cruise back to base, with an in-flight refuelling needed to provide enough JP-7 fuel for the trip. The DF-9 would be equipped with a reaction control system to maintain attitude during exoatmospheric flight.

For Mach 10 cruise missions the vehicle faired over the linear aerospike rocket engine, though left it in place rather than removing it. It utilized the same cargo bay, but carried only 10,000lb... either recon equipment or nuclear strike systems. It would be able to cruise at Mach 10 for a distance of 7,390 nautical miles. Cruise altitude was not given, apart from being in excess of 110,000ft. As with the space launch missions, after deceleration and descent the DF-9 could meet up with a KC-10 in order to refuel the JP-7 and cruise subsonically to a friendly airbase. Range was sufficient that using just two continental US air bases, Vandenberg, California, and Langley, Virginia, only the Indian subcontinent and the Indian Ocean would be inaccessible.

The DF-9 would use a 'cold' structure for the fuselage, where the large liquid hydrogen tanks formed an integral part of the structure. The liquid hydrogen would actively cool the fuselage structure. The wings, fins and nose would be 'hot structures' made of titanium matrix composite with zirconium diboride leading edges. The nose would have an additional active cooling system.

The DF-9 was still being described in 1998, a year after McDonnell Douglas had ceased to be an independent company and was by then a division of Boeing. The concept doubtless survived into the 21st century in some fashion. And in fact while the DF-9 was not built, the configuration did lead to the X-43 Hyper-X subscale scramjet test vehicle. Three of these research aircraft were built and flown, using almost exactly the same geometry as the DF-9, just scaled down substantially.

Carried under the wing of an NB-52 and boosted to speed and altitude by an Orbital Sciences Pegasus booster, they were incompletely successful as the first test flight ended in a booster failure. Still, the second and third flights were successes, the third reaching a maximum speed of Mach 9.64 for all of about ten second before running out of fuel.

GD/NASA Mach 5 Cruise Waverider

Throughout much of the 1990s a design from 1992 was repeatedly publicized in various papers and reports from

Boeing DF-9
SCALE 1/300

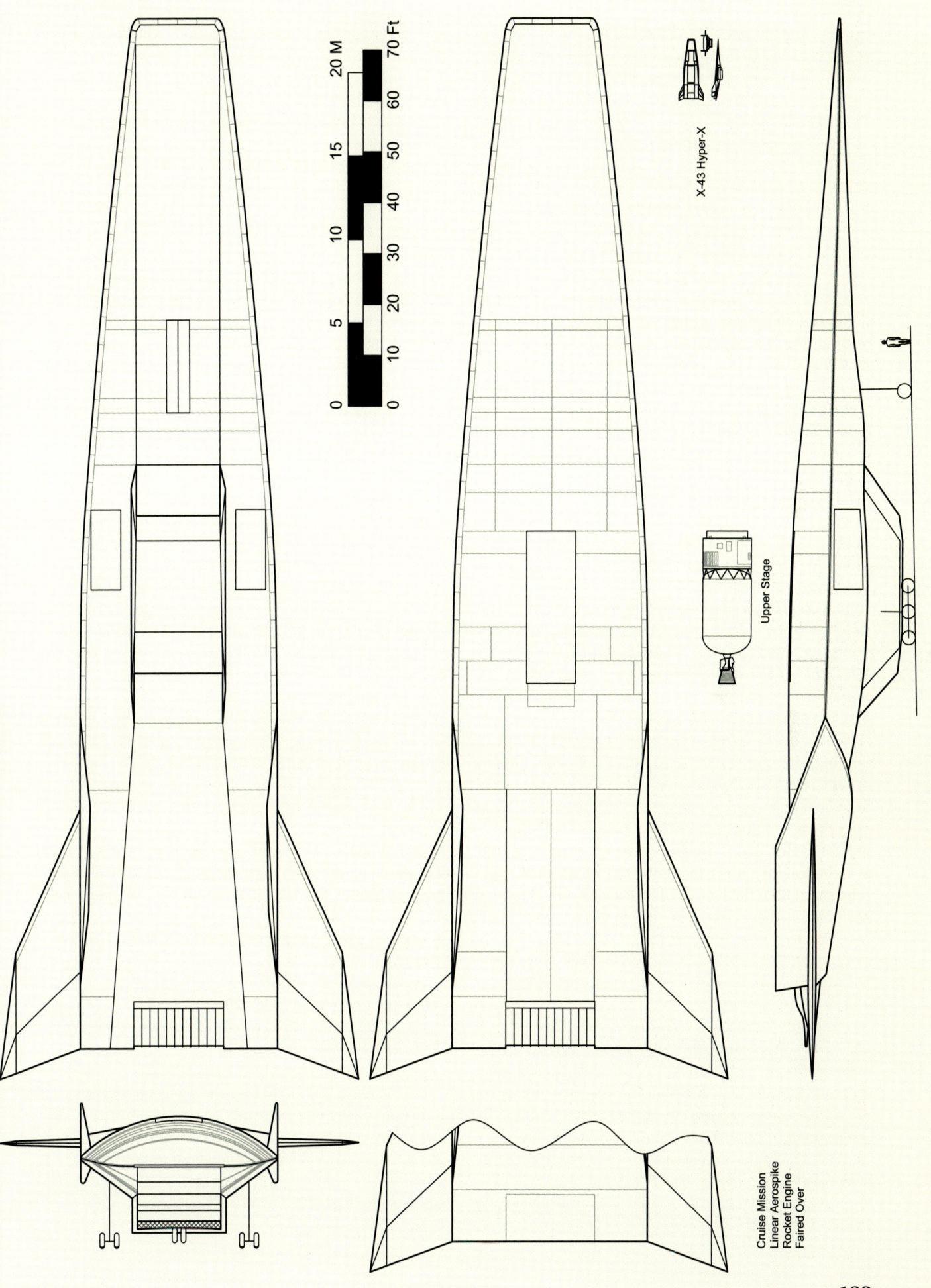

X-43 Hyper-X

Upper Stage

Cruise Mission
Linear Aerospike
Rocket Engine
Faired Over

NASA. The design was the result of a collaboration between NASA Langley and NASA Lewis and several major aerospace corporations. Pratt & Whitney was responsible for the propulsion systems while General Dynamics took care of the airframe structure, all based on a NASA waverider configuration.

The aircraft design shown (no name or designation seems to have been made public, though it is very likely that this was another result of the INCAAPS programme) was a first pass concept, with no optimization. It was analyzed based on its established configuration and was found to be adequate for the role envisioned. That role was reconnaissance/strike, using tanker aircraft at both the beginning and end of mission.

The mission was said to begin at Mach 0.8 and 30,000ft altitude where the Mach 5 cruise aircraft would rendezvous with a tanker aircraft which would transfer aboard a full load of fuel. The fuel in this case was unconventional; since the fuel would be used to provide airframe cooling during the aerothermodynamically hellish Mach 5 cruise, a high flash point for the fuel was needed, driving the use of a paraffin fuel.

After separation from the tanker aircraft, the Mach 5 cruise aircraft would first accelerate to Mach 1.2, then climb to 90,000ft while accelerating to Mach 5. After cruise, which would include a turn over the target to return home, the aircraft would begin a very long, gradual descent back to another tanker aircraft. This would in some ways be a harder part of the trip. The structure used fuel for coolant, but during descent the fuel consumption would drop, reducing its ability to serve as a flowing coolant.

The aircraft would use endothermic fuel for structural cooling. Unlike a liquid hydrogen fuelled aircraft, which transfers structural heat to the hydrogen fuel which simply grows warmer in the process, in an endothermic cycle the warmed fuel is passed over a hot catalyst (usually coating the structure to be cooled) which promotes a chemical decomposition of the fuel. The fuel usually breaks down into a combination of methane, carbon monoxide and hydrogen, and in the process absorbs more heat than it otherwise would have; additionally, the fuel is now a relatively low molecular weight gas which will combust more quickly when injected into the engine.

The engines planned were an over/under turboramjet. At lower speeds the duct would be shaped so that the air would pass through a relatively conventional afterburner-equipped turbojet, but as airspeed climbed the duct would mechanically reshape itself to direct the flow through a lower ramjet. At high speed the entire forward fuselage served as an inlet; the underside of the rear fuselage, a large exhaust nozzle.

A single relatively small (2,000cu ft) payload bay was located behind and below the single-seat cockpit. It's unclear if any thought was given to how opening such a bay and deploying a weapon would affect the airflow into the engines.

This design was shown in numerous open sources, and may in some small way have contributed to the notion of the supposed 'Aurora' hypersonic recon aircraft that many people claimed was flying at the time.

Lockheed-Martin Hypersonic Cruise Vehicle

Begun in 2003, the joint DARPA/Air Force 'Force Application and Launch from CONUS' (FALCON) programme was meant to develop global-range prompt strike capabilities with both nuclear and non-nuclear warheads, using systems less expensive than expendable ICBMs.

FALCON was split into two main sub-programmes: the Small Launch Vehicle (SLV), aimed at developing low-cost orbital space launch systems for small payloads, and the Hypersonic Weapons System (HWS), which would develop global-range manoeuvrable strike systems. The HWS effort was itself split into two areas: the CAV (Common Aero Vehicle), a manoeuvrable glider which could be loaded with a wide variety of nuclear or conventional warheads up to 1,000lb, and the HWS itself. This would be a large airbreathing hypersonic aircraft capable of carrying a number of CAVs and other weapons, able to strike targets 9,000 nautical miles from a launch site in the continental US (CONUS) within two hours of launch.

Three contractors received Phase 1 study contracts for the HWS in 2003... Lockheed Martin, Andrews Space Inc., and Northrop-Grumman. In 2004, Lockheed won the Phase 2 round.

The Lockheed-Martin Hypersonic Cruise Vehicle as revealed publicly was an unmanned scramjet powered aircraft, capable of prompt aircraft-like operations and global range. Details on it are scant, with dimensions being determined solely from a crude scale comparison with the B-52. Inward-turning inlets fed the propulsion system... a turbojet to about Mach 3, a scramjet to above Mach 6.

A weapons bay was illustrated along the vehicle centreline, with artwork showing the vehicle launching CAV warheads identical in configuration to the HTV-2. A patent on the inward-turning inlets provide good configuration diagrams.

All leading edges were sharp, greatly reducing supersonic drag but requiring advanced materials. The waverider-configured craft would be optimized to fly at one altitude and velocity (somewhere in the vicinity of Mach 6 to 8); at that design point, performance would be adequate for global range.

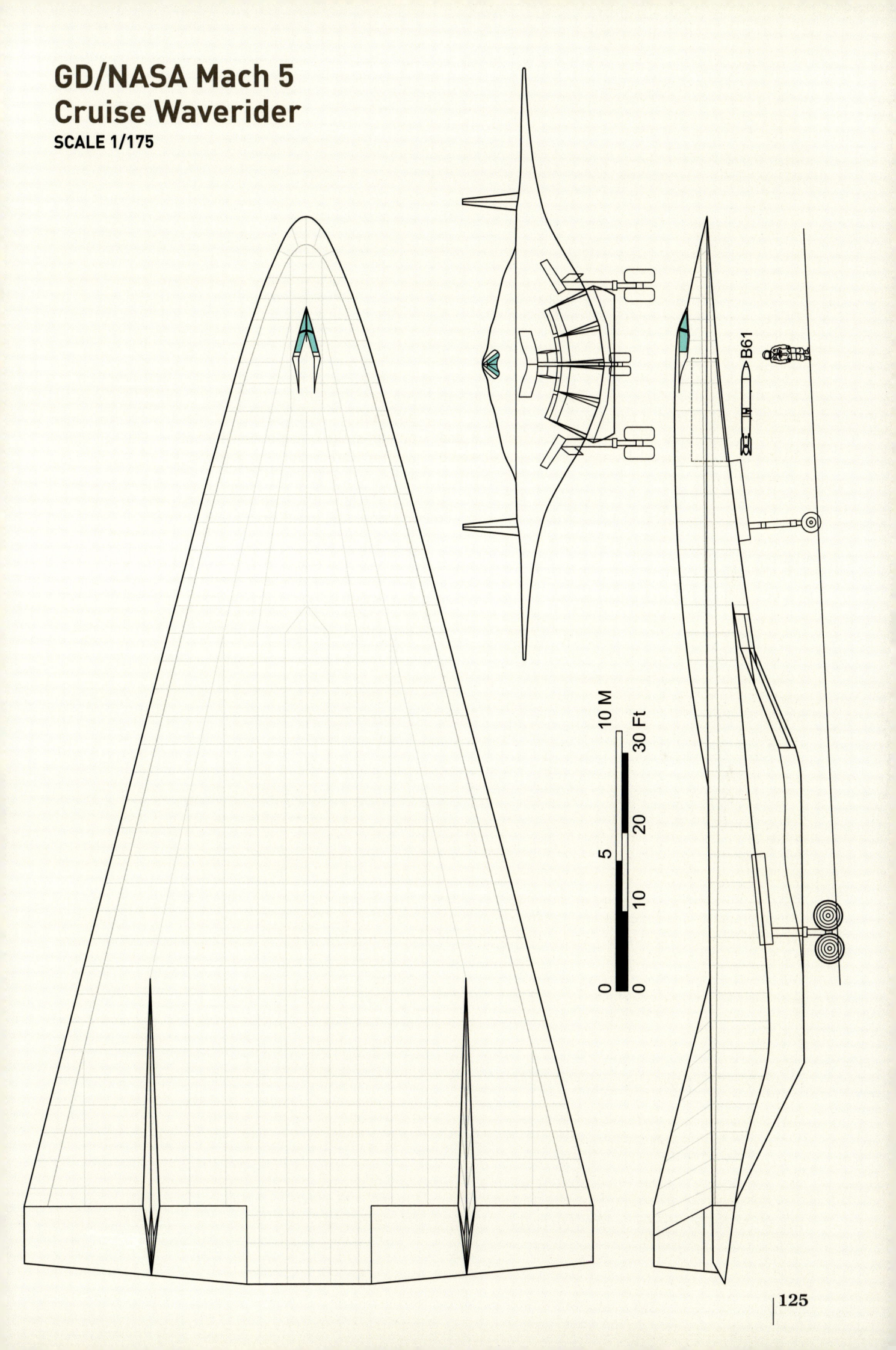

GD/NASA Mach 5
Cruise Waverider
SCALE 1/175

125

GD/NASA Mach 5
Cruise Waverider
SCALE 1/175

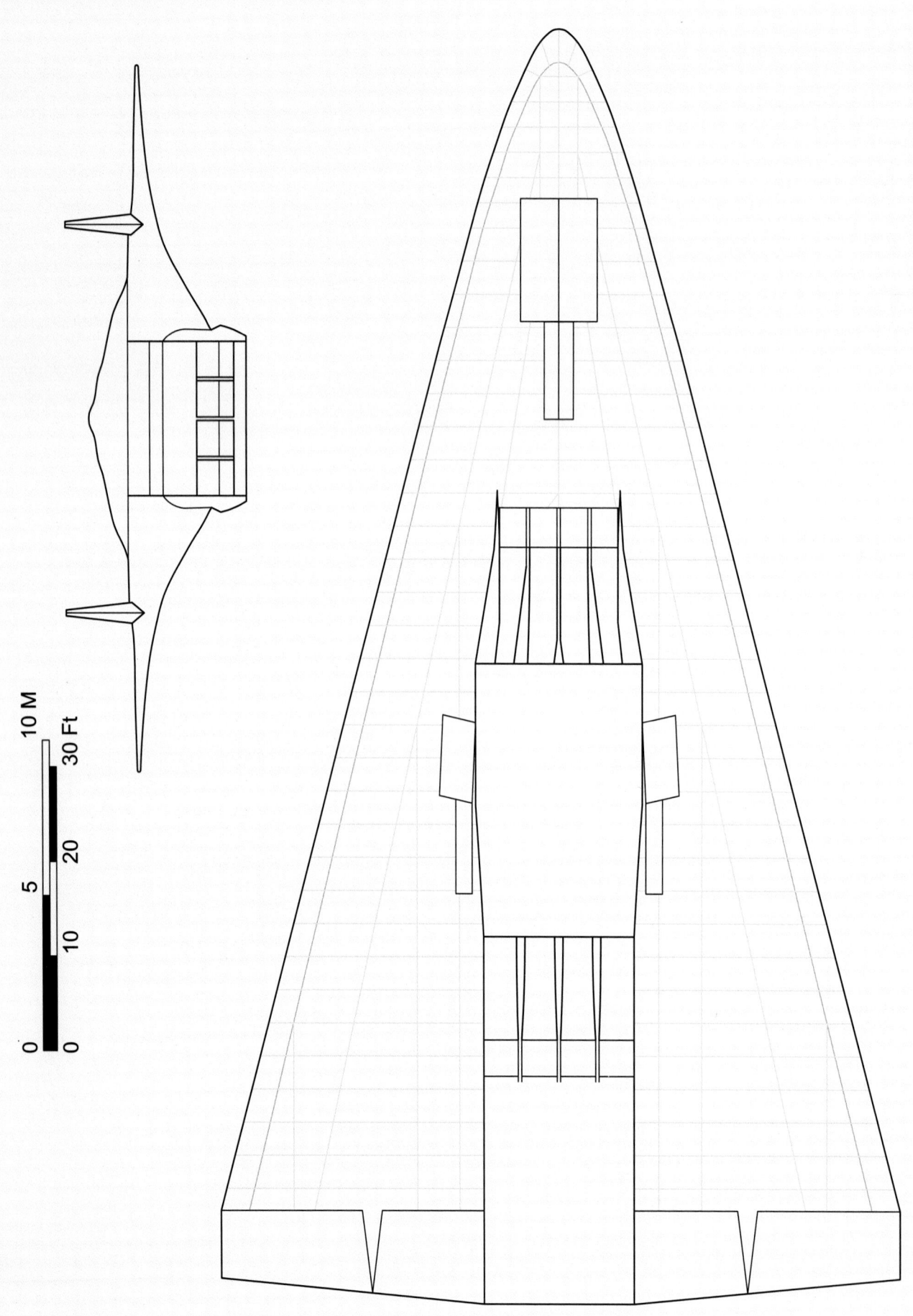

126

Lockheed Falcon HCV
SCALE 1/250

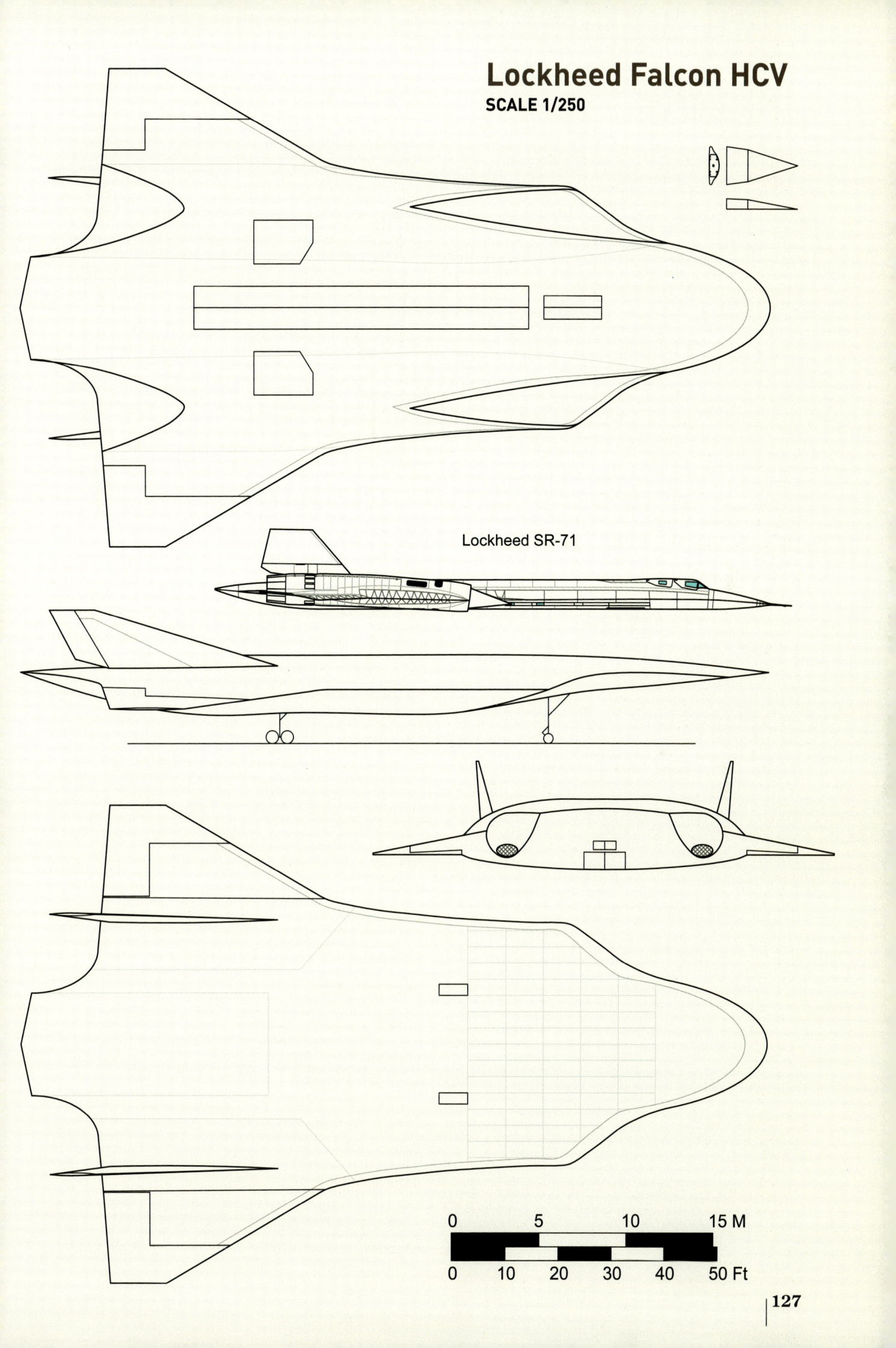

Lockheed SR-71

0　　　5　　　10　　　15 M

0　　10　　20　　30　　40　　50 Ft

References

Chapter 1: Nuclear
"NEPA Project Quarterly Progress Report for the Period April 1 – June 30 1950," NEPA Division Fairchild Engine & Airplane Company, Report No. NEPA 1484, 1950

Manson, S., Wachtl, W. "A Design and Performance Study of the Nuclear Direct-Air-Cycle Supersonic Airplane, Including the Effects of Operating Temperatures and Fuel Plate Material and Thickness," Langley Aeronautical Laboratory, NACA RM E53C18, 3-27-1953

"Investigation of a Sodium Vapor Compressor Jet for Nuclear Propulsion of Aircraft," Atomic Energy research Department, North American Aviation Inc., NAA-SR-134, June 25, 1953

"Advanced Configuration Study Power Plant Description and Comparison," Aircraft Nuclear Propulsion Department, General Electric, XDC-60-2-2, February 29, 1960

"Advanced Configuration Study, Design," Aircraft Nuclear Propulsion Department, General Electric, XDC-60-2-3, February 29, 1960

"ANP Program Review," Convair San Diego, ZP-313, September 1960

"ANP New Naval Applications," Convair San Diego, ZP-M-116, March, 1961

"Aircraft Nuclear Propulsion Application Studies, Comprehensive Technical Report," General Electric Flight Propulsion Laboratory Department, APEX-910, April 30, 1962

Chapter 2: Seaplanes
Olson, R., Bielat, R. "An Aerodynamic and Hydrodynamic Investigation of Two Multijet Water-Based Aircraft Having Low Transonic Drag Rise," Langley Aeronautical Laboratory, NACA RM L55A11a, February, 1955

"Water-Based Aircraft: An Analysis of Their Potential: Attack Missions," The Glenn L. Martin Company, ER No. 6602, 30 April 1955

McKann, R., Coffee, C. "Limited Hydrodynamic Investigation of a 1/15-size Model of a Modified Nose-Inlet Multijet Water-Based Aircraft," Langley Aeronautical Laboratory, NASA RM L55J19, February 3, 1956

"Feasibility Study of Seaplanes as Strategic Bombers," Convair San Diego, Report No. ZP-177, Contract No. AF 18(600)1608, 31 December, 1956

Morse, A., Woodward, D., Blanchard, U. "An Investigation of the Hydrodynamic Characteristics of a Dynamic Model of a Transonic Seaplane Design Having a Planing-Tail Hull," Langley Aeronautical Laboratory, NACA RM L56C28a, June 19, 1956

Bielat, R., Coffee, C., Petynia, W. "Aerodynamic and Hydrodynamic Characteristics of a Deck-Inlet Multijet Water-Based Aircraft Configuration Design for Supersonic Flight," Langley Aeronautical Laboratory, NACA RM L56H01, December 5, 1956

Blanchard, U. "Hydrodynamic Investigation of a Model of a Supersonic Multijet Water-Based Aircraft with Engines Exhausting From the Step," Langley Aeronautical Laboratory, NACA RM L57F20, August 23, 1957

Petynia, W., Hasson, D., Spooner, S. "Aerodynamic and Hydrodynamic Characteristics of a Proposed Supersonic Multijet Water-Based Hydro-Ski Aircraft with a Variable Incidence Wing," Langley Aeronautical Laboratory, NACARM L57G05, October 23, 1957

"The Convair Hydro-Ski Supersonic Attack Airplane," Convair San Diego, ZO-P-017

"Single Ski Supersonic Attack Aircraft," Convair San Diego, Report No. ZO-P-015

Coffee, C. "Hydrodynamic Characteristics of a Model of a Proposed Six-Engine Hull-Type Seaplane Design for Supersonic Flight," Langley Aeronautical Laboratory, NACA RM L58E13 June 14, 1958

"Preliminary Study Mach-4 Attack Seaplane J58 Powered," Convair San Diego, ZP-214, July 25, 1958

Petynia, W., Pearson, A., Fournier, R. "Aerodynamic and Hydrodynamic Characteristics of a Proposed Supersonic Multijet Water-Based Hull-Type Airplane with a Variable Incidence Wing," Langley Research Center, NASA TM X-249, December 2, 1959

Wornom, D. "Transonic Aerodynamic Characteristics of a Model of a Proposed Six-Engine Hull-Type Seaplane Design for Supersonic Flight," Langley research Center, NASA TM X-246, March 15, 1961

McKann, R., Blanchard, U., Pearson, A. "Hydrodynamic and Aerodynamic Characteristics of a Model of a Supersonic Multijet Water-Based Aircraft Equipped With Supercavitating Hydrofoils," Langley Research Center, NASA TM X-191, March 15, 1962

Chapter 3: Nuclear Seaplanes
"Feasibility Study of Seaplanes as Strategic Bombers," Convair San Diego, Report No. ZP-177, Contract No. AF 18(600)1608, 31 December, 1956

"ANP Program Review," Convair San Diego, ZP-313, September 1960

"ANP New Naval Applications," Convair San Diego, ZP-M-116, March, 1961

Raithel, Capt. Albert "Nuclear Patrol – Attack Seaplane Studies, Martin Model 331," Journal of the American Aviation Historical Society, Fall 2006

Chapter 4: VTOL
"Characteristics Summary – VTOL D188A," Bell Aircraft Company, 28 February 1958

"Presentation Summary of the V/STOL Fighter Bomber – Republic Model AP-100A AP-100B," Republic Aviation Corporation, ERD-AP100AB-901, 15 July 1959

"VTOL Fighter Program, Description and Technical Data for Mock-Up Inspection," Bell Aircraft Corporation, Report No. 2000-927006, 6 February 1959

"XF-109 V/STOL Tactical Fighter Weapon System," Bell Aircraft Corporation, Report No. 2000-953001, 17 February 1959

"V/STOL Tactical Fighter Weapon System," Boeing Aircraft Company, D2-3021, 1959

"V/STOL Tactical Weapon System Studies," Boeing Airplane Company, D2-4470, June 1959

"Lockheed CL-407 Design Study – V/STOL Strike-Reconnaissance Weapon System 1964-1970," Lockheed, July, 1959

"Tactical Design Studies – Interim Report," Boeing Airplane Company, D2-4918, October 1959

Kartveli, A. "Spectrum of Supersonic Aircraft," Republic Aviation Corporation, Presented at the Institute of Aeronautical Sciences National Meeting, San Diego, California, August 1-3 1960

"A new V/STOL Technology," Ryan Aeronautical Company, Report No. 65B015, 19 March 1965

Chapter 5: Hypersonic
"Design Study, Strategic Bomber, Model 813-1032," Boeing Airplane Company, D2-2850-1, 1958

"SR-170 Extended Range High Speed Strategic Bomber Study," Boeing Airplane Company, Project 7990-79501 Contract AF 18(600)-1786, 1959

Morris, R., Brewer, D. "Hypersonic Cruise Aircraft Propulsion Integration Study, Volume 1" Lockheed California Company, NASA Contractor Report CR-158926-1, Contract NAS1-15057, September 1979

Krumm, N. "NASP-Derived Hypersonic Cruise Vehicles," General Dynamics-Fort Worth Division, 13 November 1991

Pegg, R., et al "Design of a Hypersonic Waverider-Derived Airplane," NASA-Langley Research Center, NASA Lewis Research Center, Lockheed Engineering and Science Company, Sverdrup Technology, Inc. AIAA-1993-0401, January, 1993

"Mach 10 Hypercruiser," Lockheed presentation, 1995

Hunt, J. L., Eiswirth, E. "NASA's Dual-Fuel Airbreathing Hypersonic Vehicle Study," NASA Langley Research Center & McDonnell Douglas Aerospace, AIAA 1996-4591

Scuderi, L., Orton, G., Hunt, J. "Mach 10 Cruise/Space Access Vehicle Study," The Boeing Company/NASA-Langley, 1998

Scuderi, L., Orton, G. "A Hypersonic Cruiser Concept for the 21st Century," The Boeing Company, AIAA 1998-5525

Hunt, J., Rausch, V. "Airbreathing Hypersonic Systems Focus at NASA Langley Research Center," AIAA 1998-1641, 1998

Walker, Dr. S., Rodgers, F. "Falcon Hypersonic Technology Overview," DARPA/CENTRA Technology, AIAA 2005-3253, 2005

General data table

Aircraft	Source Grade	Crew	Span	Wing area (sq ft)	Length	Engines	Dry weight (lb)	Design Fuel (lb)	Design Payload (lb)	Max Payload (lb)	Gross weight (lb)	Range (n.mi.)	Cruise speed	Max speed	Ceiling (ft)
Nuclear powered															
Lockheed L-195-A-13	3	?	?	?	225'	?	?	?	?	?	?	?	?	Supersonic	?
Lockheed NEPA A-7	3	?	~142'	5,500	~297'	12 nuclear turbojets	?	?	?	?	550,000	?	Mach 1.02 @50 kft	Mach 1.12 @35 kft	?
N-3	3	?	99'	3550	180'	6 NEPA No. 7 nuclear turbojets	?	?	10,000	?	390,000	?	?	Mach 1.5 @ 35 kft	?
N-4	3	?	110'	4050	185'	10 NEPA No. 7 nuclear turbojets	?	?	10,000	?	425,000	?	?	Mach 1.5 @ 45 kft	?
North American Sodium Vapour Compressor Jet	3		98' 4"	3200	179' 2" (fuselage)	600 megawatt reactor + 5 compressor jet engines	?	?	20,000	?	400,000	?	Mach 1.5 @40 kft	Supersonic	?
NACA 1952	2	?	~86.4'	?	175' 9"	504,000 Btu/Sec reactor + 6 turbojets	?	?	?	?	480,500	?	?	Mach 1.5 @ 35 kft	?
NACA Nuclear Ramjet	2	1	69'	1,915	130'	2 GE AC-210 nuclear ramjets	?	?	10,000	?	214,810	?	Mach 4.25 @71.5 Kft	Supersonic	?
Lockheed L-285-815	3	5	138' 11"	?	184' 0"	3 P&W TJDLA13-5 nuclear turbojets / 2 P&W TJDLA13-5 chemical turbojets	?	?	?	?	?	?	?	Mach 2.75	?
Lockheed L-286-665	4	5(?)	85' 8"	?	168' 10"	2 GE ACJ nuclear turbojets / 2 GE X-61 chemical turbojets	?	?	?	?	?	?	?	Supersonic	?
Lockheed CL-293-64	4	?	135' 8"	4600	212' 9"	P&W NJ-2: 1 320 megawatt reactor+ six turbojets	?	?	10,000	?	?	?	?	Supersonic	?
Lockheed CL-315	3	?	128' 6"	?	222' 1"	4 nuclear + 4 chemical turbojets	?	?	?	?	484,000	?	?	Supersonic	?
GE Supersonic System 6X	3	5	~57.6'	5460	144	6 nuclear turbojets	?	?	?	?	?	?	?	Mach 3.5 @ 60 Kft	69,000
Convair WS-125A	4	4(?)	113.92'	?	221.41'	4 nuclear + 2 chemical turbojets	?	396,303	?	?	620,000	22,000	Mach 0.9+	~Mach 2.0	?
Boeing Model 722-209	3	?	134'	?	219' 4"	4 nuclear + 2 chemical turbojets	?	?	?	?	?	?	?	Supersonic	?
Lockheed CL-319	3	?	74' 3.8"	1800	161' 3.5"	2 P&W JT9A-20	95,640	?	10,000	?	255,600	1,660 @ 55Kft	?	~Mach 2.5	?
Lockheed CL-326	3	?	122' 6"	2500	149' 4"	P&W NJ-2: 1 300 megawatt reactor+ six turbojets	322,770	15,000	?	?	337,770	?	?	Mach 0.9 @ 20 Kft	?
Boeing Model 726-1	3	4	73.0'	1333	132.17'	1 GE AC110 nuclear turbojet	173,370	?	?	?	205,370	?	?	Supersonic	?
Boeing Model 726-3B	3	?	~58.25'	800	~133.75	1 GE AC110 nuclear turbojet	?	?	?	?	136,930	?	?	Supersonic	?
Boeing Model 726-13	3	?	~59.15'	?	~116.35	1 GE AC110 nuclear turbojet	?	?	?	?	?	?	?	Supersonic	?
Boeing Model 726-20	3	?	~91.6'	2102	132' 11"	2 GE AC107 nuclear turbojets	217,000	?	?	?	239,000	?	?	Supersonic	?
Boeing Model 813-1034	3	3	94' 5"	5625	180' 10"	1 450 megawatt reactor + 2 184" nuclear ramjets + 4 P&W J-91 turbojets	306,000	50,000	10,000	?	366,000	?	Mach 3 @ 62 Kft	Supersonic	?
Republic M=4.25	4	2	110' 0"	4860	150' 0"	2 nuclear ramjets + 3 J-79 turbojets	?	?	?	?	350,000	17,000+	?	Mach 4.25	?
Convair Carrier Based Attack Recon	4	2	50' 5"(stowed)	2434	112' 6"	1 P&W 200 megawatt reactor + 2 nuclear turbojet + 2 nuclear ramjets	121,850	8,900	5,000	?	136,930	16,000	Mach 3 @ 70 Kft	Mach 3.7	?
Convair Carrier Based Combined Engine	4	2	50' 5"(stowed)	2030	100' 0"	1 P&W 200 megawatt reactor + 2 nuclear turbojet/ramjets	120,570	8,900	5,000	?	135,650	16,000	Mach 3 @ 70 Kft	Mach 3.8	?
Pluto	4	0	~143"	>	~878"	1 Tory II-C/AF	?	?	?	?	~55 Klbs	~10,000	Mach 2.8 @ 1000 ft	?	?
Seaplanes															
Convair Betta	3	2	632'	1202	1333'	3 GE J53 turbojets	?	?	10,000	?	?	?	?	Supersonic	?
Martin M-275	3	?	86.9'	1882	160'	4 Curtiss-Wright J67 turbojets	?	?	?	30,000	160,000	?	?	Mach 1.13+	?

129

Aircraft	Source Grade	Crew	Span	Wing area (sq ft)	Length	Engines	Dry weight (lb)	Design Fuel (lb)	Design Payload (lb)	Max Payload (lb)	Gross weight (lb)	Range (n.mi.)	Cruise speed	Max speed	Ceiling (ft)
Martin Model 316	3	?	90.0'	2000	163.0'	4 Curtiss-Wright J67 turbojets	?	?	?	30,000	200,000	?	?	Mach 1.35+	?
Martin Model 329 C-1	4	3	74.15'	1835	143'	6 Orenda PS-13 turbojets	109,420	101,415	6,400	16,000	220,000	2000	Mach 085 @ 52 Kft	Mach 2.32 @ 45 Kft	?
Martin Model 329 C-2	4	3	73'9"	1800	146'	6 Orenda PS-13 turbojets	120,460	140,150	6,400	16,000	270,000	2790	Mach 085 @ 50 Kft	Mach 2.32 @ 45 Kft	?
Martin Water Based Attack aircraft	3	1	33'	320	56.6'	1 GE XJ79 XX-24A turbojet	17,073	2072			28,313	1200	530 kts @ 38 Kft	748 knots @ ~40 Kft	?
Convair Combat Seaplane Delta Wing - Single Engine - Ski	4	2	46'1.2"	750	~86'8"	1 Allison 700 B-3 turbojet (J-89)	?	?	1,700	?	54,335	1,600	Mach 0.9 @ SL	Mach 3 @ 60 Kft	?
Convair Combat Seaplane Delta Wing - Double Engine - Ski	4	2	~44'10"	750	~88'0"	2 X-275A turbojets	?	?	1,700	?	?	1,600	Mach 0.9 @ SL	Mach 3 @ 60 Kft	?
Convair Combat Seaplane Delta Wing - Single Engine - Canard-Ski	4	2	46'1.2"	750	~81'4"	1 Allison 700 B-3 turbojet (J-89)	?	?	1,700	?	?	1,600	Mach 0.9 @ SL	Mach 3 @ 60 Kft	?
Convair Combat Seaplane Delta Wing - Single Engine - Hull	4	2	~40'5"	550	78'4"	1 Allison 700 B-3 turbojet (J-89)	?	?	1,700	?	?	1,600	Mach 0.9 @ SL	Mach 3 @ 60 Kft	?
Convair Supersonic Attack Airplane	4	3	78'4"	?	125'0"	6 GE J-79 turbojets	?	?	3,000	?	?	3,400	?	Mach 1.25+ @ 35 Kft	?
Convair Water-based B-58	4	2	67.5'	1542	120'	4 GE J-79 turbojets	61,647	72,235	~10,000	?	170,194	4,600	?	~Mach 2	70,000+
Convair Hydro-Ski Supersonic Attack Airplane	4	2	49'4"	860	68'4"	2 GE J-79 turbojets	26,743	20,000	2,000	2,000	49,693	1,600	Mach 0.9 @ 40-48 Kft	Mach 1.49 @ 35 Kft	?
Convair Mach 4 seaplane Config 1	4	2	54'3"	2360	118'9"	3 P&W J-58 turbojets	80,350	112,735	6,000	?	200,000	3,350	Mach 4	Mach 4 @ 80 Kft	?
Convair Mach 4 seaplane Config 2	4	2	54'3"	2360	118'9"	3 P&W J-58 turbojets	78,250	114,835	6,000	?	200,000	3,350	Mach 4	Mach 4 @ 80 Kft	?
Convair Mach 4 seaplane Config 3	4	2	54'3"	2360	123'6"	3 P&W J-58 turbojets	83,840	109,245	6,000	?	200,000	3,350	Mach 4	Mach 4 @ 80 Kft	?
Convair Mach 4 attack-recon	4	2	51.4'	2640	151'2.4"	2 turbojets	?	?	?	?	?	?	?	Mach 4	?
NACA TMX-191	3	?	72.5'	1500	158.3'	4 advanced Orenda Iroquis turbojets	?	?	?	?	225,000	?	?	Mach 2.0	?
Nuclear seaplanes															
Martin Model 331-B3	4	3(?)	102'8"	2000	170'2"	1 GE AC110 nuclear turbojet + 2 Orenda PS13 turbojets	256,606	38,000	6,400	?	296,831	15,700	~Mach 0.9 @ 28 Kft	Mach 1.5 @ 35 Kft	?
Convair Model 23A	4	3	76'4" (theo.)	2000	153'10"	1 GE AC110 nuclear turbojet + 1 60 Klbf rocket	?	?	?	?	268,100	?	?	~Mach 2	?
Convair Model 23A-3	4	3	85'10"	1850	152.08'	1 GE AC110 nuclear turbojet	?	?	?	?	?	?	?	~Mach 2	?
Convair Model 23B	4	5	115'0"	3312	204'2"	4 PWA NJ-2B nuclear engines	?	?	?	?	383,520	?	?	~Mach 2	?
Convair Model 23B-1	4	5	115'0"	3312	204.16'	2 GE AC110 nuclear turbojets	?	?	?	?	?	?	?	~Mach 2	?
Convair 6-Engine Nuclear Powered Attack Seaplane	3	5	155'	5700	~274'4"	6 PWA NJ-2B nuclear engines	?	?	?	?	?	?	?	~Mach 2	?
Convair WS-125 flying boat	4	4	134'	5140	232.16'	2 GE AC-110 nuclear turbojets + 2 P&W JT-9A turbojets + 1 60 Klbf rocket	423,989	?	10,000	?	647,686	22,000	Mach 0.9+	Mach 2.2	?
Convair Submersible nuclear ramjet	2	3 (?)	~24.7'	?	~140'	1 nuclear ramjet	~240,000	?	20,000	?	~350,000	?	?	Mach 4 @ SL	?
VTOL															
Boeing Model 809-1012	3	2	53'9"	2550	126'0"	4 GE X279E turbojets + 24 GE J-85 turbojets	?	97,900	3,000	?	200,000	?	?	Mach 3.0	?
Boeing Model 809-1013	3	2	54'0"	2000	105' (fuselage)	8 GE X279E (1.1 scale)	?	98,000	3,000	?	200,000	?	?	Mach 3 (?)	?
NACA VTOL	3	?	~32'	?	~112'	6 30Klbf turbojets	65,000	?	?	?	175,000	?	?	?	?
Boeing Model 818-104,-105	3	2	35'0"	660	77'3"	12 GE growth J-85	?	25,000	1,500	?	52,000	3290	Mach 2.5 @ 55 Kft	Mach 2.6	?
Boeing Model 818-159	3	2	24'	560	80'	2 GE TF35-X220C + 6 GE J-85 (SJ-117D)	39,500	13,900	1,000	?	54,400	1240	Mach 2.5 @ 71 Kft	Mach 2.5	?